Joyful Babel

APPROACHES TO TRANSLATION STUDIES
Founded by James S Holmes

Edited by Henri Bloemen
　　　　　 Dirk Delabastita
　　　　　 Ton Naaijkens

Volume 22

Joyful Babel
Translating Hélène Cixous

Edited by
Myriam Diocaretz
and
Marta Segarra

Amsterdam – New York, NY 2004

Myriam Diocaretz is Head of the Digital Culture Research Programme
at the European Centre for Digital Communication/Infonomics,
in Maastricht.

Marta Segarra is Director of the *Centre Dona i literatura* (Center of
Women and literature) and Professor of French and Francophone literature and cinema at the University of Barcelona.

The paper on which this book is printed meets the requirements of "ISO
9706:1994, Information and documentation - Paper for documents -
Requirements for permanence".

Le papier sur lequel le présent ouvrage est imprimé remplit les prescriptions de "ISO 9706:1994, Information et documentation - Papier pour
documents - Prescriptions pour la permanence".

ISBN: 90-420-0989-6
©Editions Rodopi B.V., Amsterdam - New York, NY 2004
Printed in The Netherlands

Contents

Preface MYRIAM DIOCARETZ   5

Acknowledgments   6

Critical Introduction MARTA SEGARRA   7

PART I: Translating *other* Discourses

Translating the Enigma:
Hélène Cixous's Writing Notebooks SUSAN SELLERS   25

Betrayed VERENA ANDERMATT CONLEY   39

PART II: Translating 'as if Other', or Translation in Difference

Nearly Reading Hélène Cixous:
The "Equivocal Vocation" of Translation ERIC PRENOWITZ   47

La coupe des mots. Notes on the Italian Translation
of *OR Les lettres de mon père* MONICA FIORINI   61

Translation's Infinite Spiral:
Reading, Translating, Reading Cixous LYNN K. PENROD   75

"Without your breath on my words, there will not be
any mimosa". Reflections on Translation SISSEL LIE   93

Desvelo MARA NEGRÓN   101

The Betrayal of Textual *Différance* (of the *Voiles*): a
Translational Analysis of *Savoir* MARIBEL PEÑALVER VICEA   111

PART III: Translating Sexual Difference

Transreadings NADIA SETTI   133

Problems in Translating Hélène Cixous
into Japanese Feminine Language ISAKO MATSUMOTO   153

PART IV: Translating Other's Culture, or Translating Words into Bodies

"Translating HC/Writing the self" (*L'Indiade*
and the Replication of an Elusive Dream) ANU ANEJA   165

Translating Hélène Cixous's *Tambours sur la digue*:
The Ineffable on Stage JUDITH G. MILLER   183

Hélène Cixous, Translator of History and Legend:
"*Ce transport vertigineux*" DEBORAH JENSON   197

Beyond the Text, into the Realm of Live Performance:
Working on the *Portrait de Dora* LILIANA ALEXANDRESCU   205

Bibliography   217

Preface

For several years I had had the vision and the intention but seldom the time to initiate this much needed collection. I first wrote to the translators of Hélène Cixous in 1999 to ask them to participate in this project. The response was enthusiastic; however, there were a few among them who could not contribute at that moment, or later, because of previous commitments and/or heavy workload. One outstanding translator who was just beginning to work with Hélène Cixous's texts is present in spirit among the contributors for he departed this life: Brian Mallett. Brian, you will be remembered for your talent and professional dedication, wherever you may be now.

A few other translators, dispersed and mobile, often moving from one continent to another, could not be reached. It is our hope that in the subsequent volume those that could not contribute will join us. Yes, it is comforting to know that translating Cixous signifies plurality and dissemination, for there are more translations of our author that are forthcoming, and more being started. Therefore, we can confidently state that we hope that in the coming years other critical editions will follow *Joyful Babel. Translating Hélène Cixous*, with new contributors or additional perspectives.

Leaving the future aside, the present volume stands on its own, as a representative of the field of translation in its cross-disciplinarity, as a zone within cultural studies, as a crossroads between writing in or for particular geo-cultural spaces and the inner spaces of writing, as a dialogic encounter between the translators and their own audiences and readerships, between the translators and the discourses of Hélène Cixous, and at another level, with us, the implied addressees or readers of their reflections.

I am grateful to Marta Segarra for accepting to join me in this project in 2001. The present volume was prepared in harmony with Hélène Cixous; the editors are grateful to the author for helping us to contact or locate her translators. However, the editors worked independently from the author, and assume full responsibility for the overall choices in the volume.

Myriam Diocaretz

Acknowledgments

The Editors wish to thank professor William Charles Phillips and Sarah Cornell, English copyeditors of the volume. We also thank Esther von der Osten-Sacken, who was engaged in this project in its early stages. Eric Prenowitz kindly corrected some French quotations translated into English.

Critical Introduction

Marta Segarra

> Translating is, after all, madness (M. Blanchot)
> Translation is the most intimate act of reading (G. Ch. Spivak)

Translation studies are by now recognized as a crossroads of various disciplines – linguistics, literary criticism, philosophy, and even anthropology, according to Venuti (2000: 1) –, and thus a field that corresponds to our own historical times (Díaz-Diocaretz 1998). This sole fact justifies the interest of a volume dedicated to theoretical and practical reflections made by translators. But why "translating Hélène Cixous"? Why focus on a single writer, and why Cixous? The first part of this question is easy to answer: we focused on the translation of a single writer because we thought that it would be a good way to present new explorations of the theory and practice of translation; that is why all contributors are translators of Cixous's texts. But still, why Hélène Cixous? First, because her work is translated into a wide range of languages, including English, Japanese, Italian, Spanish, Dutch, Norwegian, and Hindustani – all of them represented in this book. Moreover, because we think that translation itself, literally or metaphorically, is a constant presence in Cixous's writing. In the following paragraphs I will examine some of the most illuminating metaphors that translation theorists have established to think about translation, in order to prove that they are also essential images in Cixous's world.

The first metaphor would be an erotic one. Since the XVIIth century, translation has been assimilated to a "beautiful but unfaithful" woman in a traditional phrase (*les belles infidèles*). An also traditional debate among translators is between fidelity and infidelity: as formulated by Sissel Lie in this volume, would it be better to read a "beautiful but unfaithful" translation or a "tedious and faithful" one? Would we agree with Borges, who celebrates the "happy and creative infidelity" of a translation of *One Thousand and One Night* (1935: 45), or with Nabokov, who defends "literal translation" with "copious footnotes, footnotes reaching up like skyscrapers" (1955: 83)? This resembles the bourgeois erotic distinction between the faithful and tedious wife and the beautiful but maybe treacherous mistress. Jacques Derrida (1985: 176) alludes precisely to the bond of marriage in order to evoke the relationship between author and language. More explicitly, George Steiner (1975: 298) refers to the "Augustinian *tristitia*" that follows the act of erotic love to describe the "sadness" implicit in the act of translation, a sadness produced equally by success and by failure, and that we could relate to the act of "mourning" mentioned by Mara Negrón in her article in relation to the translator's task.

The erotic metaphor, mentioned by several of the contributors, turns sometimes – some could argue that this is perhaps because most of them are women – to the maternal, as we read in Susan Seller's and Anu Aneja's texts, which describe translating as "giving birth". Most of them are aware too that this love is intimately interwoven with "hate" (Derrida 1985: 176). Translating implies "commit[ting] abuses" (Derrida in Lewis 1985: 39) to the original text, some type of violence. Cixous herself evokes "the blind violence of translation" (1991: 22-23). This is logical if we agree with George Steiner that translation is a "demonstrative statement of understanding", and that understanding is a "violent" act, according to Heidegger (Steiner 1975: 297). Here comes another metaphor tied to love and hate, that of nourishing and devouring: both apparently contradictory actions are associated with translating. In fact, the Brazilian writers Haroldo and Augusto de Campos compare translation to a "cannibalistic act" – an image that we can find in some of the articles of the volume such as Aneja's –, and Hélène Cixous herself uses this metaphor to talk of love (in Godayol 2000):

> I think we are above all wolves. It is known that love is devouring. It is the great drama of love: we want at once to devour the other and not to devour the other. [...] We must perform this double movement all the time. One must desire above all, be ready to kill for it, and at the same time be able to renounce the satisfaction of one's desires *in extremis*. In extremis. Just before destroying. (Cixous 1997: 111)

In this fragment, Cixous develops one of her most usual themes, the relation to the Other, frequently trapped in a double bind between nourishing and devouring, between love and hate, between protection and aggression. Most theorists supporting this belief assume that translation is the arena of a battle – or an embrace – between the original and the translated text, or between the two languages and cultures involved. As Antoine Berman expresses it (appropriating an expression by Heidegger), "translation is the trial of the foreign" (in Robinson 1997), which consists of "receiving the Foreign as Foreign" (Venuti 2000: 288).

Berman's famous book, of the same title (1984), examines how the history of translation has been just the opposite, one of "naturalisation" or "domestication" of the original's "strangeness" to the target culture. Myriam

Díaz-Diocaretz (1985) created the most useful concept of the "translator-function" to account for the mechanisms at work in this process, the ideological regulations (such as "didactic", "corrective" or "preventive" turns) that reign in a "hegemonic" conception of translation. All this leads to a logical conclusion – but not as widespread as it should be – that Díaz-Diocaretz was one of the first to stress: translating has an ethical dimension, which has been traditionally hidden behind its technical aspects. Most of the contributors of this volume are widely aware of – and frequently torn by – these ethical implications of the choices they must make. Here, Cixous's writing proves again to be a breeding ground for this theorizing, because of its inner "strangeness" or "foreignness", this is to say its marvellous work on language. Venuti – in his *Rethinking Translation* (1992: 4) – maintains that translated texts should not fear "non-linear syntax", "plurivocal meaning", unusual "rhythms", etc. But Cixous's original writing is already full of these "foreignizing" features: it contains an inner otherness in a permanent Bakhtinian dialogue. This is another one of Cixous's perceptive insights: others are not outside but inside *me*.

This ethical dimension of translation has also political implications; as Díaz-Diocaretz (1998) stresses, the translator's historical times are our own – as Europeans, because European cultural identity will be based on "unity in diversity" (*ibid.*), or as Americans, if we believe Venuti (1995: 20) when he says: "Foreignizing translation in English can be a form of resistance against ethnocentrism and racism, cultural narcissism and imperialism, in the interests of democratic geopolitical relations". Cixous's texts, especially her dramatic work, also resist "ethnocentrism and racism", taking in other cultures and other languages into them. But, as I already stated, they show above all that otherness is inextricably tied to oneness, and that we should thus look to ourselves "as if other" (Derrida 1985: 175). As Maurice Blanchot (1971) puts it, not all works permit what we could call – playing with Joseph Graham's title – "translation in difference". Blanchot says that only those writings which already contain difference, which are able to be "different" or "strangers" to themselves can lead to a true and enriching translation (1971: 71). Cixous's work is one of them, as it clearly shares this "strangeness of origin" (*ibid.*). If translation is a "hermeneutic of trust", Cixous's texts inspire this feeling with their "radical generosity" (Steiner 1975: 296).

The idea of trust is close to another current metaphor for translation, which would be in the field of economics, that of a contract – the translator "takes" from the original and must "render" or "compensate" for this taking – or a "significant exchange" (Steiner 1975: 302), and, more originally, that of a debt. It is Derrida who develops the latter, in a commentary on the well-known essay of Walter Benjamin on translation. For the French philosopher, the translator is not simply an "indebted receiver" (Derrida 1985: 179) of some original text that s/he has to give back more or less equal to itself after manipulation; the original is also indebted to the translator – or, more exactly, to the translated text – because it has appealed to it. Derrida states that "translated texts never say the same thing as the original text. Something new always happens"; in other words, "the same text doesn't exist" (Derrida 1999a: 62-63, my translation from Spanish). Eric Prenowitz, in his essay for the present volume, comes to perceptive conclusions following Derrida's statement. The translated text must be an "echo" (Steiner 1975: 301) of the original one, but we must understand here "echo" not as a vain and mechanical repetition, but as an allusion to Echo overcoming her curse when she repeats the cry of loving Narcissus: *"veni"*[1].

Steiner develops his mythological metaphor to its logical extension, the very Narcissian mirror: translation should be a "mirror which not only reflects but also generates light" (1975: 301). We enter here another semantic field, that of the gaze, to describe the process of translation. This should be either "transparent" – Benjamin says in his thought-provoking essay that "a real translation is transparent; it does not cover the original, does not black its light, but allows the pure language [...] to shine upon the original all the more fully" (1923: 21) – or recognize the fallacy of transparency and not pretend to be "invisible" (Venuti 1995). Benjamin's phrase on covering and letting light pass evokes a powerful image in Cixous's (and Derrida's) world: the veil, which is a leitmotif in the articles by Mara Negrón and M. Peñalver Vicea. As a Tunisian woman writer puts it, the veil "serves for showing as for hiding: the most important is to show that one hides" (Bel Haj Yahia 1991: 54, my translation from French). The veil is thus a paradoxical image, which integrates these two apparently contradictory moves, of showing and covering, and of self-protection and self-aggression. It is comparable to the "hymen" for Derrida (1985: 191-192), as an image of what remains "untouchable" when the "communicable meaning" of the text has been "extracted" by the reader-translator, who has "penetrated" it to honour the contract. We return here to the erotic metaphor with which we started.

The semantic field of the gaze permits the use of other visual metaphors, such as "myopia", which Cixous turns into a meaningful concept in *Veils*. This enables Peñalver Vicea to mention the "glasses" as a simile for the translator's attitude to the original, and to state that translators should always be "myopic". David Robinson proposes another metaphor in the same line, borrowed from neurology:

> The translation would be the prosthetic device – an artificial, mechanical contrivance designed to replace a textual limb "lost" through the target language reader's inability to read a text in the original language – that comes to feel real, native, strong enough to "walk on" or live through, when a proprioceptive phantom is incorporated into it. [Proprioceptive phantom = "some nexus of felt experience that charges the text, any text, with the feel of reality, of 'one's-owness'"] (Robinson 1997: 119)

I am sure that Hélène Cixous would like this image, so close to some of her loans from medical language and practice. Robinson's picturesque claim for this "phantom limb" that one feels after the loss of this extremity, graphically renders the double bind inherent to translation, made of loss and of gain, of triumph and of defeat. That makes translation, after the fall of the tower of Babel, "both necessary and impossible", according to Jacques Derrida (1985: 174). But does translation work to rebuild this tower, as Blanchot says, commenting on Benjamin? Benjamin thinks, in fact, that what inspires the translator's task is "integrating many tongues into one true language [...], allowing his language to be powerfully affected by the foreign tongue" (1923: 21-22). All the target languages which are present in this volume, affected by Cixous's particular "idiom" in French, would then merge to constitute a unique and "true language" (*ibid.*: 20), that we could call Cixousian.

With regard to idioms and languages, the editors chose to translate all the quotations present in this book into English, thus unifying the *joyful* multiplicity of languages also existing in it. But we should also draw attention to the fact that the English used in this collection is an *impure* one, permeated by the tongues and idioms of every one of its contributors, and especially of those for whom English is not their mother tongue – among whom I count myself. Myriam and I think that this crossbreeding of languages is a fertile ground for dialogic exchange.

We have divided the volume into three parts: the first section is devoted to **"Translating *other* Discourses"**, and includes two innovative articles that comment on the possibility of translating *special* discourses – Cixous's notebooks preceding her fictional writing and the writer's Paris seminars – into a written one.

Susan Sellers (2004) has edited and translated into English Cixous's "Notebooks" in order to study the creative process between the first 'notes' and the final book. These are notebooks that Cixous wrote parallel to one of her latest "fiction". The translation of these notebooks is particularly difficult because the concision of the notes, taken sometimes in a hurry by Cixous, deprives the translator of the context that normally shapes her choices. That gives Sellers a larger freedom, with all its "privileges" but also its problems. As translator, she tries to resist the temptation of looking to the fiction for "clues", because the notes are prior to the final text and must be translated as such.

The abbreviations used by Cixous in her notepads are also illustrative. Sellers chooses the significant example of the article *'un'*, *'une'*, symbolised by number "1" in them. This single form for masculine and feminine seems to erase the sexual difference, rather surprisingly in an author like Cixous whose work is entirely based on it, but it can also be interpreted as the existence of a non-gendered or neutral zone in the first steps of the creative process, a space where gender cannot be determined and is maybe "unimposable". Likewise, the passage from handwriting to a printed edition erases the characteristic subjectivity of the original text, and Sellers turns it into a metaphor for translating itself, which consists also of a kind of depersonalisation of the author's text. Finally, Sellers takes one of Cixous's favourite metaphors, giving birth, so as to illustrate the translator's task: "*reculer pour mieux sauter [...] c'est le meilleur moyen de faire des accouchements*" says the "*sage-femme*" or wise-woman: it is sometimes necessary to draw back a few steps in order not to force the "mother-text" into a "damaged result". "Translation cannot be hurried".

Verena Andermatt Conley, who translated more than 6.000 pages from oral recordings of Hélène Cixous's seminars into English, underlines in her essay that every translation is a betrayal. When translated, words and expressions evoke different images than in the original text, therefore causing a different kind of emotion on the reader. As Cixous's writing is already a translation of emotions – and not simply of ideas – into words, it is impossible, according to this translator, to re-produce the same performance in a language other than the original French. But the process of reading itself is also a betrayal, because the reader deciphers the text guided mostly by her or his own emotional experience. Conley argues that in order to translate successfully such a "poetic text" as Cixous's, an "empathy" must be established between the translator and the writer. Translating cannot be a mechanical process without any affectivity involved: the translator must implicate herself or himself into the task, even if there is a risk of mistaking her or his own affectivity for that of the writer.

The translation of Cixous's seminars proved to be very difficult, because it implied multiple levels: these ones are oral texts, and their transcription in written French is already a kind of translation; besides, in her academic work, Cixous constantly refers to other writers such as Joyce, Lispector, Kafka or Bernhard, so translating their texts into French. The translator, concludes Conley, must then try to minimise the betrayal of these multiple transitional operations.

The next section of the volume is entitled **"Translating 'as if Other', or Translation in Difference"**, and contains some theoretical contributions that reflect on translation as an experience related to a dialogue with the Other, to difference, to the foreign, and which possesses thus an ethical dimension. As Monica Fiorini suggests explicitly, Cixous's conception of language conveys this type of ethical content, as the writer seems to give an essential freedom to language, not "mastering" the words but letting them associate and transform freely. Therefore, the translation of such writing invites a defamiliarization of the translator's own language.

Eric Prenowitz, in the article that opens this section, focuses on *OR, les lettres de mon père* – a book where Cixous poses the question of reading – in order to show, following Derrida, that reading is never a "hermeneutic process of uncovering a content inherent to the text". The text's truth, in other words, does not exist. This has a direct consequence on translation, as it can never be a *direct* rendering of this non-existent single truth. Translation is also, states the author of this insightful piece of work, "a doubly performative and thus a doubly violent gesture": it stresses "the absence of the original", in the sense above mentioned, and also "constitutes the reader" of the new text, and constitution always implies some violence. But this violence is also a "hospitality", in the Derridean sense. This ambiguity between violence and hospitality, and the possibility of reading, are precisely the most important themes of *OR*. In his book on Hélène Cixous *H.C. pour la vie, c'est à dire...*, Derrida points out the untranslatability of many Cixous's expressions, but this impossibility springs from an "excess of translations": many options are equally appropriate. Believing in a translation that could maintain this "semantic multiplicity" of the original is "the impossible dream of translation", according to Prenowitz.

Monica Fiorini's essay also centres on *OR Les lettres de mon père*, of which she made the Italian translation. Due to the "latent multilingualism" (French echoes with German, English and other languages) and the multiplicity of discourses (orality, intertextuality, etc.) which lie in Cixous's texts, the translator must have a close look at the "literality" of this writing to keep its plurality and richness. *OR* is also a book entirely concerned with translation: the narrator asks herself how to read or *translate* the father's letters to the mother so as to "translate" his being. It is never a question of reproducing these letters in their words. The title of this book already poses a major problem. In French and in the textual world of Cixous, "*or*" means, of course, 'gold', but these "letters" can also be found in "*orange*", "*oran-je*", "*or-en-je*" ['Oran-I', 'gold-in-I'], and are central in the father's name, "*GeORges*" (also "*je-or-je(s)*" ['I-gold-I(s)']). The translation of "*OR*" by "*ORO*" in Italian limits all these polysemic possibilities; it might be preferable, then, to play with other words like "*ORA*" (which means mainly 'now' and 'hour') to ensure the polyphony of the text. This could be considered an "unfaithful" translation, but Fiorini maintains that in order to be faithful to the original text, the translation should respect the "performativity" of it as a unique event, and not try to give a word for word translation.

Another example of the difficulty of translating Cixous, and at the same time of the semantic richness of her writing, is the expression that Fiorini chose as her title: "*la coupe des mots*". In French, "*coupe*" means both 'cut' and 'bowl' (and a 'bowl of fruits' evokes the German word for fruits '*Obst*', which leads us to 'obstetrics', and so on). Fiorini sees in this expression a metaphor for the "textual body" of Cixous's writing: in it, one cannot consider the word as a unit of sense, cut and isolated, as each word contains – like a "bowl" – a multiplicity of other words, sounds, and letters (as for "*or*"). Thus, a type of translation based on the ideal of "a word for a word" does not apply to Cixous's writing.

Lynn K. Penrod convincingly argues for her part that translation, understood as a close and creative reading of the original text, is a necessary step to any "interpretation" of Cixousian writing. Following Lewis (1985) – whose theory is itself inspired in Derrida –, Penrod states that a good and not "servile" translation of this type of texts must always be "ab-usive", that is, not condescending to the "*us*-system", "the chain of values linking the *us*ual, the *us*eful, and common linguistic *us*age". Nevertheless, translation must always respect some norms; from her own experience as translator of *La fiancée juive de la tentation* by Cixous, Penrod comments on five of these points as defined by A. Martin. First, it is necessary for the translator to reach a deep and complete "understanding" of the text in order to translate it. In the case of Cixous, that includes identifying her intertextual allusions to other texts or even historical figures such as Saint Francis of Assisi in the beginning of *La fiancée*. Second, there is a question of "loyalty" or "equivalence": the polysemic use of words and expressions by Cixous is often impossible to keep or equate in translation, and the use of footnotes is not a good solution as it breaks the rhythm of the text, according to the translator. Rhythm is also an important feature, and Penrod, as other contributors of this volume, refers to the particular "undulating" rhythm – "flow" seems to be in the original sense of the Greek word for rhythm – of Cixous's writing. But it is also important to bear in mind the "target language quality", in this case English, which does not offer the same chances as French, especially to play with the gender of words.

Finally, the author discusses the relationship between *La fiancée juive* and Rembrandt's painting "The Jewish Bride", which demands also an active collaboration of the observer, because they both work with the "in-between", "the simultaneously visible and invisible", which is visually represented in the painting by the "reclining figure-eight" that stands for infinity. Penrod uses this figure to metaphorise the never-ending process of "reading-translating-reading" Cixous.

It is a frequent statement that the translator is first of all a reader of the original text, but a special reader who creates a new writing in her or his own language. Sissel Lie argues in her impassioned essay that one of the most important things this new text must keep from the original one is its rhythm, not only its meaning. Antoine Berman says that in order to respect this "kinship" between different languages (the concept comes from W.

Benjamin), the translator has the possibility of using several techniques, such as creating new words in his or her own language, and "compensating" for the lack of a good translation of a word or expression, placing it in another part of the text than in the original, amongst others. Lie gives some examples of her use of these techniques from her own translation of Cixous in Norwegian. She also warns against the excessive use of footnotes where translation seems impossible, in order not to "destroy the poetry" of Cixousian writing. Therefore the dilemma for the translator would be between a "beautiful and unfaithful" version and a "tedious and faithful" one. The danger of the first possibility is to "lose the memory" in the way between one language to another; the second instead obliterates the literary value of the text.

The translated text should then be a "work of art in itself", in the tradition of its own language, such as the Norwegian version of Proust, which was fundamental to the creation of modern Norwegian. The translator should not try to "master" the text but to "feel" it with her body and senses, and then create a "new literary text" close to the original one. The strangeness of Cixous's writing – already in French – can be perceived by target-language readers as a bad translation, but the translator must restrain herself from "normalising" Cixous's own language. Sissel Lie hopes that her translations of Cixous could even make Norwegian a "richer" and "less laconic" language.

The Spanish word *desvelo* (which means sleeplessness, but contains also the word '*velo*' ['veil']), in the title of the contribution by Mara Negrón, who translated *Voiles* into Spanish, represents metaphorically to her the attitude of every translator, who must be "awakened and ready to play between languages". Derrida's and Cixous's texts are moreover written in "a plurality of languages and voices". Derrida (1985) suggests that the translator estranges himself from his own language in contact with the original one; Negrón understands it as a defamiliarization of her own language, which becomes "*unheimlich*". The translator loses her own language (which entails a sort of "mourning"), and then there is a "rebirth" in the space of the Other.

Negrón compares the texts by Derrida and Cixous, which she translated, stating that they both use a "veil effect" that must be preserved in translation. She gives several examples of this operation, which begins in the title, *Savoir* ['to know', 'knowledge'], usually translated into Spanish by '*saber*' but which in her translation becomes *Sa(v)er*. She created a neologism with the aim of keeping the multiplicity of semantic nuances and echoes of the original word, and especially the meaning of '*voir*' ['to see'; in Spanish: '*ver*'], a central image to Cixous's text. In a similar way, she recuperated an old Latin word for 'worm' in Derrida's title [*Un ver à soie*: 'A silk worm'], which became in Spanish *Un verme de seda*, evoking powerfully the image of the gaze. "*Ver-me*" contains also the first person of the reflexive pronoun ['to see-me'], preserving thus the polysemic echo of the French '*soi(e)*'. This is a beautiful example of the possibilities of translation just where it seems most difficult. Referring also to the etymological origin of the word, Negrón concludes that translation means to displace the translator's language, to situate it in an "unstable" and "invisible" place between languages, in order to keep the sense eternally in motion and not to settle it in a solid position.

Maribel Peñalver Vicea meticulously analyses Negrón's translation of *Savoir*, specifying some linguistic procedures, and starting from the notion that translating means "betraying the *différance*". The first one is "transcoding", which is facilitated in this case by the fact that Spanish and French derive both from Latin, and then they share many etymological roots. Peñalver Vicea describes the richness of the title *Savoir*, successfully rendered in Spanish as *Sa(v)er*, as we have already seen. On the other hand, the gender ambiguity of the general title of the book, *Voiles* (which means both 'veils' and 'sails' in French, depending on its gender, obliterated in its plural form), is impossible to keep in Spanish. The translator must choose one option between '*velos*' or '*velas*', and this is qualified as a "castration". Neologisms, a "poison" and at the same time a "potion" to language's health, are also examined by Peñalver Vicea, as well as the loss of sound games, very outstanding in Cixous's writing, not only from an aesthetic point of view but also from a semantic one. For instance, the sound 'v', contained in '*voile*', '*savoir*', '*juive*' ['Jewish woman'], '*voler*' [both 'steal' and 'fly'] and other privileged images in Cixous's world, connects all of them, reinforcing their metaphorical sense, and this is inescapably lost in Spanish or any other language but French.

The translation of metaphors is another tricky problem; M. Peñalver Vicea takes some of the most important ones in *Savoir* and applies them to the activity of translating, stating, for instance, that the translator should always be "myopic" so as to keep the uncertainty of the original text, which should not be "unveiled" by univocal choices. Following the same metaphor, the author concludes that translating is the only way to "unveil" some linguistic procedures of Cixous's writing, but it conveys also the risk of "veiling" the ambiguity and so the richness of the original text. Translating means castrating, but this is a fertile castration as it engenders a new text in the target language.

The third part of the book is devoted to **"Translating Sexual Difference"**, and contains two contributions that pursue the practical and theoretical reflections on translation, giving a special stress to the question of gender. As her starting point, Nadia Setti affirms the importance of "writing the sexual difference" in the work of Cixous. This is not a question of changing the grammatical structures of the French language but a much "larger and complex strategy", involving also syntax, rhythm, sound and sense. And this ambitious project is simultaneously explained and performed by Cixousian writing; performance may even precede rational explanation, creating an "other" language inside French. Cixous writes in French as if it were a "foreign" language to her, thus enlivening it, treating it as a "living" material in continuous movement and not petrifying it in definitive and stable choices. The translator must be aware of this "indecision" of Cixous's idiom in order not to assimilate its otherness to sameness, and not to reduce the original text's strangeness in its own language(s). This plural is explained by the fact that Cixous definitely operates in various languages, from her "m'other" language, German, to the multiple intertextual inferences from the authors she reads. But the intrusion of other languages into French is not here a violent disruption or conscious "babelisation" such as Joyce's in *Finnegan's Wake*. It is more likely an unconscious and poetical reference to this "m'other" language, "more voice than grammar", made of rhythm, music, and breath. This is a "vocal substance" which depends moreover on each reader's interpretation – or "translation", says Setti – of the text.

This is why Cixous's writing defies a word for word translation and demands a "textual" one, which considers the text as a whole and examines first its rhythm patterns – Setti argues that each Cixousian piece of writing has its own – in order to reveal the "rules of the game". And the translator must play following these rules, but with different cards. It is impossible to keep in the translation exactly the same way of disseminating the meaning as in the original text; in other words, its "particular way of signifying". On the other hand, that also means having the freedom to continue the game in further ways. Translation thus reveals what is ambiguous in the original text, and what is forcibly lost when one translates it. But in its economy there is also a place for gain: Setti attributes to the "textual generosity" of Cixous's writing the large "benefits" that its translation can give to the target language.

The particularities of Japanese grammar make translation from European languages a highly difficult task. The example chosen by Isako Matsumoto in her article is the use of personal pronouns: 'I' and 'you' can be translated into Japanese in more than twenty different ways, depending on the degree of politeness, affirmativeness, on the social status, the age or the gender of the speaker – and of the interlocutor. Moreover, Japanese speakers, who use the third person or simply make impersonal sentences, generally avoid first and second personal pronouns. Japanese verbs are not conjugated by subjects either; the author puts this reluctance of the "consciousness of building up a subject" down to the influence of Buddhism and Zen in Japanese mentality. On the other hand, sexual difference is patent in the use of pronouns, adverbs, and particles, which end the sentences, forming a "masculine" or a "feminine" language depending on the gender of the speaker. A "neutral" register is only possible in special discourses such as academic essays or lectures. Women's language tends to be polite and respectful to the other, showing the traditional submissiveness of women in Japan. The feminine "I" in "The Laugh of the Medusa", translated into Japanese by Matsumoto, is not that of the passive and subordinated woman, but the 'I' of a new and assertive feminine subject. The translator could not then use the traditional Japanese women's language, but a new "unconventional" one, not too "mannish" but not too "feminine" either, because the latter would mean adhering to the usual sexism in Japanese society. Matsumoto opted first to use the neutral form, but finally chose a "woman's language", rendering it more "powerful" by making use quite often, for instance, of the first personal pronoun.

The difficulty was even greater when translating *The Conquest of the School at Madhubaï*, because in a play there must be a "vivid, spoken language", and in spoken Japanese sexual difference cannot be erased. The first and faithful translation by Matsumoto was rewritten by a Japanese playwriter, who used a very masculine – and even "macho" – dialect for Sakundeva's lines, underlining her "masculine" side, as a bandit and a killer. The author opposed this choice, as it failed to convey other feminine aspects of the character such as her symbolic maternity.

The themes brought in by Matsumoto take us to the last section of the volume, devoted to **"Translating Other's Culture, or Translating Words into Bodies"**. From her own experience of translating Hélène Cixous's *L'Indiade* into Hindustani, Anu Aneja poignantly raises postcolonial issues. She elaborates first the metaphors of the erotic in translation, and of the translator as a mother: translating means yielding to the seduction of the other's text; and to combine the other (text or language) and the "flesh of your own words" implies becoming "the M/other". Recalling her first attraction for the French language as a gateway to another world and another culture, Aneja is also aware of the colonial implications of any European language in India. Likewise, she stresses the violence that translation always carries, especially when it consists of rendering a postcolonial text into a European language. Translating *L'Indiade* into Hindustani is a particularly complex case because this text is already, in a certain way, a translation from Indian culture into French. Cixous took some historical and mythical Indian figures in order to turn them into "metaphors", not only of recent Indian history but also of sexual difference, among others.

For instance, one of the characters in this play is the historical person of Gandhi. Cixous's Gandhi is a *translator* himself, transposing his dreams into reality, and dreaming about a land without borders between countries, between genders, between religions. But the historical Gandhi was also a man who supported a traditional and passive image of Indian women, as the Sita of the *Ramayana*, whose main purpose in life was to preserve her chastity, her "lack of desire". Although Sita is also an image of the woman who crosses the line, the limits imposed on her desire, and the border between masculinity and femininity. Aneja's beautiful essay also transgresses boundaries, blending personal memories, political reflections, and images of her sculptural work related to the issues discussed in it, such as mothering.

Judith G. Miller's contribution, full of insight and honesty, is a self-criticism of a first translation that she did of a Cixous's dramatic text, and also a homage to the translator Brian Mallet[2], who helped her to re-write it. Miller recognises the weight of her professional activity as an American stage director in her translation of *Tambours sur la digue*. The influence of American theatre, based mostly on a vigorous and assertive realism, made her transform the puppets imagined by Cixous in this play into "characters", by ascribing to them a colloquial language which gave the puppets a more human presence on the stage. She examines several passages of her first translation and compares them to the second version made in collaboration with Mallet in order to demonstrate this point. For instance, Miller's first translation of the title was *Duan and the Drummers*, giving more protagonism to people than to the objects evoked in the original title, finally rendered as *Drums on the Dam*, because the drums are more central to the play than the drummers themselves. By trying to translate more accurately the images created by Cixous, and by renouncing the colloquial tone of the first, in the second version the translators succeeded in preserving the highly metaphorical and even "spiritual" content of the original play and its "ceremonial quality". Puppet theatre allows the author to spare psychological motivation, and, choosing such a genre, Cixous stressed the universality of the action, which is "the cruellest of farces", and thus capable of showing the inexpressible genocide. Miller concludes that, in her case, and perhaps due to the "incompatibility" between Cixous's and her own theatrical language, the latter being "vigorous and forthright" in contrast to the first, which is "polysemic" and "playful", the only way to subdue her "writer's ego" and respect the force of the original text has been working together with another translator.

Deborah Jenson begins her argumentation showing that many readers of Cixous's early theoretical texts – especially in the United States, where they were enthusiastically received – were disconcerted by her later plays and asked themselves how both types of writing could be reconciled. After her own translation of *The Conquest of the School at Madhubaï*, Jenson brilliantly relates Cixous's own "translation" from history into legend as effected in this play (whose protagonist is the contemporary Indian woman "bandit" Phoolan Devi) to the "global maternity" and the "writing of the body" developed in these theoretical texts. The violent death of Devi, which occurred while Jenson was revising her translation of the play, led her to reflect on the contact between "reality" and fiction in a work so "anti-realistic" as Hélène Cixous's. The writer herself considers theatrical writing as a "vertiginous transport" of a real body and (hi)story to the stage. This process is a translation in the etymological sense of "transporting" or "transferring", in this case, life into writing, and real persons into actors. Cixous has also expressed her fascination for the real bodies of the actors engaged in performance, seeing that as a kind of "depossession of the self". Jenson argues that this attraction might have been decisive for the literary engagement with contemporary history that Cixous makes through her plays.

On the other hand, Phoolan Devi and her family mostly contributed to the transformation of her life into legend or myth, but Cixous defends in a text – which accompanies the play – that legend can provide a chance to escape the destiny "programmed by the great social machines". Developing the metaphor of the "writing of the body", Jenson concludes that Cixous's translation of history into legend allows readers to find a securing place, compared to a maternal womb, to retreat from these implacable "social machines".

The last article is by Liliana Alexandrescu, who staged a version of *Portrait of Dora* in Dutch and also translated this text into Romanian. Alexandrescu speaks of translation in a theatrical and cultural sense: if writing a play is already a "translation of passions", says Hélène Cixous, putting a written text on the stage is also a translation, from words into bodies, here complicated by the *real* or linguistic – and cultural – translation from the original French into Dutch. The relationship between the actor and the character is also an important factor in this sort of theatrical translation. Alexandrescu talks vividly about a certain "vampirism" that characters exert on actors, who get "into the skin" of these fictional beings, an expression that evokes for her "Mayan ritual sacrifices". Moreover, in the particular case of Dora, body language is far from negligible, as it sometimes supports and at other times negates her spoken discourse. This, together with the fact that three different time levels coexist in the play (the "past of memory and dream", when Dora was still a child; the "present of scenic dialogue" between the analyser, Freud, and grown-up Dora; and a "closer present" of Freud's comments on "Dora's case") convinced the director to employ two different actresses to incarnate Dora as a child and as a young woman. Both Doras are on stage at the same time, one acting as the *Doppelgänger* of the other. For instance, while the adult Dora talks to Freud, Dora the child is engaged in physical actions. This implied for the director a division of the text in order to attribute to it two different persons. Occasionally they talk at the same time (this is reflected in the book by two different letter types), and in the last scene, both Doras intervene simultaneously. So, the "translation of passions" is itself translated by means of the staging.

We expect that all these reflections made by Cixous's translators not only will contribute to the emergent field of translation studies, but that they also present new insights on Cixous's fictional and theoretical world. As a mode of understanding Cixous's discourses her translators have often become engaged in writing criticism as well. Thus, several translators participating in the present *Joyful Babel* were among the contributors to the first international collection of essays on the author's work (van Rossum-Guyon and Díaz-Diocaretz 1990). Moreover, Borges's statement (1935: 39) that *One Thousand and One Nights* has an "intensity that is not [usually] tolerated in prose" applies also to Hélène Cixous's writing. Hers are texts written "in the limits of translation" (Derrida 1999b: 44), which cannot thus be "appropriated" by the author nor by the reader/translator (Derrida 1999a: 53). Nevertheless, as Walter Benjamin suggested, a good translation makes the work of art "not simply live longer" but live "more and better, beyond the means of its author" (Derrida 1985: 179). The editors of this volume hope that it will then be another brick in the building of this joyful tower of Hélène Cixous's oeuvre, too.

---

[1] I follow here the interpretation of this myth that Derrida makes in his Preface to *Voyous* (Derrida 2003).

[2] B. Mallet was also going to contribute to the present volume; unfortunately he passed away in 2000.

References

Bel Haj Yahia, Emna. 1991. *Chronique frontalière*. Paris: Noël Blandin.
Benjamin, Walter. 1923. "The Task of the Translator" in Venuti (2000): 15-25.
Berman, Antoine. 1984. *L'épreuve de l'étranger*. Paris: Gallimard [partial English translation in Venuti (2000)].
Blanchot, Maurice. 1971. 'Traduire' in *L'amitié*. Paris: Gallimard. 69-73.
Borges, Jorge Luis. 1935. 'The Translators of the *Thousand and One Nights*' in Venuti (2000): 34-48.
Cixous, Hélène. 1991. *Coming to Writing and Other Essays* (tr. S. Cornell, D. Jenson, A. Liddle, and S. Sellers). Cambridge, MA: Harvard University Press.
Cixous, Hélène and Mireille Calle-Gruber. 1997. *Rootprints* (tr. E. Prenowitz). London and New York, NY: Routledge.
Derrida, Jacques. 1985. 'Des Tours de Babel' in Joseph Graham (ed.) *Difference in Translation*. Ithaca, NY and London: Cornell University Press. 165-207.
—. 1999a. 'Lo ilegible' in *No escribo sin luz artificial*. Valladolid: Cuatro.publicaciones. 49-64.
—. 1999b. 'En el límite de la traducción' in *No escribo sin luz artificial*. Valladolid: Cuatro.publicaciones. 37-48.
—. 2002. *H.C. pour la vie, c'est à dire...* Paris: Galilée.
—. 2003. *Voyous*. Paris: Galilée.
Díaz-Diocaretz, Myriam. 1985. *Translating Poetic Discourse: Questions on Feminist Strategies in Adrienne Rich*. Amsterdam-Philadelphia, PA: John Benjamins.

—. 1998. *European Culture and the Intersection of Culture/Multiculture*. Unpublished lecture notes. Symposium on the Translator as Reader and Writer, Ariane Project, Maison Descartes (Amsterdam).

Godayol, Pilar. 2000. *Espais de frontera. Gènere i traducció*. Vic: Eumo.

Lewis, Philip E. 1985. 'The Measure of Translation Effects' in Joseph Graham (ed.) *Difference in Translation*. Ithaca, NY and London: Cornell University Press. 31-62.

Nabokov, Vladimir. 1955. 'Problems of Translation: *Onegin* in English' in Venuti (2000): 71-83.

Robinson, Douglas. 1997. *What is Translation? Centrifugal Theories, Critical Interventions*. Kent, OH, and London: The Kent State University Press.

Sellers, Susan (ed.). 2004. *The Writing Notebooks of Hélène Cixous*. London and New York, NY: Continuum (forthcoming).

Spivak, Gayatri Chakravorty. 1992. 'The Politics of Translation' in Venuti (2000): 387-416.

Steiner, George. 1975. *After Babel: Aspects of Language and Translation*. London: Oxford University Press.

Van Rossum-Guyon, Françoise and Myriam Díaz-Diocaretz (eds). 1990. *Hélène Cixous, chemins d'une écriture*. Amsterdam-Paris: Rodopi-PUV.

Venuti, Lawrence. 1992. *Rethinking Translation: Discourse, Subjectivity, Ideology*. London and New York, NY: Routledge.

—. 1995. *The Translator's Invisibility: A History of Translation*. London and New York, NY: Routledge.

— (ed.) 2000. *The Translation Studies Reader*. London and New York, NY: Routledge.

PART I: Translating *other* Discourses

Translating the Enigma: Hélène Cixous's Writing Notebooks

Susan Sellers

The author has edited and translated into English Cixous's "notebooks", in order to study the creative process between the first notes and the final book. The concision of these notes, taken sometimes in a hurry by Cixous, deprives the translator of the context which normally shapes her choices. That gives her a larger freedom, with all its "privileges" but also its problems. The passage from handwriting to a printed edition erases likewise the characteristic subjectivity of the original text, and is a metaphor for translating itself, which consists also of a kind of depersonalization of the author's text.
Key words: Cixous's notebooks, sexual difference, translation as depersonalization.

I am currently working on Hélène Cixous's writing notebooks, editing and translating a selection from them for publication[1]. This is a rich domain, not least because of the enormous volume of material that exists. In Cixous's fiction, *Benjamin à Montaigne: Il ne faut pas le dire* [*Benjamin to Montaigne: It Must Not Be Said*], there is a humorous sketch describing how the author begins writing on cheap notepads purchased by her mother from the cut-price store Leader Price (Cixous 2001: 28). The text relates how these discount pads gradually become a necessity to the author, and explores this feeling which arises partly from the fact that they are bought by the author's mother, partly from their cheapness, and partly from the memory of previous writing experiences on similar notepads so that it is as if the words "Leader Price" signal the gateway for writing.

Cixous writes in longhand. She does not use a typewriter or word-processor, arguing that the technology operates as an obstacle to the physical, corporeal action of writing. In *Benjamin à Montaigne: Il ne faut pas le dire*, there is the following account of writing:

> *Et voilà comment pensais-je en suivant la course de ma main sur le papier, confiante, ma main, moi en ma main, dans les forces mystérieuses qui nous soufflent le mouvement de la vie, voilà comment, partant de ces blocs Leader Price [...] je parcours en hypotaxes tous les temps sacrés et insignifiants de mon histoire.* (Cixous 2001: 29-30)

> And that is how I would think following the course of my hand on the paper, confident, my hand, me in my hand, among the mysterious forces that breathe us the movement of life, that is how, starting with these Leader Price pads [...] I travel in sentence fragments all the sacred and insignificant moments of my story.

It is the movement of the hand on the paper, the unimpeded link between hand and paper, that enables the author to follow writing's *"course"* as it propels her through life's enigmas. Cixous's preference for handwriting means that unlike many word-processed texts every trace of the writing – from first impulse through to the final manuscript complete with its corrections – remains, except for material Cixous deliberately chooses to discard[2]. The existence of these notes and drafts provides a wealth of information about the process of composition.

Cixous also uses the A4-size Leader Price notepads on which she writes her fictions to record thoughts, ideas, conversations, descriptions of scenes, dreams, which may themselves become gateways or ingredients in a text. Sheets are often torn from a notepad and stored in a folder with the relevant project, so that typically a manuscript will be accompanied by many loose sheets of paper. Some of these notes will have been written before the fiction was started, others during the creation of the fiction. I was intrigued when I first began looking through Cixous's notes to discover that in addition to the plain A4 Leader Price pages there were many other sizes and types of paper – loose sheets, as well as those bound in notebooks. When I asked about this Cixous replied that she always has a notebook with her, to record as quickly as possible a word or a phrase or a conversation or a scene which strikes her, before the immediacy and truth of the moment is lost or veiled over by a lapse of time[3]. In addition to these necessarily small, portable notebooks, Cixous uses differently sized paper or notebooks alongside the A4 format of the Leader Price notepads as she works on a text. These range from very beautiful notebooks which have been given to her as presents, to pads of post-its which she can stick in a visible place on her desk or attach directly to a sheet of the manuscript she is composing. Cixous told me that paper size is important to her, since she frequently chooses a large or small page in relation to the size of the note she wishes to make[4]. One of the many, many challenges Cixous's notebooks present to a translator is that of trying to convey the impact of these different paper sizes.

The project I am working on at present is to translate the notebook material produced before and during the writing of Cixous's fiction *Le jour où je n'étais pas là* [*The Day I Was Not There*], in order to study the relationship between the notes and the completed fiction and to understand more fully the process of composition. In an interview following the publication of *Le jour où je n'étais pas là*, Cixous suggests: *"je n'écris pas des romans, j'écris ce que j'appelle des fictions, je transpose, je transfigure du vivant, je me nourris de la chair et du sang de mon entourage"* (Cixous

2000b: 10) ["I don't write novels, I write what I call fictions, I transpose, I transfigure from the living, I nourish myself with the flesh and blood of my surroundings"]. It is this transposition and transfiguration of life into fiction that Cixous's writing notebooks elucidate.

The author's mother plays a prominent role in *Le jour où je n'étais pas là*. It is the mother who accompanies the author on the walk through the woods where she comes across the three-legged dog whose presence resonates through the text and who dissuades the author from rescuing it. It is the mother who runs the maternity clinic in Algeria which provides a backdrop for the narrative. Finally it is the mother to whom the author confides the care of her Down's syndrome baby and who is thus the source of information about the baby's life and death[5]. The mother's experiences and words comprise a significant proportion of the fiction. For example, the grandmother's plea for something to end her life which parallels the story of the "mongol" baby is recounted by the mother (Cixous 2000a: 74-80). What the notebooks reveal is that whereas some of the mother's words are almost verbatim transcripts of real-life conversations included in the text with little alteration or commentary, others are the pretext for more elaborate transpositions. There is, for instance, an account in the notebooks of the way a doctor intervened at a birth with disastrous consequences for his patient:

> *il t'a déchiré il n'a pas remarqué*
> *il a sorti le placenta tt de suite*
> *ss attendre qu'il soit sorti et il a laissé 1 morceau dedans*[6]
>
> he tore you he didn't notice
> he took the placenta out straight away
> without waiting for it to come out and he left a bit inside

This notebook passage can be linked to the fiction in various ways. Not noticing, not seeing, is an important theme of the book, as is the notion that there may be other ways of proceeding, other speeds, other understandings[7]. However, perhaps the most exact echo occurs during a sequence written in the first person in which the idea of a piece of the placenta being left inside the mother's body is woven into the author's reflection on the legacy left her by the baby[8]. Here, the notebook material serves as a stimulus for poetic exploration.

One of the problems the translator of the notebooks faces is to decide to what extent to draw on the completed fiction to determine how best to translate some of the otherwise enigmatic entries the notebooks contain. Frequently, pages give two or three lines of observation without context, as in the following example:

> *Pourquoi je rêve? Façon de se lécher?*
> *de faire sa toilette –*

> *Toilette, motif très puissant de mes rêves*
> <u>Toi</u> lettre petite toile

A literal translation of this passage might read as follows:

> Why do I dream? A way of licking oneself?
> of washing –
> Washing, very potent motif of my dreams
> <u>You</u> letter small cloth

While my literal translation is reasonably accurate, it is at best impenetrable and at worst meaningless. The way in which "*toilette*" breaks down into its constituents to suggest "*toi/lettre*" is lost in the English, as is its osmosis to "*petite toile*" where the notion of "*petite*" is already contained in the ending '*ette*'. The rendering of "*toile*" as cloth in English, though sound because of the association with washing, nevertheless fails to indicate the other meanings of "*toile*", which include, vitally, 'canvas'. A translation of Cixous's notebooks needs to be faithful to the manner of their composition and their function while keeping readers in view. Careful decisions need to be made about how much to intervene. To return to my earlier example of "*toile*", the translator must consider whether to show the progression from "*lécher*" to "*toilette*" by stressing the notion of washing and hence choosing 'cloth', or to indicate the liaison between dreams and art by using a word like 'canvas'. Then there is the option of attempting to find an equivalent strategy in English that would approximate to the play and sense of the French – perhaps by working with the notion contained in "*toilette*" of 'dressing' and linking this to 'addressing' – with all the attendant dangers of imposition and infidelity.

Yet another example of the difficulty posed by the fact that French often contains dual or multiple meanings which can be translated into English by a number of different words occurs in the phrase: "*Bien sûr que j'aurais volé*"; here "*volé*" might be translated by either 'stolen' or 'flown'. The phrase occurs on its own, with no apparent relationship to what precedes it and with nothing following it. While such problems beset any French-to-English translator, they are particularly difficult to resolve when it comes to translating Cixous's notebooks where many of the considerations that normally shape one's choice are absent. For instance, when translating a fiction the decision as to how to translate "*toile*" might be determined by how it has been translated previously or by the general context in which the word appears. In the notebooks, one is most often dealing with jottings which are not part of a larger narrative and so there are fewer guides and constraints to bring to each choice. This gives the translator of the notebooks all the privileges and problems of an exceptional freedom. It is difficult to resist the temptation to look to the fiction for clues to translate a puzzling word or phrase. The pitfall is that one is then using the fiction to legislate, when in most cases the notebook material preceded the fiction and, as has been suggested, may have been further transposed and transfigured in the writing. Yet the urge to turn to the fiction for pointers or confirmation of one's choices remains strong. Translation is frequently a scary business and the task of translating Cixous's notebooks can feel particularly so.

Le jour où je n'étais pas là is the author's endeavour to revisit the birth, life and death of her "mongol" baby named after her father, Georges. The author confesses that for some forty years she has given almost no thought to this son. He is brought back to her partly through looking at the family's records – a working title for the fiction was *Livret de famille* ['Family Record Book'] – and partly through a scene the author witnesses on the Paris metro which involves the insult "*Trisome*" (Cixous 2000a: 34). This attempt to think back over the infant's short life in Algeria, the author's own birthplace, prompts a host of reflections that include questions of attachment and exile, acceptability and difference, innocence and fault, saintliness and cruelty, intention and action, crime and pardon. These are elaborated both in relation to the child and through the events and memories that occur as the author pursues her explorations, such as the encounter with the abandoned three-legged dog, the visit to the cinema to see a film about Adolf Eichmann, her recollections of her own childhood, and her mother's responses to her probings. All are crucial to the evolution of the author's feelings about the baby. Each adds a new perspective or insight to her quest to understand. The film about Eichmann, for instance, triggers thoughts about Jewishness and the Holocaust which inform her meditations on the treatment of so-called abnormal children.

Maintaining the links between all the various strands of the text is a recurring problem for translators of Cixous's fiction. The difficulty is even more acute when translating the notebooks since there is no accompanying narrative to keep other possibilities alive. Often, a way needs to be found to express different meanings within a few lines or, sometimes, a single word. This raises the thorny quandary of footnotes. While it is physically disruptive to the act of reading to include notes in the translation of a fiction, in a closely printed body of continuous text it is nonetheless possible to find a way of hiding the numbers or symbols that signal the note. The process of reading the notebooks is different from the experience of reading the fiction as passages of extended prose are comparatively rare. In some ways, this would seem to sanction the deployment of notes, since there is no intrinsic flow to the reading. However, the very different spacing of words and lines in the notebooks from conventionally printed text means that the inclusion of numbers or symbols to indicate notes can appear even more intrusive. The problem is compounded by the fact that the notebooks include their own code of numbers and symbols. Some lines, for instance, end with a number which corresponds to the page-number of the manuscript – often added by Cixous as she goes back through the notebooks to record where she has used them.

In addition, Cixous utilizes symbols such as crosses, asterisks and arrows which would confuse a system of symbols to designate notes.

I was disconcerted when I began reading Cixous's notebooks to discover that the number '1' is used to denote *'un'* or *'une'*. At first I was disappointed to come across this gender-neutral symbol in a writer who has sought to reinstate the feminine and challenge the universality of a dominant masculinity. As I worked through the notebooks however, this absence of gender distinction started to raise interesting questions. It began to seem as if in the writing there might be a realm prior to gender, a site where the marks of gender have not yet been determined and imposed – a domain, perhaps, where gender is indeterminable: even unimposable. This is particularly poignant in those pages of the notebooks which concern the "mongol" baby.

The author's thinking back over the birth, life and death of her son in *Le jour où je n'étais pas là* leads her to reflect on the difficult but essential truths that lie at the heart of the human enigma, truths which Cixous has repeatedly suggested it is the particular ability of writing to approach. This is comically figured in *Le jour où je n'étais pas là* in a scene in which the author depicts herself fighting the book she is writing over where it should end. After a series of discussions with her mother, the author inches closer to understanding how her son died. It is a difficult process, not only because of her feelings about her child but because she is brought to re-examine her mother's role. The author realises that there is a correlation between the grandmother's request for something to end her life without being told and her own interrogations about the baby. The recognition forms the final line to a paragraph. The next lines are qualifications prompted by the book: "*'Pensai-je' dit le livre. 'Ajoute ces mots' dit le livre. 'Elle sait peut-être, et toi tu ne sais rien' dit le livre*" (Cixous 2000a: 187) ["'I was thinking' says the book. 'Add these words' says the book. 'She knows perhaps, and you know nothing' says the book"]. The intervention forces the author to admit that she would rather believe what pleased her: "*Finir dans le secret j'aurais aimé*" (*ibid.*: 187) ["To have finished in secrecy is what I would have liked"]. It is the writing that pushes her past her preferences to encounter the truth. The book is a "*non-moi*" (187) ["not-me"] which propels the author to pursue an investigation she might otherwise have curtailed.

One of the notebook pages discloses the first traces of this struggle. The page opens with:

moi je laisserais tomber
ms le livre ne veut pas

le livre = juge

me I'd let it go
but the book doesn't want to

the book = judge

The page heralds two major obstacles to translating Cixous's notebooks. As has been indicated, the notebooks are handwritten. Translating handwriting is a very different experience from translating type. There are frequently places where the words are hard to read. Here, the formation of the word "*juge*" looks as if it could be "*piege*", since the 'j' is written as a bar which might be the start of a 'p', and the second stem of the 'u' is looped so that it is possible to construe the letter as an 'i' and an 'e'. Translating Cixous's notebooks involves the sometimes difficult task of deciphering a personal hand often written at great speed with copious abbreviations. I confess that it was recourse to the fiction that resolved the issue in this case, since the following line appears shortly after the passage cited: "*On ne peut pas imaginer l'autorité d'un livre: c'est un juge*" (2000a: 188) ["One cannot imagine the authority of a book: it's a judge"].

The hurdle of decipherability includes other complications. We have all had the experience of reading a handwritten document where we are able to guess a word from its overall shape, even though we are unable to identify the individual letters. This is perhaps especially true of signatures. My father, who had to sign many papers on behalf of the company he worked for, had a signature which tailed into a mark that was frankly indistinguishable from a curved line. In the notebooks, words or lines are frequently written quickly so that some letters remain unformed, and while it is possible to construe their meaning they nevertheless retain an aura of mystery about them: an enigma which transcription and translation obliterates.

In *Le jour où je n'étais pas là*, the author explains how she records her mother's testimony: "*Tout est interprétation, traduction d'un ton de voix. [...] Il faut une minutie. À côté du récit je note chaque inflexion. L'essentiel est dans l'intonation. Selon la couleur, bonheur, malheur*" (2000a: 148) ["Everything is interpretation, translation of a tone of voice. [...] One needs to be meticulous. Beside the account I note every inflection. The essence is in the intonation. Depending on the shade, happiness, misery"]. This description, in its account of the necessity of adhering to how a thing is said, is pertinent to translating the notebooks, where the handwriting reveals so much about what is written. In the page cited above, for instance, it is clear from the formation of the letters, from the abbreviations and use of arrows and dashes to stand in for words, that it was written fast. It is impossible to convey this sense of speed, which leaps out from the handwritten page, in any typed translation. The handwriting in the notebooks conveys whether the writing came quickly, flooding out as the writer sought breathlessly to keep up with it, or, conversely, falteringly, accompanied by many crossings-out and rewritings. While translation can yield the result of the writing, it veils this disclosure of the process. There are also different styles of handwriting in the notebooks. The lines cited above are written in large, open letters, while the lines that follow are written in a much smaller, tighter hand. Looking at the page, it is as if the opening lines are a title or heading to what follows. The blank space left round the phrase "*le livre = juge*" and the size of the writing reinforces this impression: it is as if the words dominate – judge – the rest. There are crossings-out which it is impossible to render, since the scoring makes what is beneath impossible to decipher accurately. This, too, poses problems for the translator, since one must decide whether to ignore the deletion, or whether to attempt to indicate it in some way – perhaps through an intrusive note.

My own handwriting is looped and rounded. Shortly after I learned to write I changed to a school where the style taught was italic. I was extremely proud of my new accomplishment and was reluctant to change to the undecorated straightness of italics. My unwillingness was compounded by my dislike of my new teacher, who was fierce and had a tendency to shout. Inevitably, traces of this early grounding remain. I continue to love looped writing as I loved my first English teacher. Handwritings are personal, in a way typed lines are not. The fact that the notebooks are written in Cixous's own hand colours one's reading. It is easy, as one works, to feel that – like a letter – the handwritten lines are addressed to oneself alone. It is important to guard against this sense of intimacy. It means, paradoxically, that one has to work harder to keep the necessary, respectful distance. Translation is always a matter of finding a way of bringing the other into one's own language without obliterating their distinctiveness – a task that is made more complicated in the case of Cixous's notebooks by the apparently personal call of the handwriting.

There is a further aspect to Cixous's handwriting in the notebooks which causes problems. It is very difficult to decipher the punctuation. While there are places where it is clear that a full stop is intended and other places where there is evidently a dash, there are many places where it is hard to tell which is meant. The mark is somewhere between the two – as if the words require a breath which has neither the finality of a full stop nor the expansiveness of a dash. I have no comparable symbol on my keyboard. Occasionally in the notebooks, there is a slightly wavy line drawn next to a group of phrases, rather like an exaggerated parenthesis. It is impossible to know exactly how to *translate* this mark. It isn't a bracket, it isn't an asterisk. Its function seems to lie in suggesting that the lines might stand together in some way while at the same time drawing attention to them.

The shorthand can also create dilemmas. Cixous frequently abbreviates words in the notebooks. The ending '*-ment*', for example, is repeatedly designated by a single "t", '*sans*' is often written as "ss", and '*tout*' as "tt". These abbreviations can have a bearing on the effect of a passage, particularly where the use of a single or double letter echoes the make-up of surrounding words. One recurrent shorthand symbol I have found it impossible to replicate on my word-processor in my transcriptions is the abbreviation of '*même*' to an "m" topped with the circumflex accent. These are tiny points. They are nevertheless one more reducing grill the notebooks must undergo in the course of being translated.

Writing in longhand means that one can arrange words and lines on a page as one wishes. One is not bound by the conventions of a computer or even the traditions of narrative but can envisage the space creatively. Cixous's notebooks give full rein to this freedom. Unlike the draft manuscripts of Cixous's fictions, there are very few pages in the notebook material where the prose is written continuously. Most often, the sheets have a few lines followed by a gap, then more lines grouped together in clusters. Copious blank space might be left at either side of a note as well as above and beneath it. As suggested earlier, some of the words or lines on a page will be larger or formed differently to the rest. This contrasts radically with the draft manuscripts where the writing and spacing between the lines are remarkably even. On some sheets of the notebooks, words are inserted between lines, or there will be phrases written in the margins – often at angles to the original. It is relatively easy when translating the notebooks on a word-processor to insert spaces between words or groups of lines, but arranging for different type-sizes or for text to be set at angles is more complicated. It can be done, although it is hard to do accurately and the result lacks the instinctive feel of the handwritten sheets.

That these issues of the way words are written are important is highlighted in *Le jour où je n'étais pas là*. At one point in the narrative, the author describes how she notes down what her mother tells her: "*J'écoute, rivée aux mots, me demandant comment ponctuer, si je dois mettre virgule ou point ou enlever les tirets ou les blancs, comment interpréter son discours*" (Cixous 2000a: 101) ["I listen, riveted to the words, asking myself how to punctuate, if I should use a comma or a full stop or take out the dashes or the spaces, how to interpret her speech"]. As she listens to her mother, the author realises that the truth lies in the beating of an eyelid, the way her mother turns her head, as much as in what is said. Handwriting contains equally revelatory gestures, all of which are lost in the transfer to type.

One of the many points of interest in the notebooks are the frequent repetitions of words. These occur most often in records of conversations, replicating the way spoken language operates. For instance, in one passage a vet talks about his life, emphasising its high stress-levels as he ponders a colleague's suicide. Though the passage does not appear directly in *Le jour où je n'étais pas là*, the vet's narrative of a lack of concern in the medical profession and meditation on childhood illusions versus adult reality reverberates in the fictional text. The words "*vétérinaire*" and "*stress*" occur repeatedly in the passage, as the following lines demonstrate:

> *le stress, voila le mot du vétérinaire, la vérité c'est le stress, l'animal est stressé, les maitres sont stressés, de stress en stress... je suis devenu vétérinaire par vocation comme tous les vétérinaires, à quatre ans je voulais être indien et cela m'a mené droit à vétérinaire.*
>
> stress, that's the vet's word, the truth is stress, the animal is stressed, the masters are stressed, from one stress to another... I became a vet by vocation like all vets, at four I wanted to be an Indian and that led me straight to being a vet.

Cixous has suggested that one of the ways writing can enable a writer to approach the truth is by attending to the additional richnesses and strangenesses writing itself can bring. Like the "mongol" baby, writing has "*d'autres savoirs et d'autres consciences et d'autres sciences*" (Cixous 2000a: 116) ["other knowledges and other consciousnesses and other sciences"], which contribute to the writer's store[9]. For Cixous, these other knowledges are transmitted primarily through the French language, and would operate differently if she were writing in English or German. An example is the possibilities suggested by the signifying operations of language, which can indicate stresses or generate meanings the writer may not have anticipated. Such patterns are enormously problematic for the translator, even where, as here, "stress" is identical in French and English, and the English word 'vet' contains at least some of the elements of the French '*vétérinaire*'. In the first line of the passage quoted the close echo between "*vétérinaire*" and "*vérité*" is striking. The reiteration of the '*vé*' and 't' and 'r' sets up a dynamic between the two. The dynamic both equates the vet with the truth and at the same time puts the vet's truth into question: is this the truth – "*la vérité*", or simply the vet's truth – *la vérité vétérinaire, la véritérinaire*? All this is hidden in an English translation where the vet has no such relation to the truth[10].

The movement between "*né*", "*niais*" and "*nez*" in *Le jour où je n'étais pas là* provides a striking illustration of the way writing's own operations can initiate connections and insights the writer's limitations may have prevented them from seeing. In the text, the author's realisation that her newly-born ("*né*") child looks simple ("*niais*") shades through its close homophone – "*nez*" – to the memory of her mother's insistence when she was an adolescent that she should have her nose shortened in order to appear less Jewish. The link is reinforced by the fact that it is partly the baby's flat nose which gives it such a "*niais*" look. In this way, the child's disability is set in the wider context of the author's Jewishness. While such operations are vital to the text, they are frequently problematic for the translator. The following lines from the notebooks serve as an example: "*(c'est une question de nez, de nouveau nez ds la famille*" ["(it's a question of the nose, of a new nose in the family"][11]. If one opts to translate the second phrase into English as "new nose in the family", then the full force of "new-born" which chimes so strongly in the original is obscured.

Cixous has repeatedly argued that dreams are the "*moteurs puissants*" ["powerful motors"] of her writing (Cixous 2000a: 10). She keeps paper and felt pens by her bed and tries to write a dream down as soon as possible so as not to lose any of its force. If she wakes from a dream while it is still dark, she writes without turning on the light so as not to interrupt the train of the dream. This dream material frequently infiltrates and propels the fiction she is working on. When I talked to Cixous about the dream-writing, she stressed that she regarded it as both the most potent and the most true. While there are recorded dreams in many of Cixous's fictions, what the notebooks indicate is that these are rarely given verbatim but are most often used either as inspiration for a textual dream or as a source for the writing. In the notebook material for the writing of *Le jour où je n'étais pas là*, there is the record of a dream which can be seen to have a profound relation to the text. The dream begins with the author and her two "children" – "*mon nouveau bébé et ma chatte*" ["my new baby and my she-cat"]. The cat complains that the baby is scratching her – protestations which evoke the author's fears in the text that her cat will object if she brings the three-legged dog home. What is striking about this passage and the dream in general is the way the cat and the baby change places with each other. Here, it is the baby and not the cat who scratches – or so the cat insists – and the slippages between the two continue so that at points it is difficult to determine whether it is the cat or the baby that is indicated. There are also various phrases in the dream which highlight the slippage, such as "*ss cesse s'échangent*" ["continuously interchange"] and "*l'une est l'autre aussi*" ["the one is also the other"]. This exchange is clearly a precursor to the complex relation between the cat and the "mongol" baby in *Le jour où je n'étais pas là*[12]. In the notebook dream, the writer imagines taking her "children" to the airport with her. She puts the baby on a "*petite étagere*" ["small shelf"] while she tends to the luggage. This recalls the mother's account in the fiction of the niche in the cemetery containing the baby's remains, which the author comes to realise is a fabrication and not the baby's final resting place (Cixous 2000a: 180). The dream ends on a beach. The author carries the baby which still needs to be dressed in her arms. She reproaches herself for not having dressed the baby sooner and promises that as soon as she has done this she will set the baby down on the sand. The dream ends with the words "*elle doit pouvoir tenir tte seule*" ["she must be able to stand by herself"]. This is an interesting phrase, partly because the feminine "*elle*" seems to indicate the "*chatte*" rather than the (masculine gender noun) "*bébé*". It recalls the three-legged dog as well as the "mongol" child. I translated the word "*tenir*" in the phrase as "stand", a word which chimes with all the various references to disability, and particularly limping or being deprived of a leg, in the fiction. However, the dream also hinges on the fear of abandonment and so connects to this strand in *Le jour où je n'étais pas là*, from the story of the orphaned Irina, to the author's guilt, implicit in the title, at not being there for her baby.

To invoke this in my translation, the sense also present in "*tenir*" of being able to manage, to hold on, to survive, would need to be signalled. This is yet a further instance of the difficulties posed by the fact that French words frequently contain dual or multiple meanings which need to be indicated by different words in English, and points once again to the complicated relationship between the notebooks and the fiction which translation cannot ignore.

There is a final, ethical hindrance to translating Cixous's notebooks. Whereas in the fictions, the personal material has undergone transformation and has been approved by the author as ready for publication, in the notebooks there are many, many personal facts about which there is no guide – bar asking Cixous herself – as to what can be made public and what should remain private. These are delicate questions. Is it permissible for the translator of the notebooks to release the name of Cixous's own Down's syndrome baby, for example, or should this be *translated* to the name that appears in the fiction? The issue extends to all the various references to living people in the notebooks, particularly in dreams where names may act as cloaks or covers and hence have little connection to an actual person.

In a recent talk, Cixous argued that "each speaking must be located and dated"[13]. A record of a conversation or thought must be embedded in its wider context if it is to be meaningful. In the case of *Le jour où je n'étais pas là*, the truths that emerge from the author's explorations are specific and shifting. As the author notes at one point: "*cela est une question de point de vue et d'occasion*" (Cixous 2000a: 72) ["that is a question of point of view and the occasion"]. Even when facts are not in dispute, they can still be interpreted in different ways. This is perhaps most obvious in the author's reflections on the rightness of her mother's action in allowing the "mongol" baby to die. While the author comes to believe that her mother knew exactly what she was doing and consequently sees her intervention as heroic, her brother insists that their mother was not fully cognizant of the consequences. The realisation has implications for the insights that emerge from the author's reflections on her Jewishness and the Jewish genocide, the plight of the disabled and disadvantaged, and the political and social situation in Algeria. By embedding the quest for answers in her own experiences, by locating and dating her interrogations and discoveries, Cixous is able to avoid the institution of an abstract Truth divorced from its context with all its accompanying evils, and advance closer to the truths – particular, complex, fragile – that comprise the human enigma.

In the notebook description cited above of the birth in which a doctor intervened too early, tearing the vagina without noticing and forcing the placenta out too quickly, both the mother and the baby suffer. The passage continues with the following lines: "*Moi j'ai tjs dit: reculer pr mieux sauter/Il faut ralentir pr donner le tmps/au muscle, c'est le meilleur moyen/de fair des accouchts*" ["I've always said: you have to back up in order to jump higher/You have to slow down to give the muscle time, that's the best way/to give birth"]. This advice could be a maxim for translators. It is essential in all acts of translation that one notices and takes the time to notice, otherwise one risks cutting the mother-text and producing a forced and damaged result. Translation cannot be hurried: as the "*sage-femme*" ['midwife']¹⁴ wisely knows one must give the muscles time to work. As in the medical profession, errors occur when overburdened schedules mean that procedures are rushed. It is the translator's challenge to ensure that the method of delivery works with and not against those in their care. Sometimes one needs to draw back from a text and return to it afresh to see how it might best be conveyed. The translator needs to be attentive to the wishes and rhythms of the body they are tending. They must accomplish the difficult act of becoming (the) patient, while at the same time employing their skills and experience to ensure a healthy offspring. It is vital that the text is born intact. Above all, like the baby, it must emerge from its delivery into the other language: breathing, kicking, alive.

---

[1] I would like to acknowledge The Leverhulme Trust, whose award of a research fellowship has made my work on Cixous's writing notebooks possible.

[2] The evidence of Cixous's archive suggests that very little – if anything – is discarded. All Cixous's manuscripts, together with a considerable number of her writing notes, are now lodged in the Bibliothèque Nationale de France.

[3] An example are the notebooks Cixous carried with her during a visit to India, where each page is approximately 9 cm x 12 cm, which contain records of conversations, many in English, and reflections on the political, economic, social, educational and religious situation of the country as she explores it. These notebooks provided source material for the writing of Cixous's play *L'Indiade ou l'Inde de leurs rêves*.

[4] However, it should be noted that this practice is not always adhered to. For example, there are many instances of A4-size sheets having just a few words written on them.

[5] The author rejects the medically acceptable "*trisomique*" in favour of "*mongol*" (Cixous 2000a: 67). I have accordingly adopted this term here.

[6] I have endeavoured to transcribe the notebooks as accurately as possible and where Cixous does not mark an accent I have similarly left the word unmarked.

[7] For example, the theme of not seeing appears in the insistence that "*on ne peut pas tuer ce qu'on voit*" (Cixous 2000a: 120) ["one cannot kill what one sees"], a phrase which derives from reflections on the fate of battery-farmed chickens and the Jewish genocide. The belief that there are "*d'autres savoirs et d'autres consciences et d'autres sciences*" (*ibid.*: 116) ["other knowledges and other consciousnesses and other sciences"] is the lesson the "mongol" baby teaches.

[8] The passage can be found on p. 97 of *Le jour où je n'étais pas là*.

[9] The movement between the "mongol" baby and writing is a complex one in *Le jour où je n'étais pas là*, present, for instance, in the author's renunciation of writing when the "mongol" baby is born and return to writing after his death. The close correlation is also indicated in the textual language, of which the following is an example: "*Je suis toujours à sa page. Toujours sur sa mystérieuse Culture*" (Cixous 2000a: 117) ["I am always turned to his page. Always on his mysterious Culture"].

[10] A play might be attempted in English using the less common 'verity', though it would sit awkwardly with the colloquial style of these lines.

[11] There is no closing bracket to this phrase, which gives the impression that it continues.

[12] See, for example, *Le jour où je n'étais pas là*: 116, 177.
[13] The phrase is taken from a talk Cixous gave at the Jewish Book Fair in London, England, on March 3rd 2002.
[14] "*Sage-femme*" literally means 'wise-woman'.

References

Cixous, Hélène. 2000a. *Le jour où je n'étais pas là*. Paris: Galilée.
—. 2000b. 'Hélène Cixous: "La langue est le seul refuge"' in *La Quinzaine littéraire* (1 octobre): 10-11.
—. 2001. *Benjamin à Montaigne: Il ne faut pas le dire*. Paris: Galilée.

Betrayed

Verena Andermatt Conley

The author, who translated 6.000 pages from oral recordings of Cixous's seminars into English, states that, when translated, words evoke different images than in the original text, therefore causing a different kind of emotion on the reader. The translation of these seminars proved to be very difficult, because these ones are oral texts, and their transcription in written French is already a kind of translation; besides, Cixous, in her academic work, constantly refers to other writers such as Joyce, Lispector, or Kafka, so translating their texts. The translator, concludes Conley, must then try to minimize the betrayal of these multiple translations.
Key words: orality, multiple languages, affective translation, Cixous's seminars.

To write, states Hélène Cixous, is to translate emotions into words. Texts are the genesis of words, and genesis the beginnings of emotion. The author emerges from the movement of translation. Cixous holds that there is no preexistent subject that consciously sets out to write a text. Her writings are invariably texts of genesis that treat of the genesis of the text. The author is an effect of such a chiasm, a fugacious but singular figure with a tag bearing the name Hélène Cixous. She writes blindly, without any aim that would seek to prove or to validate a pre-given hypothesis. Her writing performs and reflects its own creative process, and as a result it finds and locates itself at the intersection of what she calls "her own story", the space where she is when and where she is impelled to write, and of the greater site of Western History. The latter, "his story", what is inherited from the paternity of official chronicle and what is heard in "history", an incontrovertible register of facts, is affected by "her story".

By means of a verbal economy affiliated with the art of James Joyce, born in part from her monumental dissertation on the style and form of the Irish novelist, a new inflection is given to writing that concerns the construction of the self in historical time. The inflection is drawn from the sum of forces that have destined the world to be the way it was in the time she was brought into it (in 1937) and the way she has lived it ever since, in a state of immanence. The events in her life resemble those of any and every one of our lives. These events (birth, adolescence, marriage, childbearing, discovery of writing, a drive to perform and to play in the world and to change it for the better) are tied to those that we have witnessed since the aftermath of the Second World War (holocausts, degradation of the planet, shrinkage of space and compression of time, effects of liberation from the violence of religion and ideology and its terrible return).

Historical events become the stigmata or, if an oxymoron is permitted to describe the writing, *fertile wounds* that inspire a mode of writing understood not as a transcription of an idea or the register life's dilemmas and paradoxes, but as a sustained performance. The latter is at once intransitive and ongoing. Cixous writes fiction from the points where she feels that history has marked (indeed, wounded or even scarred) her in her life. What would be painful or traumatic in the sphere of everyday existence becomes creative matter, especially in the drive to turn writing, traditionally seen as masculine and virile, an attribute of "his-story", in another, of her own. She draws on other fiction to turn the pain or poverty of individual experience into rich, dazzling and singular creations. They are crafted first and foremost from sensation, but no less from literary traditions of different nations and canons, as well as from new intensities born of the dialogue of the language of others and that of her own voice.

It almost goes without saying that her work bears strong emotional charge. Emotion, a substantive that is historically rooted not in psychology but in movement, is felt as constant passage and metamorphosis. Words given to be seen and heard on the printed page turn into new and different shapes that, once discerned in new forms, suddenly shift and turn into others, and so on. The stories and novels she writes are driven by emotion. The language she uses is ciphered. Comprised of the aftereffects of diurnal speech, inspired by the remembrance of poetry and great literature extending from Homer to modern writers, it is located between dream and waking. Her language belongs to a condition of trance, of a mystical state, born at the intersection of other writers' trances and her own. But at the same time, as the substantive indicates, its state of suspension owes to the crossings and meanders – the transgressions, transitions, transports – it makes in the duration of its creation. The result is a kind of dense and highly oneiric writing that requires its readers to abandon the frame of a mimetic or realistic tradition that would require that writing be a faithful and veracious transcription of fact.

What then, when faced with such a text, is the task of the translator? As Walter Benjamin has stated in a famous article that was appended to his own translation of Baudelaire's poetry, the translator considers words in the form of graphic figures. They are pieces of a hieroglyph that needs to be transposed into another shape, no less composite in its design, in which speech and image are melded. To translate, Benjamin reminds us, is to transpose from one language to another, to move words and also, etymologically, to betray them. The words do not resonate the same way from one language to another; they do not evoke the same images. Or as Cixous's fellow traveler Jacques Derrida argues, *se donner la mort* in French is translated as "to take one's life" in English. Yet to give or to take does not have the same valence. If, once translated, words or expressions conjure up different images, what happens to the emotion that generates the writing? For, as Cixous has said, "[m]y business is to translate our emotions into writings. First we feel. Then I write. This act of writing engenders the author. I write the genesis that occurs before the author. How does one write the genesis? Just before? I write on writing" ("Writing Blind", in 1989b: 143). Emotion emerges from the different valences obtained between feeling and the shifts and gaps among different idioms.

Since Cixous deals with words of genesis and the genesis of words, it almost goes without saying that her writings are translations of translations. She translates the movements that inaugurate perception, as did Freud, by *translating herself into* the creative state of other writers and their texts. Her reader becomes, too, a translator compelled to account for this double translation, in which the multiple cipherings of language can be seen and heard in every one of her words. If the reader of Cixous is required to *decipher* words that invoke movement and genesis of consciousness it follows that she conceives of her writing as a form of *inscription*. The text stages the labor of inscription in such a way that the reader is required to perceive the dynamics of exchange, of push and pull, of stylistic thrust, percussion, and even of oscillation and undulation in the rapport that the writer holds with the body of her writing.

The reader is required to translate herself or himself into the writer's state of being as it is evinced on the printed page. A fundamental question posed by the text concerns the degree to which translation is indeed cognition. In official Translators' Schools, students are taught to remove themselves entirely from the material they translate. Any affective relation with the material – any reflection on the logic of the choices being made – is proscribed. At the school I attended briefly at the University of Geneva I was given to memorize long lists of words in a foreign language. I felt as if I was living in a state of linguistic narcosis. I transferred into programs in literature when I understood that in an efficient sense to translate meant to be entirely detached from words and to have no affective relation with them. The overriding irony of fate has been that I have since translated several hundred pages of Hélène Cixous's seminar. From the outset of the labors I asked myself the question, would I betray myself while mechanically substituting one word with another? Would I have to remove myself entirely from the material and render the words according to the dictionary and to my technical skills? The question was answered when it became clear that I already held an affective proximity with her writings. They have *moved* me. Something in them has touched a nerve and makes me want to share her writings with other readers.

The affirmation has led to an issue of broader concern that stands at the center of this essay: if reading, writing and translating are of the same order, how can the emotion they generate be controlled enough to make sense of literature, if not of translation as a mode of cognition? To read Hélène Cixous's texts is a form of affective translation, but what does that effectively mean? I translate the affective charge I receive from reading, a kind of *punctum* as Roland Barthes had put in *Camera lucida*, his posthumous essay on photography, into words. I read her texts the way Cixous herself reads Clarice Lispector, Ingeborg Bachmann or Thomas Bernhard in order to produce a reading or writing of my own. That writing is already a transposition and a translation at the intersection of her own writings with my affective being, which leads to the genesis of my own writing. Cast in this way, the process of reading-as-writing is by its very nature a performance. It is also a form of betrayal. I do no render the original as original. I inflect it with the movement of my own emotion, with the stigmata on my flesh and the words that I have learned and crafted in the course of my life.

To translate or render someone else's text from one language into another denies the freedom of relating with inner emotion. Yet, in the case of a writer like Cixous, translating presupposes a kind of empathy or *Einfühlung* nourished by that relation. To translate such a written text successfully, there needs to be a proximity of thinking with the writer. Without it, affective and poetic texts such as Cixous's cannot be translated. This empathy does not mean that the translator identifies with the writer or sacrifices himself or herself to her. Rather, the text that is destined to be translated must touch a nerve in the translator if it is to be translated with the wit and invention it requires. If not, the text will be mechanically rendered, with help of the dictionary, the school grammar, or the lists of words and their correct equivalents similar to what I was asked to assimilate and to master at the Translators' School in Geneva. Extreme proficiency will not render any of the stigmata or the *puncta* of the text.

Of course, the question can be asked, whose affect? That of the writer or the translator? And what if the translator mistakes her own affect for that of the writer? The text in translation will never be the same and cannot be as the primary text. The latter is, therefore, always betrayed for the simple reason that it has been pulled across a distance, *traduit, traductum*, both a transposition, an affective conduct but also a betrayal. That betrayal can be at the level of expression or affect. Jacques Derrida who, like Cixous, writes in densely ciphered prose, anticipates these betrayals when he punctuates his writings with the question: "How will they translate this?" The philosopher argues that a single date, a single event in an "author's" existence undoes any attempt at generalizing or at rendering him in "*fiches lexicales*" [lexical notecards]. A singularity like that of a creative writer's work, is never reducible to a generalization and is always, de facto, untranslatable. He or she is so not only on account of the difficulty of vocabulary or expression but also because of the ciphered language and the many secrets to which the translator will always remain blind.

Yet if I invoked the affect of the writer, I also mentioned that of the translator. The latter too translates blind. She (or he) translates at the level of the genesis of words and writings. However, the translator has to be more like the good psychoanalyst who listens carefully (even if distractedly) to the words of the analysand and senses the inflections, silences, instances and emphases. The words and their spacings are taken with empathy but at a real remove. The art of translating Hélène Cixous is not different from that of the psychoanalyst who is required to listen closely and be aware of his or her own affective reactions (and fantasies that come in response) to what is being said. It is a difficult task of the kind that no computer or product of a professional translator's school can readily achieve. Given the density of Cixous's prose and her psychic mobility, any translation cannot fail to be a betrayal. Yet different from a reading of or writing on (or with) Hélène Cixous, the translator, in addition to the linguistic and poetic skills required of her, has to have a sense of empathy and be able to efface herself *within* the words of the translation or *between* those of the original and those of her own idiom. Unlike the writer or the poet, she cannot let herself be carried off in rhetorical flourishes. She cannot write in trance but needs both to enter the text and identify with its form and content; but also, no less, to withdraw and think through the many linguistic and poetic challenges the original poses for each and every reader.

My own experience of translating Hélène Cixous was no doubt unique. Translating Cixous's seminars, I dealt with oral texts that had been recorded and transcribed into writing. Cixous's oral prose had elements of writing in speech. Having attended her seminars, I could hear the inflection of the voice when reading the short prose sentences. As a writer, her speech has a poetic density and estranging effects that are difficult to ascribe in English with the same resonance at the same points of articulation in the French original. A major problem consisted in the rendering of the ubiquitous '*il y a*' (French) and '*es gibt*' (German). The most logical English rendering, 'there is' (on first sight an utter banality) bears no trace of the element of giving and of unfolding heard in the formulas studied in the seminars. Similarly, the absence of adequate punctuation – what Cixous calls these delicate tattoos, so important for her – made it difficult to get a sense of the rhythm or the *breathing* of the text. As translator, it forced me to reconstruct the rhythm of the text and, as a result, to do violence to the text. The transcriptions of these oral seminars were already a kind of translation.

Cixous's readings and writings of Blanchot, Joyce, Kafka, Kleist, Lispector, Tsvetaeva and others, were the effects of events in her own life and in history. Over time, her readings change and so do her relations with the works with which she had shared many affiliations. Similarly, not only as a reader but even as translator, I cannot remove myself entirely from my own history (hardly the mystery of a 'my story') or my own geography. I will be closer to some readings at certain moments. Cixous's readings of other writings will speak to me more urgently at a particular juncture in time and space. They may, of course, speak to me for all the wrong reasons. My reading can be a translation and betrayal before any official translation. With the latter, I might betray Cixous's text even further. At the same time, if I remove myself from the translation and give myself over entirely to the primary text, I will betray myself and be unaware of how I have effaced myself in obedience to her.

To sum up: the art of translating a text like Cixous's, a text that is already based on multiple personal and professional translations of other texts from Joyce, Lispector to Kafka and Thomas Bernhard, entails going beyond a simple academic exercise in stylistics or transposition of words. In order to translate Cixous I need empathy. I need to feel the affect in her writing, become aware of its rhythms and different speeds, even before I deal with the difficulty of rendering a French word or an expression in English.

The task of the translator is to minimize the betrayal of oneself and of the text while opening oneself to the ductility of language and the mobility of words that move from one idiom to the other.

References

Barthes, Roland. 1980. *La chambre claire*. Paris: Cahiers du cinéma.
Benjamin, Walter. 1969. *Illuminations*. New York, NY: Schocken.
Cixous, Hélène. 1976. *The Exile of James Joyce* (tr. Sally Purcell). New York, NY: David Lewis.
—. 1989a. *Readings with Clarice Lispector* (ed. and tr. Verena A. Conley). Minneapolis, MN: University of Minnesota Press.
—. 1989b. *Stigmata* (tr. Eric Prenowitz). London and New York, NY: Routledge.
—. 1991. *Readings: The Poetics of Blanchot, Joyce, Kafka, Lispector, Tsvetaeva*, Verena Andermatt Conley (ed. and trans.). Minneapolis, MN: University of Minnesota Press.
—. 2001. *Portrait de Jacques Derrida en Jeune Saint Juif*. Paris: Galilée.
Derrida, Jacques. 1999. *Donner la mort*. Paris: Galilée.
Derrida, Jacques and Geoffrey Bennington. 1991. *Jacques Derrida*. Paris: Seuil.

PART II: Translating 'as if Other', or Translation in Difference

Nearly Reading Hélène Cixous: the "Equivocal Vocation" of Translation

Eric Prenowitz

Translation is "a doubly performative and thus a doubly violent gesture": it stresses "the absence of the original", and also "constitutes the reader" of the new text, and constitution always implies some violence. But this violence is also a "hospitality", in Derrida's sense. This article focuses on *Portrait de Jacques Derrida en Jeune Saint Juif*, where Cixous demonstrates that Derrida's thought is inseparable from its linguistic expression in French, consequently defying translation into any other language. Finally, some examples from Cixous's writing are read as a manifestation of this "resistance to the unavoidable translation" which characterizes her work.
Key words: reading, truth, Derrida, violence, hospitality, resistance to translation.

> *attention, vous verrez ce que vous verrez, vous lirez ce que vous lirez.* (J. Derrida, "H. C. pour la vie, c'est à dire...")
>
> *Mais qu'est-ce que ça veut dire, lire?* (Hélène Cixous, *OR*)

Letters travel, of course. The letter's voyage is the very trope of translation, its favorite figure. And to change places, it goes without saying that the letter itself must remain, immutable. However this is precisely what makes it forever defy translation. The text of a letter can only travel but the letter of a text will never translate. This apparently insoluble paradox, where the tractable and the intractable are conjugated in every *tractate,* is perhaps the simplest form of what I would hope to get across here. Surely a letter can always not arrive at (its) destination. But where does this take the translator?

"H. C. pour la vie, c'est à dire...", Jacques Derrida's major text on "Hélène Cixous", can be read as a treatise on translation. The "equivocal vocation" of Cixous's texts, Derrida says, "calls for a translation that it forever defies" (Derrida 2000: 21). But why should the problematic of translation so haunt Derrida here when he seems, at least, to be writing about Hélène Cixous in "her" language?[1] Why does *reading* Hélène Cixous seem in and of itself to entail "translating Hélène Cixous"?

Derrida's title already suggests that what is at issue is indeed translation: "*c'est à dire*", which we might wish to translate as 'in other words', is itself a paraphrase or a periphrase if not a metaphrase for translation. And so this title, which would thus be rendered "*H. C. pour la vie,* in other words...", seems to be proposing to translate the "nearly untranslatable" phrase "*H. C. pour la vie*". Yet there is ellipsis *in the place* of the announced translation. Where does this little trail of dots lead? Will Derrida, in the end, have translated or will he not have translated "*H. C. pour la vie*"? The question is all the more pressing in that the expression "*c'est à dire*" also signifies, according to another equally necessary translation, 'it is yet to be said'. As if Derrida, in reading "Hélène Cixous", were calling for a translation forever still-to-come. Because if the singularity of Hélène Cixous's texts lies in their radical resistance to a translation that they simultaneously demand, Jacques Derrida also reminds us that "translation always and only translates the untranslatable" (2000: 17).

I'll first read a brief passage from *OR, les lettres de mon père.*

First, I shall read, let us first read. Such might be the *mot d'ordre* of a paradoxical tract on translation. Where the *ordre* of this watchword or rallying call would say at once the imperative command and the temporal or spatial organization. First, in the first place, to read. But is it possible to read *first,* without any a priori? Without any order, out of order, without obeying any order? Are we not always already reading – and read – *before* any beginning? This is one of the great questions of *OR,* a book all about reading and not reading. And in fact one of *OR*'s premises or lessons, perhaps its very condition of possibility, is that not reading is not the polar opposite of reading. To translate this comment into more explicitly philosophical terms – as an example, insofar as Hélène Cixous's texts are continually begging the question of their own philosophical translation – I would propose a series of inferential remarks. 1) There is no simple truth to a text, insofar as the textuality of a text is not an objective *thing* visible to the seeing eye; it can never be made fully present to consciousness. 2) Therefore reading cannot be a hermeneutic process of uncovering a content inherent to the text, of revealing and thereby presenting what is in any case present in it. 3) Yet rather than serving as an alibi for the relativist renunciation of any reading decision – how can I choose one interpretation over others if there are no objective criteria for measuring how close the interpretation comes to discovering such a content? – this is precisely what makes the irreducible mark of reading possible. That reading should not be in its most essential movement a process of measurement, of objective, computational evaluation, is a necessary precondition for it to be invested – as process – with any moral or political urgency.

The "letters" named in the book's subtitle (literally, in a word to word translation among others, *The letters of my father*) are no doubt those of the title, O, R, and of the father's name, Georges, but they are also a series of letters written by a fiancé to his fiancée. The couple would later marry, and their first child would become the narrator-author of this book. So the letters in question are love letters, and one might even say that they are what make this rather unlikely marriage, and all that would ensue, including the book in question, possible. Thenceforth genealogy and authorship cannot be disentangled. Furthermore, the marriage of Georges Cixous, a Sephardic Algerian Jew of Spanish descent and Eve Klein, an Ashkenazi German Jew, depended not only on the letter-writers and their letters (though only his survive, it would appear), but also, for instance, on the French postal system linking North Africa and the *Métropole*, and thus on all of European colonial history, etc.

Elsewhere, Derrida describes this genealogy, "in the oeuvre of Hélène Cixous", as being "miraculously unique" (1996: 113). In this case, at least, descent has everything to do with language: "This great-French-Sephardic-Jewish-from-Algeria-writer who reinvents, among others, her father's language, *her* French language ["*sa* **langue française**"], an unheard-of ["*inouïe*"] French language, it must be recalled that she is *also* a German-Ashkenazi-Jew by the 'mother tongue'" (*ibid.*: 113-114). She reinvents a language that she also inherits, transforming it into an *unheard* language, that is, a language which cannot have been inherited. Even the possessive adjective "*sa*", which accords with the object, hesitates here: is it *his* language or *hers*? So while Hélène Cixous is no doubt the 'product' of certain events and above all certain *letters* which inscribed her text-body *before* she was there to add or drop a line, at the same contratemporal time, as we will read, she is *herself* the author of her own authoring.

The letters – and particularly the writing or the sending of the letters – thereby constitute a sort of primal scene before the primal scene, an *Ur-urszene,* so to speak. And this scene will have an unruly effect of indissemination. Decades later, long after the letter-writer's death, and long after the letters have been forgotten by their apparent addressee, they "arrive" again – but this time at the narrator-author-daughter's house. This is the *event* that will induce the birth of *OR*. Will the narrator receive the letters? Will she read them? What does it mean to arrive, to receive or to read? The stakes in this real postal fiction could not be higher, as the book opens onto a logical abyss. On the one hand, the very existence of the narrator-author, and indeed of her offspring *OR*, depends on the (past) success of the letters as part of the courting process which would lead to the primal scene, the daughter's conception, etc. And yet on the other hand the letters' journey is still under way, the succession is still in progress, and so to receive the letters, to read the letters, and thus to put an end to their peregrinations, might imperil the very history of what had already arrived or happened: the conception, the birth, the untimely death, the writer, the writing – at least as it takes place, *literally* for the first time, in *OR*. What is more, it might imperil the future itself, the narrator-author's future, whose dead father is in dire jeopardy, threatened by the arrival of a new father, the "true" father and author of the still-unread letters. And might thereby imperil the future of literature insofar as each of Hélène Cixous's books, up to and including *OR* at least, can be seen to have been inspired by this *dead one,* that is, this dead and returning father, or by this *death,* the untimely death of this beloved father. So the unexpected, seemingly extemporaneous return or arrival of the father with "the letters of my father" constitutes an unprecedented threat to Hélène Cixous's oeuvre and writing career, past, present and future. It is in the ambiguous space opened by this threat – the father both there and not there, the letters both read and not read – that the book *takes place.*

However before actually reading, a note, and a quasi-confession of something that cannot simply be forgiven: writing in English about translation, about "Translating Hélène Cixous", thus about translating from French to English, I have left a certain number of French passages evidently *untranslated.* Now to avoid translation would no doubt mean to avoid a certain violence. Indeed, translation is a doubly performative and thus a doubly violent gesture. On the one hand, a translation intervenes in the target language-world, necessarily altering it through the intrusion of the readable text the translation must be. This intervention is perhaps all the more disturbing due to its abyssal uncanniness: if a text is never simply present, a translation redoubles this effect of present absence, in that the absence of the original text is itself made present by the translation. Before it translates even a single letter, a translation spells the absence of the original. On the other hand, the translation, by opening the possibility of a reading of the foreign text, constitutes the reader as such, and this implies the performative violence proper to any constitution. And yet for its double violence, translation is of course also a double scene of hospitality: welcoming a text into a foreign language-world, and welcoming readers into a foreign text.

Such a double scene of hospitality, literally speaking, takes place at a certain moment in *OR,* "20 May 1995, toward the end of the morning", to be precise, and yet this moment, like the place, will turn out to be double. The narrator is in her office with the box of as-yet-unread letters – or so it seems.

> At this moment (20 May 1995, end of the morning) I feel totally foreigned [*étrangée*]. The strange thing is that I "see" that he is with me in my office here in this city he never visited – I am not saying that "I see him" – but I am saying that in truth he is here. [...] But I am with him over there in his room 53 rue Philippe second floor May 1935 where I would enter later on to live when I was little, I am therefore in my own

> simultaneity, [...] the rooms are simultaneous in one I enter before my birth in the other I receive my father when he is no longer here. (Cixous 1997: 80-81)

Like a translation, the letters go both ways: they bring the other (person, time, place) to "me", and they transport "me" to the other. The word "foreigned" here ("I feel totally foreigned") is a translation of the neologism, "*étrangée*". Although this word cannot be found in any French dictionary and is certainly a hapax, appearing here for the first time, it is nonetheless *recognizable* as an adjectival past participle of the feminine gender based on a non-existent French verb, '*étranger*'. As a masculine noun (meaning 'foreigner') and a masculine adjective (meaning 'foreign'), '*étranger*' is a familiar word, as is the adjective '*étrange*' ['strange' or 'foreign'], such that this phantom verb, a sort of reverse back-formation from '*étrange*', could only mean 'to foreign' or 'to strange'[2]. Thus the non-existent verb almost exists, it seems as if it must exist, it could well exist, and once it has been created, it's clear that it always virtually did exist. Such that the word 'neologism' is not quite appropriate to name what happens here with "*étrangée*" if we wanted to create a new word we might call it a quasi-neologism. Or the familiarly unheard-of product of some generative lexicology. It has a spectral, uncanny status (the canonical French translation of *unheimlich* is indeed '*inquiétante étrangeté*') that effects in the text the duplicity of the scene of translation in which it figures.

The letters go both ways, as I was saying, bringing the other to *me*, and *me* to the other. This strangeness or foreignness, the foreigner of the self, the foreigning of the self that this "simultaneity" and its double scene of hospitality implies, will not be resolved, domesticated, appropriated in this book. We never know if the letters will have been read; they remain *strange*, as they must, when the last page has been turned. The father is only "with" his daughter, through the letters, in the foreign form of the unread letters. As if the letters themselves serve in this book like a foreign text that the narrator carefully avoids translating – so as to guard their foreignness, to maintain them in their unappropriable foreign form.

Of course, in the face of this translational duplicity, one could argue that there is no reason why a text *about* translation should necessarily *do* translation. Is it not possible that a discourse *on* translation could itself remain entirely within the bounds of one particular language? Or that, in discussing this process of crossing linguistic bounds, such a discourse should adopt a trans-lingual stance, a meta-linguistic position from which both languages would be perceived in a common light *and yet, simultaneously*, each would be read in its own terms? From this lofty point of view the order of seeing and the order of reading would not be mutually exclusive. The bi-lingualness of such a discourse on translation, and its own non-recourse to translation would be only a logical consequence of the very condition of possibility of translation: in its traditional acceptation, translation presupposes a meta-lingual plane of discourse. After all if translation is to translate anything at all, anything at all after all, that *thing* must surely remain, as it is translated, the same thing. For all its purported migrancy, for all its unbridled investment in the *trans,* there is something terribly stationary about translation. In its most essential movement, translation must be wholly given over to the cause of a stubborn unbudging sameness. And it is this objective sameness, the imperious cause of this *thing,* that would take root beyond the reach of language, at least beyond *any one* language, and would therefore make itself available as such, unveiled, to the seeing and unblinking eye. So the unflinching resistance to translation that takes hold at the heart of Hélène Cixous's texts does not represent a linguistic solipsism, a cause for the reinforcement of impermeable borders (national, cultural, intellectual...). On the contrary. It is the only movement possible. It is precisely what, in the language, cannot be appropriated by the language. Cixous's untranslatable idiom inhabits the French language, and yet it defies and overwhelms the French language, outpacing it, escaping from its grasp, *within* the French language.

In other words, if there is no meta-linguistic plane, translation must pervade all language: there is no simple inside to (a) language but always a system of multiple and relative insides and outsides such that all discourse must grapple in an essential way with intra-lingual translation. But also because such a transcendental discourse would itself have to be grounded outside of language, outside of any particular language and therefore out of language – whereas language must be the very element of discourse. Language can only be read: it can only be looked at *through* language. And this is what makes translation so impossible. At best one can hope to leap back and forth from one to the other, but there is never an assured neutral or common ground. And this must also be true about writing *on* translation: where translation is at issue it must also be at work.

In his ever recommencing and seemingly endless lecture, "H. C. pour la vie, c'est à dire..,", Jacques Derrida begins by reading.
Or rather, he begins *to* read.
But before reading, he tells the story of the first time he ever "read" a text by Hélène Cixous: "I read the manuscript of what would be called *Le Prénom de Dieu,* her first book which did not yet have a name" (Derrida 2000: 18). But what he read there, or the reading he did of it, seems above all to have problematized (the) reading itself.

> I asked myself already what was happening here [*ce qui arrivait là*], the landing in full flight or the take-off lights ablaze of an unheard-of language [*une parole inouïe*], the appearance of a non-identifiable letter and literary object. What is this? I asked

myself more or less. What is happening here? What is happening to me? What genre? Who could ever read this? Me? (Derrida 2000: 18)

In the course of this account of his inaugural inquiry, of these first questions he asks himself in the face of the text as if he were giving voice to the text itself, in this first undecidable (non)reading, Derrida repeatedly has recourse to insoluble aporias of self-contradiction: how can one hear a "*parole inouïe*"? how can one identify something as "non-identifiable"? how can one produce a reading of a text that would show the text read to be effectively unreadable?

Of course Jacques Derrida does not simply affirm that Hélène Cixous's texts are unreadable. In the first place, it is a conversation with himself that he recounts here, and at each of its articulations (the "what" and the "who") the interrogation is turned back upon the interrogator as if the question of the unrecognizable or the unreadable could never be universalized, as if it necessarily hinged on a particular reader and reading. And while reading and seeing must be mutually exclusive[3], it is impossible to trace a line once and for all between reading and its other: there must always be non-reading in any reading, and vice versa.

In the second place, Derrida suspends the question, leaving it forever unanswered. But he even suspends the questioning of the question itself, which takes a perfectly undecidable, perfectly untranslatable idiomatic form: "*Qui pourra jamais lire ça?*" In this sentence, the adverb "*jamais*" flips back and forth before our incredulous eyes between a positive and a negative construction: Who will ever be able to read this? But also: Who will never be able to read this, Who will ever be able to avoid reading this? Such irresistible resistance to reading that inhabits the very process of reading forms one of the recurrent leitmotifs of Derrida's text: when he speaks of Cixous's oeuvre which "I read as I breathe, which I read and forget and *oublis* all the time" (Derrida 2000: 30), or of "recognition *as* avoidance, avoidance *in* recognition (which is happening again here, in the end)" (*ibid.*: 107), or the "resistance from the inside," of "those who do not read her, even if they declare themselves to be her allies or friends in all fields (political, academic, editorial, theatrical)" (124)[4].

So here too, the stakes are high when Jacques Derrida begins at last to read Hélène Cixous – for the first time: "So I shall read her, but while trembling, having never read her aloud in public" (20)[5]. And once again, the translation betrays the text: this declarative clause, "*Je la lis*", is in the present indicative, literally 'I read her' or 'I am reading her', and can only take on a future value by virtue of its contextual situation. So even here, in what seems to be the most insignificant of compositional formulas, the reading is both present and yet to come, accomplished and deferred.

And in fact Derrida rapidly interrupts this first citation pronounced or performed aloud – read –, precisely in order to propose a reading, or perhaps a non-reading, in the form of an attempt at translation. The quote is taken from the very last page of *OR:* "*Maintenant je suis seule avec mes proches morts*" (Cixous 1997: 199). The narrator is in her office. She had just opened one of the letters, at long last, to be swept away by the first sentence, when the door opens and her mother's head interrupts. The very living mother wants her daughter to go shopping with her. But the daughter declines and the mother exits as she entered, "*toujours actuelle*". Now the daughter is 'alone', or rather, 'alone with', on the other side of life in the gregarious solitude of her office. The book is about to slip away, in just a few lines.

This is where Derrida begins to read, to do a reading: "'*Mes proches morts', on ne saura jamais si ce sont les siens ou les siennes, ses proches* dead ones *ou* deaths: *intraduisible*" (Derrida 2000: 20). Jacques Derrida's text is in French and he is citing Hélène Cixous in French: a citation from the French in French in a French text. And yet this first comment has to do with translation: the phrase is "untranslatable", Derrida says in sum. Why is Derrida's very first act of *close reading,* in this text on "Hélène Cixous", concerned with translation? And if the untranslatable is, as he says much further on, "readable unreadable" ("*lisible illisible*", *ibid.*: 135), why does Derrida begin reading by making a comment on reading, on the impossible possibility or the possible impossibility of reading? And above all why does Derrida, himself, *break into translation* here? Why does he translate, why does translation seem impossible to resist even, and perhaps especially, where the bottom line is that translation is impossible?

Derrida interrupts this citation of a French text in French to propose a reading or the beginning of a reading, to point out a linguistic play, a certain work of and on the signifier that takes place in the sentence by Hélène Cixous he has cited: "*morts*" in this construction can be either a masculine or a feminine noun, meaning either 'dead ones' or 'deaths'. It is precisely because one word in French says two things, or rather because two things are said in French with one word, that recourse to the foreign language can help to isolate in a particularly economical fashion what is singularly French in this French construction. As if Derrida were suggesting that in its most solitary singularities a language can only return to itself, can only belong to itself, can only belong to the self that it may long to be, *by way* of another language. As if there were a silent translation whispering in the ear of every idiomatic insularity. As if without the possibility of the impossible translation the language itself would be unable to speak.

The two possible readings Derrida proposes of the noun, the two meanings, the two signifieds for the signifier '*morts*', suggest two distinct directions for translation: 'Now I am alone with my near dead ones' or 'Now I am alone with my near deaths'. Derrida gives two translations and then concludes that the word or phrase in question is "untranslatable". As if, at least in this case, untranslatability resulted not from a lack but from an excess of translations. There *are* translations, hence there *is* no translation. As if 'no translation' meant 'no one translation': when there are more than one there is none. As if the very question of translation were weighing in the balance of this strange arithmetic whereby one and one add up to zero. To put it another way, insofar as translation is a process of reproduction, recreating a text in another language, it is a jealous reproducer: itself a double, a translation will not suffer to be doubled. This is translation's impossible dream: to constitute the original's *unique double* in a given language. And yet this implacable law of numbers is itself a problem of translation – of the word 'translation', of what this word signifies. If the phrase "*mes proches morts*" is "untranslatable" according to Jacques Derrida, this is not because any one of its meanings by itself defies translation. Rather, it is because no translation could translate the equivocal, multi-vocal role of the one French word "*morts*" as it is taken up in Cixous's sentence.

We could describe this situation in formal terms by saying that "translation" is itself more-than-one and in particular polysemous, having at least three different meanings: 1. when translation translates a meaning (for example when "*morts*" is translated as "dead ones"); 2. when it translates a word's economy or role (what does not happen for example when the idiomatically economical multi-vocalness of "*morts*" is *not* translated even though each of its meanings can be translated – or what does happen, at least as far as the semantics of these three different meanings are concerned, when 'translation' is translated into French as "*traduction*"); 3. when translation translates a text: what I called the impossible dream of translation whereby semantic multiplicity and idiomatic thrift (as well as phonetic resonances, etymological links...) would be taken over without compromise into the target language.

This is an example, of course, in one, two, three parts. An example of the analytical work "translation" might seem to require of its translator: breaking the text up or breaking it down into its component parts. Whatever else it may involve, translation invariably comprises an analytical phase in which the text is meticulously dissected – in the hopes that the parts, if not the whole, can be smuggled across the linguistic border. And even though there is no intact undissected original whole: here, for example, in reading and in order to read the phrase "*mes proches morts*", Derrida immediately separates out two meanings of "*morts*". In fact, insofar as a translation generally implies a choice in such a situation, insofar as a translator of *OR* might well translate this "*morts*" either as "dead ones" *or* as "deaths", we can say that the translation itself is (or will have been) more intact, perhaps more *original*, than the original. But Derrida does not choose. Indeed his *point* here, the singular point of his comment and his reading, is that there is no (one) translation of the passage in question. And to demonstrate this point all he has to do is show that it can take more than one translation. Derrida translates, he writes "dead ones" in English and "deaths", only to show that translation is impossible. He does not attempt to evaluate the relative felicity of "dead ones" and "deaths" as translations of "*morts*" in this sentence, he does not calculate and he does not choose.

Derrida refuses to decide. He translates two meanings to show that the idiomatic economy of the text is untranslatable. And yet through this non-decision he intervenes, he makes a choice, and he leaves something out. In other words he reads, which is to say he writes, he signs, he signs "something else" (*ibid.*: 127) even as he "countersigns" what he is reading.

Because there is a third possible interpretation of the word "*morts*" in this sentence: not as a noun, either masculine or feminine, but as an adjective. In this case, "*proches*" would be the noun, meaning 'close ones' or 'near' as in 'near and dear'. The sentence in question would then translate more or less as follows: 'Now I am alone with my dead near-and-dear', or perhaps 'with my near ones who are dead'. One might even be tempted to see this translation, and thus this reading decision, as having a certain privilege over the others. For several reasons.

1. Because the syntax of this construction, with the noun preceding the adjective, corresponds to the French grammatical norm. Inversion of a noun phrase is of course possible, but at the very least the *normal* gloss of the sentence ('Now I am alone with my near ones who are dead') is as plausible as the others.

2. We could argue that this nominal use of '*proche*', and particularly in the plural, "*proches*", and especially in a possessive construction, "*mes proches*", is itself near to the heart of Cixous's writing. The nearness in question, the nearness that defines these "*proches*" as such, is of the order of what Derrida might call a paleonym: a proximity that deconstructs the opposition between near and far. Generally speaking, the "*proches*" in Cixous's texts are *others,* other than *myself,* sometimes very distant in temporal, geographic, cultural terms, sometimes very distant in literary, linguistic or syntactical terms (although what is the textual status of the otherness of an other *within* a text?), but who are vitally important to the self, to the narrator, to the writing '*je*'. And to the writing, to the writing of the *je* who writes. The *proches* are *Dedans,* of course, but this *inside,* not unlike the self itself, is marked by internal divisions, oppositions, contradictions. They form a sort of family around the writing '*je*' formed of her elected authors, texts and relations, dead or living (father, mother, brother, "sister", "friend"...).

3. In fact, these "*proches morts*" recall some other "*proches*" who or which are also "*morts*", at the other end of the book in question, *OR, les lettres de mon père*. The sentence Derrida cites to begin with is taken, as I

said, from the very last page of the book. The narrator is finally alone with the letters, "*les lettres*" of the subtitle ('the letters of/from my father') and which are literally named in the following sentence ("*J'avais toujours pensé que je finirais par ne pas lire ces lettres*": "I had always thought I would end up/finish by not reading those letters" (Cixous 1997: 199)). And yet we close the book without knowing if she will read them – or if she has read them – as Derrida himself notes:

> she says in an undecidable tense, that she had thought she would end up/finish by not reading them, that she will end up/finish by not reading them, without letting us know if, *in the end,* she will have read them. (Derrida 2000: 20)

I have hesitated in translating the expression *finir par* because this ambiguity is vital to these *last* moments of *OR*. On the one hand this is a comment about the book-writing process and how the book will end, as if the narrator-author were saying: "While writing the book I always thought I would finish the book by not reading the letters", or "with a non-reading of the letters". In this case the non-reading would in some sense constitute the book's ending. But on the other hand, this is the voice of a narrator and perhaps of the book itself who will not necessarily be finished with the end of the book, but will continue beyond its material limit, and end up reading or not reading the letters outside of the contingent space of the book that has been given to us to read. And indeed the book "ends" with an *unending*. It closes and it marks its close, its closing if not its closure, it comes to a halt, unless on the contrary this is the very envoy of a new beginning, on the last in the linear sequence of its pages, with a reading to come, a resolution, a promise to read: "I will read them tomorrow, I said/say, out loud. I promise" ["*Je les lirai demain, dis-je, à haute voix. C'est promis*", Cixous 1997: 199). Here, in fact, the tense of the verb *dire* is perfectly undecidable: '*je dis*' can be either in the present or the past (*passé simple*) tense. We cannot know if she is saying this in the present of the narration, such that the speaking narrator knows no more than we do about tomorrow, about what will happen tomorrow, whether tomorrow will happen at all, and whether the letters will be read or not, tomorrow, or if this is the narration of a past promise, in which case the letters may already have been read – without our ever knowing.

The hypothesis I am entertaining is that the word "*proches*" in the first sentence of Hélène Cixous cited by Jacques Derrida in "H. C. pour la vie, c'est à dire..." might best be read, or at least translated, as a noun. And that these "*proches*" correspond to the "letters". Of course, once again, the "*lettres*" in the book's subtitle can be read as referring not just to letters that travel in envelopes from letterbox to letterbox, but also letters of the alphabet, the letters of the title, for example, or the father's name, or perhaps also to literature, the father's literature, the father in or as literature, the father retained, transformed or hidden in the letters of his daughter's literature. The subtitle no doubt also announces, with the plural definite article *"les"*, the father's *'lait'* ['milk'] and *'legs'* ['legacy, inheritance'] as well as *'l'être'* ['the being'] – the letters being, or not, what's left of the father. But if one were obliged to seize upon a single one of these *"lettres"* for the purposes of a translation or reading, the most obvious choice would no doubt be the letters written and sent by the narrator's past-and-future father to her past-and-future mother, and which letters show up again, decades later, etc.

The entire book takes place in the ambiguous *"contretemps"* of this sending and receiving, in the endless deferral of reading but also in the reading that has already begun before the beginning. Indeed, although on this "last" page, the letters are still to be read, the book is also, already, engaged in a process of reading them. The content of the letters – whether it is real or fictional, and here the difference between the real and the fictive is more tenuous than ever – takes on great narrative importance towards the middle of the book[6]. However, the fact that the reading of the letters has, in a certain sense, always already begun in no way negates the enormity of the event of their arrival and of the pending choice to read them or not. On the contrary.

Now this messianistic opening at the "end" of the book recalls a similar reading-to-come at the beginning of the book. This is the first line on the first page: "I am going to reread *The Gambler* I thought once again" [*"Je vais relire* Le Joueur *pensai-je encore une fois"* (Cixous 1997: 11)]. *The Gambler,* of course, is a book. And thus the book *OR* opens with an extended meditation or reflection on books, memory and (re)reading, on reading before reading, reading with/out reading, and the double reading-of-the-reader, culminating with the neologism *"oublire"*, which combines the words *'oublier'* ['to forget'] and *'lire'* ['to read']: "To reread, in other words to read, in other words to resuscitate-efface, in other words *oublire"* (*ibid.*: 16). The letters have not yet resurfaced, but this passage is all about letters. And a family of books are its only characters:

> That is why I love books.
> Because they go and come die and resuscitate here in my room, in my office, day and night. Because they are faithful like my father who is a returning spirit I can count on I believe. A row of dead ones who breathe again/still already. My delicate outsized near ones. (*ibid.*: 12)

In French, the last two sentences of this citation read as follows: *"Un rang de morts qui respirent encore déjà. Mes proches délicats démesurés"*. Here, the word *"morts"* is unambiguously a noun; in theory it could be translated either as 'dead ones' or as 'deaths'. Yet it is clear from the context that these books, which "go and come die and resuscitate", are above all dead ones like the narrator's father. This of course corresponds to one of the translations proposed by Derrida for the "untranslatable" locution from the last page of

OR, "mes proches morts". But in the case of the *"proches délicats démesurés"*, while *"délicats"* and *"démesurés"* can in theory function as nouns rather than adjectives, they are much less likely to than *"morts"*. In other words, according to this passage from the beginning of *OR,* the books are dead ones, but they are also near ones. The important distinction would therefore be between the near ones and the others, not between the living and the dead. From this perspective, the *"proches morts"* of the end of the book would in the first place be near ones – who happen to be dead.

The difference between the noun and the adjective, between "deaths" or "dead ones" that are "close" and "close ones" that are "dead", may appear to be insignificant. What's more, Derrida never proposes to constitute an exhaustive catalogue of possible translations. Nonetheless, this exclusion, erasure or repression is a symptomatic reading decision that can only be overdetermined in the context of the lecture or essay in which it takes place. "At the beginning, before even beginning [...] we know we'll always have to begin again", Derrida says on the first page, "I will only recall a series of possible beginnings today" (2000: 13). And they all have to do, in one way or another, with the end. Because Derrida's text, his reading insofar as it is one, starts in the middle of an exchange in which it thereby participates, even while attempting to account for or describe it. *Mise en abyme* of a "virtually endless", "singular dispute" (*ibid.*: 14) that pits Jacques Derrida and Hélène Cixous the one against the other. Both of them, right up against each other. It turns on death, its temporality, its place "in" life. For Cixous, whose writing "begins" in many ways with the untimely death of her father, death would be at the origin, what sets life-writing in motion; for Derrida, the ultimate eschatologist, death would orient life as its impossible end. "We die at the end, too quickly", he reminds her, and yet she "believes nothing of it" (*ibid.*: 13-14).

Perhaps, at the end of *OR,* the narrator does find herself alone with her dead ones or with her deaths. Only language speaks, after all. But if the near ones are overlooked – if they're overread – if they are lost in the translation of this "untranslatable" phrase, and if this *near reading* which is not simply a close reading leaves a certain border intact between the living and the dead, no doubt it's in the name of another, paradoxical, proximity.

---

[1] Whose language is it? Introducing Hélène Cixous for the Welleck Library Lectures at the University of California, Irvine in 1990, Jacques Derrida presented her as "the greatest writer in what I will call my language, the French language if you like" (Cixous 1993: front cover). However, in *Le monolinguisme de l'autre,* one of Derrida's voices affirms: "I only have one language, it is not my own" (1996: 13). The question of translation necessarily turns on the paradoxical *properties,* if not the proprieties, of language.

[2] *Etrangée* might have been translated 'stranged', which would have the advantage of agreeing

with what is translated in the following sentence as "strange" ("*Chose étrange*").
³ See Derrida 1994: 95-96.
⁴ In "Fourmi", a *lecture* that formed part of a dialogue with Cixous at a 1990 conference entitled *Lectures de la différence sexuelle*, Derrida had already said something similar: "I have read her as if in a dream for the past twenty-five years, forgetting and keeping everything as if it should not be, in truth should never have been, able to leave me" (1994: 97).
⁵ Once again, Derrida rebegins anew: hadn't he already "read her aloud in public" at the *Lectures de la différence sexuelle* conference in 1990?
⁶ For example: "*Tu vois mes mots mes fautes mes lapsus ma mauvaise langue mon grand nez, je n'écris pas bien je suis le premier à le dire. Est-ce que tu m'aimes?*" (Cixous 1997: 74-75). Perhaps that is Kafka's hand, or Freud's if not Stendhal's, but what difference does that make? Especially when it has H. C. written all over it. Certainly there is more than one hand stirring the pot, but we're already in the "letters": in the *inexplicable* narrative structure of the text it is *also* the father of the subtitle who is writing here, this is *also* one of "my father's letters".

References

Cixous, Hélène. 1993. *Three Steps on the Ladder of Writing* (tr. Sarah Cornell and Susan Sellers). New York, NY: Columbia University Press.
—. 1997. *OR. Les lettres de mon père*. Paris: des femmes.
—. 1999. *Osnabrück*. Paris: des femmes.
Derrida, Jacques. 1994. "Fourmi" in Mara Negrón (ed.) *Lectures de la différence sexuelle*. Paris: des femmes. 69-102.
—. 1996. *Le monolinguisme de l'autre*. Paris: Galilée.
—. 2000. 'H.C. pour la vie, c'est à dire...' in Mireille Calle-Gruber (ed.) *Hélène Cixous croisées d'une oeuvre*. Paris: Galilée. 13-140.

La coupe des mots.
Notes on the Italian Translation of *OR les lettres de mon père*

Monica Fiorini

OR Les lettres de mon père, translated by the author into Italian, is a book entirely concerned with translation: the narrator asks herself how to read or *translate* the father's letters to the mother so as to "translate" his being. After analysing some cases of difficult translations, Fiorini maintains that in order to be faithful to the original, the translation should respect the "performativity" of it as a unique event, and not try to give a word for word version. This leads to the ethical dimension of translating, an experience which has to do with our relation to the Other, and to difference.
Key words: performativity, ethics, alterity, *OR Les lettres de mon père*.

The work of Hélène Cixous, in particular the poetic texts she calls fictions, have not taken off yet in Italy. The translation of *OR les lettres de mon père* (Cixous 1997) – as yet unpublished – is the first Italian translation of a literary text by the author. Indeed, the fact of its non-publication is significant and it enables us to understand the resistance in the editorial world towards a work and a line of thought that cannot overlook the idiom in which they are written and that are characterised by a latent multilingualism and an extreme pluridiscoursivity. Cixous's *fictions*, like her shorter, and often better-known texts, belong to different genres, and question the very legitimacy of the names that can be given to the author's different writings. Are they tales? Essays? Dramas, articles, lectures? None of them answers easily, or simply, to the criteria of the classification *box* in which one tries to put them. This is one of the reasons for the lack of translations. The question is complex and requires careful examination (not only in relation to the Italian context), because it is related to the nature of literary, academic and cultural institutions that bear upon the way in which a translation is done and on its mediating role between languages and different cultural contexts. For me, despite the difficulty, it is important to begin to translate *fictions*, as a contribution also to an activation (in another language) of a practice of writing that works on language – and between languages –, and in which critical, theoretical and poetic reflections are inseparable.

The translation of *OR*, of which I shall speak in the following pages, represented for me the first attempt of an approach of this kind which is now followed by another, namely the translation of the following book entitled *Osnabrück* (Cixous 1999; It. tr. 2001). Both translations show, I believe, their difficulty and their weakness, just where they come up against the more unreadable and the more untranslatable passages of Cixous's writing, those that indicate the only possible way for a reading and a translation deserving of this name (Derrida 1994). The translation is a response to an appeal by the text and a particular form of reading and writing. One could read this assertion in the more traditional sense in that it is first of all interpretation and so, somehow looks for the meaning of the text. If, on the one hand, it is always about this (search for meanings and directions of reading) too, for me translation has been a way to get closer to the literalness, to the particular form of orality, and to the rhythm of Cixous's writing. It has become a specific practice of reading her literalness and her 'letters', understood simultaneously, as will be seen, in the sense of the 'message' and of the 'trace'. It is not a question of thinking of a cast, nor of an impossible reproduction of this literality, but of listening to how the language works and how it is capable of inspiring the greatest changes through the smallest signs. It is also a question of listening to the variations of punctuation that indicate the intervals and breath of writing. For this reason, in both translated texts I have tried to maintain as far as possible this breath, not cutting-up phrases arbitrarily and not adding full-stops when this would have broken up the rhythm too much, as one can be forced to do when trying to bring out a clearer sense. Rather, it was a question of preserving the 'obscurity' of the original, its multi-voiced nature, where the French language is forced and transformed through an interplay of the syntactic, phonetic and graphic ambivalence, in an operation that is always dangerous. The editorial market usually expects not only an easily context readable text, but also a translation that is as clear as possible.

Cixous's writing resists translation as it does reading. Not by chance does *OR* open with a scene of continual re-reading, and one of its central themes is exactly the reading and the operation of writing that dislocates and replaces the question: "what does reading mean?" (Cixous 1997: 46). Furthermore the text contains many sub-texts and its language is never a single language. How then can one avoid, as much as possible, reducing the force of its linguistic and poetic research? And also: how can one try to translate a plural language, more than one language in one? This is, without a doubt, too broad and generalised a question but one implicit in every translation.

> *Dans ma langue ce sont les langues "étrangères" qui sont mes sources, mes émois. "Étrangères": musique en moi de l'ailleurs; précieux avertissement: n'oublie pas*

> *que tout n'est pas ici, réjouis-toi de n'être qu'une parcelle, une graine de hasard, il n'y a pas de centre du monde, lève-toi, vois l'innombrable, écoute l'intraduisible* (Cixous 1986: 31)
>
> In my tongue the "foreign" languages are my sources, my agitations. "Foreign": the music in me from elsewhere; precious warning: don't forget that all is not here, rejoice in being only a particle, a seed of chance, there is no centre of the world, arise, behold the innumerable, listen to the untranslatable (Cixous 1991b: 21)

With these words, in *Coming to Writing*, a work published for the first time towards the end of the seventies, Hélène Cixous speaks of this rich fabric formed by the many foreign languages (foreign languages and literary languages) that continually weave through her language, attracting, touching, changing and blending. In this way, foreign languages disturb it, preventing it from taking itself for granted, preventing it from being "*propre*" and "*appropriée*" because they:

> *Empêchent "ma langue", de se prendre pour mienne; l'inquiètent et l'enchantent. Nécessité, au sein de ma langue, des jeux et migrations de mots, de lettres, de sons; mes textes ne diront jamais assez ses bienfaits: l'agitation qui ne permet pas que s'érige une loi; l'ouverture qui laisse s'épancher l'infini* (Cixous 1986: 31)
>
> Prevent "my language" from taking itself for my own; worry it and enchant it. Necessity, in the bosom of my language, for games and migrations of words, of letters, of sounds; my texts will never adequately tell its boons; the agitation that will not allow any law to impose itself; the opening that lets infinity pour out (Cixous 1991b: 21)

One could say that it is for just this characteristic of Hélène Cixous's writing that a reading of one of her texts highlights, with particular force, an ethical dimension fundamental in the experience of translation. In her work the translation, the passage between, and of, languages is seen as a meeting and a relationship with the foreigner and the foreign that must try to respect their difference and their novelty. That brings to mind the words of Antoine Berman who connected to the interlinguistic passage a whole series of other passages concerning the act of writing and still more subliminally, living and dying (Berman 1985: 21)[1].

Continual reading and continual translation are at the centre of Hélène Cixous's poetic work. Each word reverberates and refracts many meanings like in a prism (one of the images in *Coming to Writing*). Such an explicit multiplicity must warn whoever is reading or translating. Her words demand a fine ear so that the musicality of the language is not silenced. It is often this musicality that breaks the boundaries and the rules of grammar, together with the rich fabric of references. One could say that Hélène Cixous feels herself a guest in language. She does not *master* the writing and her proceeding often accompanies the words, repeating them, and allowing transformations, due to the movement of a letter, a homophone or a change of tone, to occur among them in the passage, by contamination. Every repetition-transformation of this type alters the sense or the possible senses, and sometimes gives rise to new terms, albeit rooted in the French lexical structure, whose refraction invests the textual fabric in its whole, giving rise to an implicit and constant deconstruction and indecidability that one cannot translate without running the risk of an essential loss. Also the spatial organisation of the text on the page of the book is used to modulate it and to create pauses and resumptions as well as changes in speed (*cf.* Calle-Gruber 1996) through an alternation of short paragraphs and of long sections divided by larger or smaller blank spaces. This aspect must not be forgotten, not even when much of the musicality of the individual words, linked to the assonance and alliteration, become transformed in Italian, so that the particular movement of the body of the text in its entirety is not lost completely. In this way, one can try to save the text from the violence of translation in the same moment in which one creates another body for it. For Hélène Cixous, "the blind violence of translation" (Cixous 1991b: 22-23) is not in fact translation, but rather the act that in translating tries to possess the other language, a very different act from that which instead begins with a journey into the foreign language through the translator's own language: "*Si tu ne possèdes pas une langue tu peux être possédée par elle: Fais que la langue te reste étrangère. Aime-la comme ta prochaine*" (Cixous 1986: 32) ["If you do not possess a language, you can be possessed by it: let the tongue remain foreign to you. Love it like your fellow creature" (Cixous, 1991b: 23)].

As a translator, it is *my* language – as well as the language of the text – that the quoted phrase invites me, then, not to possess and to maintain as foreign. This does not mean that the Cixousian text puts the translator in an impossible position of a completely unpayable due (inevitable, and, as in the case of any text-in-translation, reciprocal). Rather, the text of Hélène Cixous, untranslatable in its idiom and for this still more *translatable* (in the sense first of all that it needs a continual translation, a continual invention) offers great freedom, which is much harder to absorb. Betsy Wing speaks of this freedom in the preface to her translation of *The Book of Promethea* where she observes, speaking of all Hélène Cixous's texts: "the freedoms they offer a reader or a translator result from the demands they make" (Wing 1991). One could say that it is always a question of a freedom proportional to the effort of active participation needed, and to the risks they make you run because they are texts that open a meeting-place between "idioms". But if the meeting is always dangerous, the translation can be a way:

> *[pour] me risquer à dire ce que je ne suis pas encore en mesure d'assurer par mes propres soins. De me pousser au-delà de mes limites, de m'obliger à m'avancer où je n'ai pas pied, au risque de m'abîmer. Façon de m'engager à payer le prix. Je ne sais*

pas exactement à qui; je ne sais pas comment me dépouiller assez. (Cixous, 1979: 41) [my emphasis][2]

of venturing to say that which I am not yet in a position to ensure by my own care. Of pushing myself beyond my limits of making myself move ahead, where I haven't a foothold, at the risk of sinking. A way of committing myself to pay the price. I don't know exactly to whom; I don't know exactly how to peel myself down enough. (*ibid.*: 40)

1. How to Translate Letters?

In texts like *OR les lettres de mon père* the most refined calculation of writing and the incalculable are allied. The text itself, after all, is always in some way generated from an event that, as such, is unpredictable and marks the return of the writing. This structure is easily perceptible, because it also has a very evident thematic value, in the case of *OR* where the event consists of a return or a re-emergence (according to a recurrent metaphor) from the sea of memory, "*notre mer la mémoire*", of the father's letters[3]. These letters, believed lost for over thirty years, are one day consigned to the narrator by her brother who until that moment had been their silent custodian. The brother had never dared or had never wanted to receive the letters, and he had never wanted to read them. He had perhaps implicitly accepted the idea of reading as an act of profanation and consumption, of loss without trace. The father's letters are addressed to "Eva Klein", the fiancée, who was, at he time, neither the father's wife ("Ève Cixous") nor the narrator's mother. The fiancée has disappeared by now but the letters have outlived their addressee and are, then, offered in reading to the 'I' who writes, the daughter, through a sudden revolution of the clock that stops and changes gear, breaking-up linear time and has them arrive a second time at a different destination[4].

On the one hand, the narrator speaks of the struggle between the desire to read the letters or the desire to not read them for fear that they would destroy the interior figure of the father (the father that is the first "*revenant*" ['ghost'] of Cixousian writing). On the other hand, the struggle and the tension that one registers in the pages of *OR* bring out forcefully the appeal that the letters sent to the narrator, for which reading and writing are antidotes against oblivion and silence in all its forms, a form of renewal or of "*ravivement*". The word '*ravivement*' indicates the opening up of a wound that has already healed but in it reverberates the act of bringing back to life ("*vie*"); it thus assumes a fundamental value in a text in which the reading is always promised, and remains an inexhaustible act, never concluded with an appropriation of the contents of the letters. In fact, the letters are never shown as texts, and not even, in extremis, read by the narrator in the course of the text; the figure of the father is never brought together in a definite portrait by his letters and his signature. The theme of the promise is found at every level, and brings with it not only a reflection on reading and on writing, but also on memory and oblivion that is simultaneously a poetic reflection on the experience of translation and an operation of translation. In this sense, everything in *OR* is translation or can become a question of translation, although the text does not explicitly advance the theory of its working with the language. It is a requisite and impossible reading-translation of the father's letters and of the father's being[5]. This is impossible as a repetition of the identical, and its transcription, but not as an indispensable transformation. In *OR* it is certainly not the original sense of the being of the father that returns in itself but precisely the father's letters, his fleeting traces, kept from reading and translated in a writing that is memory of what is to come.

How can one then preserve the body of this writing in its loss, the body of a unique and singular event, in which meaning and literality are not discernible? To this question, one can only reply: reading and translating, in an act that tries to be faithful to the performativity of that which is called the original text – but above all, acknowledging receipt, as the narrator acknowledges receipt of the letters, and becoming the addressee of the dispatch, the book, in another language or between languages. All this naturally knowing full well that faithfulness and unfaithfulness entwine "brushing against each other unfailingly because there's only room for one" ["*en se frottant immanquablement l'une à l'autre car il n'y a de place que pour une*"] on the narrow stairs of writing and, passing, "they touch, they merge, they even embrace" ["*elles se touchent se mêlent vont jusqu'à s'embrasser*"][6].

2. The Gold of the Title

The title for Hélène Cixous is the element that arrives last, or at least that is fixed last, even if it has to find a precise form to take its place in the space conventionally assigned to it, according to book law. Every book has to obey this law, even though it is written before title and without title (*cf.* Cixous and Calle-Gruber 1994). For those who read or who translate, however, the title has already become the first element, the starting point, and the name of the book itself, responsible not only for identifying it, but also to highlight its contents and values. In the case of *OR les lettres de mon père*, one comes up against a strange name, in two parts: two letters, or two graphemes: "*O R*", followed by a few words that make up a nominal phrase, "*les lettres de mon père*", printed in smaller characters and in italics. Its structure keeps it in the air. If one interprets in fact "*OR*" as a conjunction, the title lacks something that should precede it and towards which it should mark a change or a turning point. Right from the start, it was clear that the title was a decisive element of the translation, the first element to oblige one to choose, and that could not be translated without having seen how it functioned in relation to the text as a whole disdaining its conventional function because it immediately questions its role. This title in fact, like every title, tries to give something to the reader, an interpretative key, a synthesis, a guide, but its elliptical form does not actually specify what will be the contents of the pages that follow, duly separated from it by a blank space or an empty page. The title by definition promises. One inevitably asks then what *OR les lettres de mon père* promises, if it does or does not maintain its promises, and if maintaining the promise here means offering the key of reading, fixing the contents, the so-called hidden meaning of the text, or if, rather, what it promises is to put in discussion, and disturb, just this type of expectation. It was already the reading of the first pages that raised these questions. It is the book itself, there, that promises, but always with the knowledge that the promise will not be maintained (if by this one means that a single solution will be found), and that declares:

> *je te donnerai, si tu m'écris, toutes les clés. Et moi je joue à courir après les clés. Je bondis, j'en attrape une après des courses où j'ai donné toutes mes forces. Alors le Livre se retire en souriant avec les millions d'autres clés.* (Cixous 1997: 14-15)
>
> I will give you, if you write (to) me, all the keys. And I play at running after the keys. I launch myself, I grab one after having run flat out. Then the Book withdraws smiling with millions of other keys.

To show then what course my translation of *OR les lettres de mon père* followed, I will pursue this title as a strange key, a clue, the first apparition, or the apparition off-text, in the margin, of the element that pervades it at every level. I consider this title an element that invites one to stay as close as possible to the literality, or better, the letters. I will try then to start again from the end.

OR les lettres de mon père became in Italian *OR le lettere di mio padre*, the two letters, 'O' and 'R' remained unchanged without resulting in one of their possible meanings, that would emerge if they were given the value of a word. Besides, these meanings, what, and how many, are they? As I have already said one cannot estimate or list all the ways in which 'O' (and) 'R', not only, and not principally as *words*, work in the text along various trajectories that constitute different semantic pathways. For this very reason, the title always remains in the air as regards a possible meaning and is undermined in its main position. It does not command the text even if it is not at all just an element outside its plot. At first sight, what dethrones it is in fact the apparent contents of the book where the letters intended as epistles are absent. The text is not a correspondence. The letters 'O' and 'R' moreover are not even the initials, "letters" or "monograms", of the father. The letters can be at the same time letters of the alphabet, letters in the sense of epistles and initials. But in this case, they are then ciphered initials, or coded because they are not placed at the beginning of the name, but are hidden in its centre, "*au milieu*", in the middle of the father's name, or better, in French, of the father's "*pré-nom*", Georges Cixous[7]. In Hélène Cixous's texts, from *Dedans* to *OR*, and including *Les commencements*, *Portrait du soleil*, and many others, this indispensable figure, Georges (Georg, Saint-Georges, Jeor, etc.), moves, re-enters, giving rise to a series of substitutions. It is used in the sense that it fructifies, and produces interest in the sense of "*revenue*" and "*revenance*"[8] entering into an infinite chain of textual pathways. "*OR*" is "l'OR-en-je" ["OR in I"], a different manifestation or inscription of the Cixousian "*orange*"-"*oranje*" (Cixous 1979). Another way to write the father's name, George(s): 'JE-OR-JE'.

In Italian '*ORO*' ['gold'] and '*ORA*' ['or', 'hour'] both reverberate through these two letters. '*ORO*' [Fr. *or*], precious metal and also the element of substitution par excellence, in as much as it is money, universal translator, factor of circulation, operator of exchange. '*ORA*' [Fr. '*or*'] is, instead, to be understood, first of all, as a conjunction of adversarial value, but also as the hour or the moment of passage. In both cases, it indicates a change of direction, the moment in which something happens, a sharp curve or a hairpin bend, a turning-in on itself of the phrase, a revolution, a syncope. One could say that the conjunction/disjunction '*or*' underlies Cixousian writing, as it is a writing that does not proceed linearly, but tumbling and re-starting, together conserving the separation and turning on itself to form a ring thrown to the reader (the alliance spoken of in the pages of *OR*, in Italian '*la fede*', fidelity, the promise, thematic crux's in all the book promised before by the title). But the significant '*OR*' also dwells in a vast number of words and through these appears distributed throughout the text, a text that never offers the reader the rules of its distribution, and does not set out its internal economy of dispersion or of dissemination (Derrida 1972). The duty of the translation seemed to me to be first of all to pursue it, to let it resound as much as possible, so as not to lose it. The problem, however, could be, initially, actually that of seeing it. If it was not pointed out by the title such an encrustation of '*OR*' would perhaps risk remaining imperceptible if not invisible, encoded, even if not veiled, exhibited but all the more elusive to a hurried, or simply fast reading, like that which Hélène Cixous's texts sometimes seem to demand, driven on by their internal rapidity and by the continual movement that keeps the meanings in suspense. In effect, if it was not for a page that draws the attention to '*ORO*', to '*ORA*', to the temporal value of '*OR*', and to "*Oracle*"[9] – to its being letter/s and message –, it would be more difficult to set off on the hunt for all its refractions. The passage to which I am referring is almost at the beginning of the book. "*OR*" appears three times. To underline its different value in these lines, too dense to be quoted here in full[10], I have decided to alternate '*ORO*' and '*ORA*'. The hour in temporal sense, in French '*l'heure*', it is, moreover, one of the points in which in Italian one can have a multiplication of the inscriptions of "*OR*". Multiplications which intensify still more in relation to an adverb among the most insistent in these pages: '*ora*' can also in fact translate '*maintenant*', that is 'now'.

Subsequently, I continued to follow the double thread of '*ORO/A*' trying to maintain it and to bring it out wherever possible, helped in this by the closeness of the two languages. Even if it is also important to consider the pronunciation of these two letters inside single words, the word "*mort*" ['dead'], for instance. In this case the orality of Hélène Cixous's writing, her work on musicality, clearly emerges and consequently an unexpected difficulty compared to the Italian where '*mort*' is translated '*morto*', a word that has the same root and almost the same form, but a different pronunciation which troubles the rhythm of the whole text. If it was unavoidable to lose '*OR*' in a few passages, in other parts, for the aforementioned reasons, it became more visible and more audible in Italian than in the corresponding part in the French text. An example of difficulty and loss is the translation of "*gorge*" (in Italian '*gola*'), which refers to "Georges" and resonates with it. The word '*gola*' conserves both the anatomical sense of throat and that of the narrow mountain passage, but not the alliteration that permits the almost immediate superimposition of the two French words through the pronunciation[11]. By contrast, in another page already rich with '*OR*', these letters are rather further multiplied in particular through the translation of the personal pronoun '*elles*' with the Italian '*loro*' ['they']. This choice has perhaps lessened the inscription of the feminine, but has helped me to bring out the two letters of the title. The translation, displacing the letters differently, even minimally, can in fact, like a revealer, a litmus paper, highlight a very precise way of working in which everything happens, in the meeting between different elements, among them and in the space between one and another. One of the images that best represents this kind of writing is without doubt that of the corner (understood as a meeting point and once again change of direction). But the same page dedicated to the corner also offers a splendid figuration of the position – difficult to experience – in which a translator finds herself at a dangerous turning point of a choice:

> *Le choix est un démon fidèle à mon chemin. [...] Il y a le choix. Il tombe sur nous. On ne choisit pas, on choisit ne pas, et finalement on est choisi. Mais selon moi qui suis née à l'angle de deux rues appelé les Deux Mondes, il y a l'angle où demeurer. Certes c'est un espace difficile à vivre, nerveux, étroit, l'on doit sauter d'un bord à l'autre sans arrêt. Chaque fois que tu choisis dit Eschyle tu fais le mauvais choix*

nécessairement, tu ne choisis pas ce que tu crois choisir. Il y a une surprise. (Cixous 1997: 67)

Choice is a demon faithful to my path. [...] There is choice. It falls upon us. One does not choose, one chooses not to, and in the end one is chosen. But for me who was born at the corner of two streets called the Two Worlds, there is the corner in which to stay. Certainly it's a space in which it's difficult to live, irritable, narrow, one must continually hop from one part to the other. Every time that you choose says Aeschylus you necessarily make the wrong choice, you don't choose what you believe you choose. There is a surprise.

The translation finds in the corner – in the crossing in which there is mutual exchange between the languages – the only place in which to stay, although then every choice must always be made starting from and towards the edge of the translator's language.

3. *La coupe des mots*

The title, from which I began, shows then the way in which Cixous's writing brings about the greatest of revolutions through the smallest of changes, not of one word but of one or more elements of a word, and through the dislocation and inversion in the interior of a word and between adjacent words linked in the linguistic fabric. For example the case of a word like '*OUBLIRE*'.

"*Oublire*" differs from the verb '*oublier*' ['forget'], in Italian '*dimenticare*' or '*obliare*'[12], only in the movement of two letters that change place: '*oublire*' and '*oublier*'. This strange linguistic entity that comes to light for the first time in *OR les lettres de mon père* is at the same time illegible, because there isn't an accepted intralinguistic translation for it, and legible because the French language permits it or at least the French of *OR* does with its idiomatic specificity. Another language, Italian in this case, in reality cannot offer any translation in a strict sense, any *word for word* translation and doesn't permit the working of an analogue transformation or fusion ('*oubli*' + '*lire*') capable of keeping together the oblivion and the reading, and what is called the engagement of oblivion and memory in the first page of the text. The isolated position of the phrase – placed between two ample blank spaces – gives it a particular breath inside the poetic reflection on reading or rereading that occupies all the first part of the book: "*Relire, c'est-à-dire lire, c'est-à-dire ressusciter-effacer, c'est-à-dire oublire*" (Cixous 1997: 16) ["Reread, that is read, resuscitate-cancel, neglect-read"].

The centrality of this passage is evident, but, unfortunately, it also represents one of the places in which the impossibility of translation, and hence also the loss, is more acute. One does not know how to transport it into another language except through an explanation and a comment that cuts up the 'word', trying to break it down and to spread it out and so losing the effect of multiplication or of empowerment that brings about their union in the text. The solution of using two verbs united by a hyphen is not in this sense a real one, much less a satisfactory solution, even if it tries to make use of the hyphen not just to mime a sort of oxymoronic union of oblivion (neglect) and reading, but also to maintain the repetitive rhythm of the phrase. Moreover, speaking of oxymoron in this case can refer us to many other points in the text in which the contrary words refer to each other. Mireille Calle-Gruber speaks of a widespread "*pratique de l'entre-deux*" (Calle-Gruber 1994: 24) where a word is and is not this word, and is also its contrary and its phonic double (*ibid.*: 33). What seems important to underline, in relation to this difficulty, is that in Hélène Cixous's texts it is impossible to count the number of words, recognise, isolate and number those lexical unities traditionally individuated as a whole stable in sound and sense. They are indissoluble unities – and at the same time the only one that can be dissolved in that act that Jacques Derrida defines as precisely that of translation: forsake the body to save the sense – of a sound form and of a concept. One cannot translate such a textuality according to an economy of translation that – at least implicitly – makes reference to the ideal of 'a word for a word', because in each word more words accumulate, different connotations and numberless denotations, a situation made only more evident by the frequent homonyms and homophones, let alone by graphically identical or similar terms even if belonging to a different language (for example in the case of 'remember'/"*remembrer*"). The word cannot be the measure of the text. In Hélène Cixous's poetic textual work it is always a question of cut/cuttable words, and so of the letter, or rather of letters, of which *OR* are but a privileged example. In the title, "letters" in the plural indicate also that in this textuality the word cannot be the cardinal element of the translation.

If the body of the Cixousian word is never an undecomposable body, it differs from itself, and is divided and multiplied because of the division, then the cut ("*la coupe*") does not mean a diminishing of the sense, nor the individuation of the parts that only once recomposed would go to reconstruct a fragmented but definite whole. The text articulates, spreads out, through the dissemination of its letters promised to reading and translation. In this sense one could say that a title like *OR les lettres de mon père* maintains its promise.

The work of dissemination, of '*coupure*'-'*coupe*'-'*couture*' ['sewing'], operates at both the most elementary level and at a discursive level, pervading all the text and all Cixousian works. "*La coupe des mots*" is, thus, in my opinion, an expression that also immediately alludes to '*coppa*' ['bowl', of words-letters]: container of fruit, bowl in olivewood ("*en bois d'olivier*") full of "*oranges sanguines, jaffa, bresil, orienge, occident, bananes, pommes, fraises*" (Cixous 1980: 194). The text is the bowl in which the words are gathered – words-fruits, with the skin or peeled, dismantled and reassembled, what Hélène Cixous calls in *Illa*, a book from 1980, "*Obst*", the German word for 'fruits', a term however that she also tends to translate as "*obstétrique*" or 'obstetrics' to indicate their value as the midwives of sense.

A book of the genre of *Obst* is fertilised by multiple gametes, it is a fruit that contains innumerable "read-fruits" ("*les myriades de fruits-lus*"), that is other texts, and gathers "in the act that reads without binding of a midwife" ["*dans le geste lisant sans lier d'une femme obstétricienne*"], in an operation that ties and unties incessantly. The word "*coupe*", in its indecidability and untranslatableness encapsulates some of the pathways of which I have tried, here, too briefly, to follow without being able to repeat the course of the translation, with its difficulties and its delights. Therefore "*coupe*", which means both 'cut' and 'bowl', without there being any evident etymological link between the two perfectly homophonic and homographic terms, is the epitome of both the economy and the fertility of Cixous's texts.

---

[1] For the ethical dimension of translating see also, in particular, pages 75 and 76 of the same text.

[2] The lines quoted are taken from *Vivre l'orange/To live the orange*, a bilingual text dedicated to Clarice Lispector. In *To live the orange* Hélène Cixous speaks of her translation of Lispector's "apple" (referring to the value that this fruit assumes in the Brazilian writer's texts) into "orange", her personal birth-fruit. It is a text about a metaphor for a reading-translation that is also recognised (and is "denounced", this is the exact word used by Cixous) as transformation, but that cannot be confused with a form of appropriation: it is rather a vital recognition of the need to translate and to translate oneself in the meeting with the language of the other.

[3] As soon as one tries to translate '*la mer*' [the sea] it changes gender (it becomes in fact '*il mare*'), and ceases to echo, musically, '*la mère*' [the mother], in Italian '*la madre*'. Writing '*ma(d)re*' ['*mare*'+'*madre*'] did not seem a solution. In the translation I preferred then to write simply "*il mare*" so that the reference to the fluid marine element, substance and form of time, was not lost.

[4] The expression that Hélène Cixous uses is '*tourner de l'oeil*' ("*l'horloge tourna de l'oeil*") that one could translate as 'faint'. In French it indicates blackout, a type of arrest or death. I translated it in a very literal and so at first sight disconcerting way to conserve the image of the eye – that in the text is a type of eye of time – that turns in on itself.

[5] Another very complex aspect is the articulation in the text of "*lettre*", "*lettres*" and "*l'être*" [the being].

[6] "*Certains croient à l'une d'autres croient à l'autre. Moi je crois à fidelité. C'est une question de fidélité*" ["Some believe in one, others believe in another. I believe in fidelity. It's a question of fidelity"] (Cixous 1997: 13). Cixous enumerates, in *Illa* (1980), the calm sciences, sisters of fidelity and sciences of translation: "slowness, invocation, trust, openness, attention or fidelity" ["*la lenteur, l'invocation, la confiance, l'ouverture, l'attention ou la fidélité*"].

[7] The fact itself that it is not the surname (guarantee of unity and transmission) but the first name also indicates how this paternal figure is not written in a patrilinear genealogy and does not function as a signifier that transcends the text. The substitutions or multiplications of his first name multiply the effects of the subject detracting its capital letter. The first collection of Hélène

Cixous's essays, entitled *Prénoms de personne* (1974), unites, not accidentally, "*pré-nom*" (first name) with "*personne*", that is at the same time 'person' and 'nobody'.

[8] *Revenance* is one of the more important neologisms that one comes across in *OR*. For the Italian translation I resorted to an ancient form, with the suffix *-anza*: '*ritornanza*', also used to translate, for example, "*néance*" [a kind of nothingness] with "*nullanza*" in another place.

[9] "*Comme un oracle [...] un message divin personnellement adressé: son or irresistible*" ["Like and oracle [...] a divine message personally addressed to me: its gold irresistible"] (Cixous 1997: 12).

[10] "*Mes rêves font tout à la tête de quelqu'un qui n'est pas la personne que j'étais quand je me suis couchée. Je pourrais m'énerver car malgré toute mon antique expérience j'attends toujours vaguement une réponse. Non pas que j'espère, c'est la machine humaine qui attend malgré moi. Mais une fois par un environ quand même il y a une lettre. Et cette lettre c'est l'Or même. Ou une fois tous les deux ou trois ans. Cela vaut bien la peine d'être mille nuits en souffrance pour une nouvelle pareille. Mais on doit supporter mille peines pour une chance, c'est presque impossible. Car cet Or n'a pas de date, il peut arriver d'une nuit à l'autre, on ne peut se faire une raison ni une patience [...]. Mais pour l'Or, pas de ruse possible, je veille chaque nuit je tisse une docilité des nerfs à tamiser une ténèbre après l'autre, le dieu vient mais rarement, il faut tenir à sa mesure*" (Cixous 1997: 25) [my bold]. ["My dreams do everything to the head of someone that is not the person that I was when I went to sleep. I could get nervous because despite all my former experience I am always vaguely awaiting an answer. It is not that I hope, it is the human machine that awaits despite myself. But about once a year at least one letter arrives. And this letter is *Gold* itself. Or once every two or three years. It is well worth suffering a thousand nights for such news. But one must endure a thousand sufferings for just one occasion, it's almost impossible. Because this *Hour (Gold)* has no date, it can arrive from one night to the next, it's not possible to live with it or to be patient [...]. But for *Gold*, no possible shrewdness, I stay awake every night I weave a docility of nerves to attenuate one darkness after another, the god comes but rarely, one must be up to it" [my italics].]

[11] The word '*gorge*' [*gola*] reconnects itself in the text to the persistence of the cough and the father's difficulty in respiration, but also to the phonetic organ and to the place where the voice and words pass. The narrator becomes "*gorge*" of "Georges": place of passage and so of translation in as much as she is the reader of the father's letters.

[12] The Italian verb '*obliare*' has now almost disappeared, there remains only the noun, '*oblio*'.

References

Berman, Antoine. 1999. *La traduction et la lettre ou l'auberge du lointain*. Paris: Seuil.
Calle-Gruber, Mireille. 1996. 'La vision prise de vitesse par l'écriture. À propos de *La fiancée juive* d'Hélène Cixous' in *Littérature* 103: 79-93.
Cixous, Hélène. 1973. *Portrait du soleil*. Paris: Denoël.
—. 1974. *Prénoms de personne*. Paris: Seuil.
—. 1979. *Vivre l'orange/To Live the Orange*. Paris: des femmes (bilingual) (2nd ed. 1989 in *L'heure de Clarice Lispector*. Paris: des femmes).
—. 1980. *Illa*. Paris: des femmes.
—. 1986. *La venue à l'écriture*. Paris: des femmes (1st ed. 1976).
—. 1991a, *The Book of Promethea* (tr. B. Wing). Lincoln, NB and London: University of Nebraska Press.
—. 1991b. *Coming to Writing and other Essays* (tr. S. Cornell, D. Jenson, A. Liddle, and S. Sellers). Cambridge, MA: Harvard University Press.
—. 1997. *OR les lettres de mon père*. Paris: des femmes.
—. 1998. 'La venuta alla scrittura' (tr. M. Fiorini) in *Studi di Estetica* 17: 10-53.

—. 1999. *Osnabrück*. Paris: des femmes.
—. 2001. *Osnabrück* (tr. M. Fiorini). Ferrara: Tufani.
Cixous, Hélène and Mireille Calle-Gruber. 1994. *Photos de racines*. Paris: des femmes.
—. 1997. *Rootprints* (tr. E. Prenowitz). London and New York, NY: Routledge.
Derrida, Jacques. 1972. 'La Pharmacie de Platon' in *La dissémination*. Paris: Seuil.
—. 1986. 'Titre à préciser' in *Parages*. Paris: Galilée.
—. 1994. 'Fourmis' in Negrón, Mara (ed.) *Lectures de la différence sexuelle*. Paris: des femmes. 69-102.
Stevens, Christa. 1999. *L'écriture solaire d'Hélène Cixous*. Amsterdam and New York, NY: Rodopi.
Wing, Betsy. 1991. 'A translator imaginary choice', preface to Hélène Cixous *The Book of Promethea*. Lincoln, NB and London: University of Nebraska Press.

Translation's Infinite Spiral:
Reading, Translating, Reading Cixous

Lynn K. Penrod

A good translation must always be "abusive", according to Lewis. Nevertheless, translation must always respect some norms; from her own experience as the translator of *La Fiancée juive de la tentation*, the author comments on five of these points. She also discusses the relationship between *La Fiancée juive* and Rembrandt's painting 'The Jewish Bride', because they both work with "the simultaneously visible and invisible", which is visually represented in the painting by the "reclining figure-eight" that stands for infinity. Penrod uses this figure to metaphorize the never-ending process of "reading-translating-reading" Cixous.
Key words: translation norms, painting, Rembrandt, infinity, *La Fiancée juive*.

> *La confusion des langues n'est plus une punition, le sujet accède à la jouissance par la cohabitation des langages, qui travaillent côte à côte: le texte de plaisir, c'est Babel heureuse.* [The mixture of languages is no longer a punishment, the subject attains *jouissance* through the cohabitation of languages working side by side: the text of pleasure is a happy Babel.] (Roland Barthes)

> Like all those whose vital substance is cut from the same fabric as writing, I am constantly impelled to ask myself the questions engendered by this structure which is at once single and double: questions of the ethical, politico-cultural, aesthetic, destinal value of this constitution; questions of the necessity of writing for myself and for others; of the usefulness, the strangeness of forever being here and elsewhere, ever here as elsewhere, elsewhere as here, I and the other, I as other, etc... Stretching out existence, enlivening it, troubling it, surprising it. Questions cross my horizon like herds of wild geese, "omens" according to Stephen Dedalus, but of what? (Hélène Cixous)

1. Translating Cixous: the Why if not the How

The mere juxtaposition of the words 'translation' and 'Cixous' elicits extreme anxiety and enthusiastic kaleidoscopic imaginings within me. Yet despite these genuine feelings of trepidation, in this essay, one that attempts to grapple descriptively with the intricate web of problematic joys and frustrations involved in the translation of texts by Hélène Cixous, I do hope to achieve two modest objectives: first of all, to convince my reader (if convincing be needed) that the entire process of translation is so intimately related to the process of reading itself that it has become a necessarily critical factor in any attempt at the *interpretation* of Cixous's work; and secondly, to retrace, if possible, through the use of my own translation experience (complete with its litany of trials and tribulations) the thorny path of the translation of Cixous's 1995 text, *La fiancée juive de la tentation*, a piece of work that remains, even as I write this essay, almost – but not quite – *finished*.

My objectives may seem slight, and entirely too personal perhaps, to be of any use to others, and yet my own experience of the textual world of Hélène Cixous has always been bound up in questions relating to both processes of reading and translating, particularly in the cultural conversations between *French* and *English* uncovered therein. In fact, reading and translation, translation and reading, are often so intertwined in my own work that I sometimes find where one begins and the other leaves off hard to ascertain.

Indeed the most apt figure I could imagine to illustrate the process of *readingtranslatingreading* Cixous would be the recumbent figure eight, the figure traditionally representative of infinity itself. In other words, the translational process cannot be separated from the reading process and vice versa; the process is both ongoing and never-ending and is the source for much of the textual energy of Cixous's oeuvre. Thus are translation and Cixous inevitably and indissolubly linked. And thus are questions and issues relating to the translation of Cixous's texts from *French* to other languages both urgent and timely. Every translator of Cixous would agree, I think, with Mary Lydon's apt observation in her 1995 essay on Cixous and translation:

> Let me remark parenthetically that the ambiguity of *Entre l'écriture*, hence the difficulty of rendering it adequately in English, usefully illustrates the immediacy, the urgency with which the issue of translation, or better, translatability, asserts itself whenever Cixous is the subject. This is so to a greater degree in her case than it is for any other writer associated [as in the minds of her North American readers Cixous, willy-nilly, remains] with what we have come to call "French feminisms". Indeed it may well be the unique challenge her writing issues to translation, that, more than anything, distinguishes it from the various other writing practices that have been grouped together under this rubric. (Lydon 1995: 91)

Cixous herself has pointed out (in her preface to Susan Sellers's *Hélène Cixous Reader*) that she possesses "several French languages" (xvi) and goes on to describe herself as follows:

> Sometimes I experience reading returning to "the author" I am in the following manner: according to the country of reading, according to the state of cultural dissemination in such a country, such a language, I am "known", defined or coded very differently and in a way that is to me unexpected. In France, I am mainly known through my seminars, and most especially through my theatrical works. (My plays have been performed at the *Théâtre du Soleil* before 150,000 spectators.) Now the theatre public may be totally unaware that in other spheres I am the author of things which are not theatrical. Inversely, in the USA, Canada, Japan... people are unaware that I am an author for the theatre, and I am often classed, sometimes even exclusively, in the category of theoreticians. This is how I appear on contemporary scenes as if I were a quarter of myself. Yet it is the whole that makes sense. That which cannot be met on one path, and which I cannot say in one of my languages, I seek to say through another form of expression. (Sellers, 1994: xvi)

Thus the why of translating Cixous must of necessity be bound to the urgency of making the "unknown" Cixous "known" to the other cultures and languages where currently there is but a partial acquaintance. This underlines as well the cultural dimension so intimately bound to reading and translating Cixous. We should never forget that the translator does not live in a cork-lined room nor does s/he have a compartmentalised mode of existence we might term 'translator mode'. Even though the work of translation requires us to process another's text – moving it, transporting it, often traducing it, into another language with nothing but the inadequate tools of language itself –, translators are constantly engaged in layers of process simultaneously. Especially when dealing with so-called "difficult" texts (and Cixous's texts certainly qualify as such), the translator's process quite quickly evolves into a dazzling, vertiginous succession of roles: reader-translator-writer-reader-translator-writer *ad infinitum*-roles that infinitely loop back upon themselves.

Of course the why of translating Cixous also involves us in the question of reading *between* texts – reading between the multiple French languages of Cixous and the multiple cultural divergences between her pluralized French and, in my case, English. As Rainer Nägele explains:

> What does it mean to read between the texts? In a certain sense we always read, when we read, "between" (the lines, for example), because reading always involves a space of presentation where the figures gesture to each other in configurations and constellations that present more than any single figure means. But the structure of the space between the figures, which is determined by them and determines them is shaped in more particular ways than by the mere universal differential relation of all signs" (Nägele 1997: 13)

I open here a brief digression into the question of translation theory and its relationship to Cixous and translation. It is quite clear that the why of translating Cixous constantly involves her translators in a kind of process we could term (following Jacques Derrida and Philip Lewis) "ab-usive."

Originally written in French as "Vers la traduction abusive", for a 1980 colloquium at Cerisy-la-Salle, Lewis's article was subsequently translated and published in *Difference in Translation* (a 1985 collection of essays edited by Joseph F. Graham) as "The Measure of Translation Effects". As Douglas Robinson points out, Lewis takes the notion of "abusive translation" directly from Derrida's "Le retrait de la métaphore": "*Une 'bonne' traduction doit toujours abuser*", or, as Lewis translates: "A 'good' translation must always commit abuses" or "a good translation must always play tricks" (Lewis 1985: 39-40).

Lewis is obviously aware of the pejorative force of the words "abuse" and "abusive" in English, but as Robinson reminds us, "he is at pains throughout the article to recuperate the word for translation theory through linguistic deconstruction" (Robinson 1991: 133). Lewis argues that "weak, servile translation" results from "a tendency to privilege what Derrida calls, in 'La mythologie blanche', the *us*-system, that is, the chain of values linking the *us*ual, the *us*eful, and common linguistic *us*age" (*ibid.*: 40). As Robinson says, "[t]his *us*-system informs the mainstream tradition of translation theory, reductive, assimilative, commonsensical, and as such constitutes the enemy, the internalized and bureaucratized master that Derrida and Lewis [...] resist through ab-use, a directionality away from use":

> To accredit the *us*-values is inevitably to opt for what domesticates or familiarizes a message at the expense of whatever might upset or force or abuse language and thought, might seek after the unthought of unthinkable in the unsaid or unsayable. On the other hand, the real possibility of translation – the translatability that emerges in the movement of difference as a fundamental property of languages – points to a risk to be assumed: that of the strong, forceful translation that values experimentation, tampers with usage, seeks to match the polyvalencies or plurivocities or expressive stresses of the original by producing its own. (Lewis 1985: 41)

So for Lewis an abusive translation would respect neither the source-language nor the target-language text (although random "abuse" is not what he advises, rather a "measured modulation of both the source-language text and the target language so as to bring about significant shifts in meaning, tonalizations, expectations, outcomes", in Robinson 1991: 133). For translators like Robinson (and myself) who may "feel constrained by the tyranny of the *us*-system, 'common usage', the way things are said and done, the only correct way to translate this or that the way you have to translate if you want to be published, read, understood [...] this is a powerfully attractive formulation. It liberates translators from the dual jail cells of fidelity to the source-language text and communication with the target-language reader" (*ibid.*: 134).

Robinson summarizes the sort of translation hierarchy as outlined by Lewis as follows:

> 1. at the bottom the weakest sort of translation, which seeks to restore or naturalize in the target language abusive turns in the source language, so that the target language text conforms to standard target-language usage, and becomes what Venuti (1994) calls "invisible" or "domesticated";
>
> 2. in the middle a stronger sort that seeks to reproduce in the target language the author's abuses of the source language, producing a strange or foreignized or visible text that manifestly abuses the target language but stands in a problematically complicitous relation to the source language text; and,
>
> 3. at the top the strongest and most forceful kind of translation, what we might call (with an uneasy glance over our shoulders at Derrida) abusive translation proper, which introduces its own target-language abuses into the abusive source-language text, generating a text that abuses both the source-language text and the target-language linguistic system. (Robinson 1991: 134-135)

In any translation of the work of Hélène Cixous the translator is always and ever acutely aware of the abuse (in its most violent sense) that one is committing to the source-language text. And yet one is always keenly aware of striving towards that "strongest and most forceful" level of abusive translation (in its most affirmative sense) as I believe is intended by Derrida and Lewis. Robinson goes on to question what he considers Lewis's "implicitly normative glorification of violence" (1991: 135) and to raise several other significant questions connected to "ab-usive" translation (as envisioned by Lewis – or later theorists like Lawrence Venuti):

> [W]ho is the abused? The source-language author, text, culture? The target-language reader, text, culture? [...] How is the abuse channeled? How does it hit its mark? What social and psychological effects does it have on its victims and its perpetrators?
> If, on the other hand, we believe or hope that abuse may ultimately be avoidable, do we then simply act as if it already were, as if we were already free of the normative abusive ideologies that brutalize us? Or must we enter into a difficult transformative process aimed at uncovering the sources and the channels of our own abusiveness and eradicating them? (Robinson 1991: 136-137)

I close this somewhat serendipitous parenthesis relating to the idea of translational "ab-use" and the significant yet, I think, basically unanswerable questions the concept raises simply to signal my own ongoing awareness as a translator of Cixous that such a process is constantly at work within me. As Nägele (1991: 11) reminds us, "[i]mplicitly and by necessity, theory precedes any praxis of reading, but in such a way, we hope, that the praxis of reading will displace any preconceptions, suspend or transform them".

The infinite spiral of reading and translating Hélène Cixous begins, ends, and takes place in the "in-between," in the "*entre l'écriture*". The why, if not the how, of translating Cixous involves all Cixous translators in theorizing, theorizing that is both open-ended and ongoing. Thus questions of reading and interpreting cross the horizon of the translator "like herds of wild geese" just as they do for the writer herself. The translator of Cixous is impelled, like Cixous herself, to consider "the usefulness, the strangeness of forever being here and elsewhere, ever here as elsewhere, elsewhere as here..." (Sellers 1994: xiv). And to move from the why of translating Cixous to the how of translating Cixous, we cite Nägele once again:

> There are other structures of the "between". There is the one that opens up, for example in the Jewish joke of Katzmann in Paris, who wants to hide his Jewish name in a good French name, only to find himself more Jewish than ever as *chat l'homme* (= *shalom*). In the intersection of two languages, between the German signifier "Katzmann" (= cat-man) and its literal French translation, a third language suddenly appears in the Hebrew *shalom* (Nägele 1997: 15)

How Cixous translators manage their interstitial lives is another story.

2. Translating Cixous: the How if not the Why

In "A Translator's View of Translation Norms", Alice Martin argues that while few translators would lay claim to such a thing as a "translation theory" (given that most of them are busy doing their work and can seldom take the time required to formulate even a practice-based "theory" – especially if their work seems to be acceptable to the target culture), they are nonetheless usually aware of the "norms" under which they work. Martin's "norms" should be classified, in my opinion, more properly as "working goals" for translators, given that she in no way lays claim to rule-bound prescriptive norms either for herself personally nor does she suggest them for others. Rather, however, Martin has attempted to organize the practicality of the "how" of translation practice; and in so doing her "norms" quite neatly organize and illustrate the how, if not the why, of translating Cixousian texts.

Martin describes the translator as having three "alternating and co-existing roles: reader, professional, and artist" (Martin: 1). For her the translator-reader's job is "to establish relations with the work as an ordinary human being: finding the emotional footing on which the source text and consequently the translation process stands, something that needs a little time to mature and may get overwhelmed by practical problems if not given time" (*ibid.*: 2). The translator-professional (the translator in working mode, I would say) involves that part of the translator in constant awareness of some kind of loosely organized translational "norms". (I will return to some of those suggested by Martin in my discussion of the process of translating Cixous's *La fiancée juive*.) Martin's third function, that of the translator-artist, is also, of course, extraordinarily important for anyone involved in the translation of Cixous. Even though Martin is fully aware, as a working professional translator, that like it or not, norms are always present and at play as the translator works, she also reminds us that not everything in the translation process can be accounted for by norms. "[V]alid principles are occasionally overruled by what might be named pursuit of the reader's happiness – something that could itself be called a translation norm, since a translation overlooking it is often a failure" (*ibid.*: 3-4).

Martin identifies six areas within the translation process that serve as guideposts for translators, five of which prove extremely useful when tackling the thorny issues related to translating Cixous. They are (1) understanding, (2) accuracy, reliability, loyalty: a question of equivalence?; (3) target language quality; (4) rhythm; (5) quotability; and (6) harmony between translation and illustration (*ibid.*: 5-13). In the remainder of this essay, then, I should like to take each of Martin's suggested areas (except for quotability) and discuss their applicability to some of the specific problems related to the translation of *La fiancée juive*.

2.1 Understanding

No translator would disagree with Martin when she reminds us that reading the text to be translated as an "ordinary reader" is never enough for the translator. "It is necessary to develop a professional way of reading in order to analyse the text in as much detail and depth as possible. While it is not part of a translator's job to explain the work to outsiders, let alone be as vocal about it as a literary critic might, understanding or at least not misunderstanding is vital" (Martin: 5). Understanding for Martin also covers matters of style.

> Metaphors and symbols need to be recognized: metaphors taken literally usually reveal themselves in translation. A particular form of the norm of understanding is that the translators should strive to grasp what function an element has in the [source text]: having found it out, s/he is on surer ground in seeking the corresponding element for the [target text], whether it be a twisted Shakespeare allusion of a clue to the murderer's identity. It seems worth paying relentless attention to passages which are initially puzzling, because it is often here that the traps are, and the keys as well. (*id.*)

In translating Cixous's *La Fiancée juive* one encounters numerous examples of extratextual gesturings that pose "understanding" or "knowledge" problems for the translator. Perhaps to illustrate this we could simply have a look at the very first paragraph of the text:

> *Réveille-toi, réveille-toi, il va arriver le Pauvre, vite lève-toi, mets ta force. Je sursaute. Le voilà qui passe en courant comme un fou devant moi, mille ans ne le fatiguent pas. Vite mets tes beaux vêtements! – Ne les mets surtout pas! Il n'aime pas*

> *les ornements. Ah! Je le reconnais. Courir comme un fou, en avant, en avance des années, des années. Me voilà qui court comme une folle derrière lui.* (Cixous 1995: 7)
>
> Wake up, wake up, he's coming, the Poor One. Quick, get up, put on your strength. I wake with a start. There is he, running by me like a madman. A thousand years have not tired him out. Quick now, put on your best clothes! No, don't do that, certainly not! He doesn't like adornment. Oh! I recognize him. Running like a madman, out in front, ahead of the years, the years. And here am I, running like a madwoman behind him.

Now at first glance this paragraph does not seem, in terms of "understanding" or "knowledge" at least, to be particularly "difficult". There is obviously some kind of dialogue in progress as the text begins. Someone is asleep and is being awakened in anticipation of the arrival of "*le Pauvre*". But here, of course, we encounter our first difficulty. Who is this "poor one"? A *real* person? A fictional creation? Some kind of hybrid? On my first reading of the Cixous text, I have a vague memory of Francis of Assisi wandering around in the woods doing good deeds and being thought a bit mad... Did he live in a cave for several years? Was it Francis who called the body "Brother Ass"? Francis of Assisi? Where to check this? Will I need a note? I recall this early internal "reading dialogue" here simply to illustrate what makes translating Cixous very much a concurrent process of "reading" and "interpreting".

Several hours of research (and a rather complicated foray into the world of the visual arts as I tracked down paintings of Francis of Assisi, tapestries depicting the saint, and the like) finally yielded me the small nugget of information that indeed Francis at the age of 24 (in 1205) had been given the message by the crucifix of Saint Damien that his duty would henceforth be to restore churches that had fallen into disrepair. And indeed, after breaking with his family in 1206, Francis did spend the following two years caring for lepers and repairing chapels. And finally in 1208, he received the message that he needed to devote himself to a life of poverty. Of course, Cixous's text itself also provides the reader-translator with further "understanding" when much later the narrator tells us: "*D'ici je vois très bien François courir dix ans autour d'Assise pieds nus sur les montagnes déchiquetées en attendant*" (Cixous 1995: 103) ["From here I can see very clearly Francis running along the jagged mountain paths around Assisi for ten years while he waited"].

This one tiny example, however, serves to put the translator of Cixous on notice that even in a text calling for a certain amount of "ab-usive" treatment (in every sense of the term) there remain vast areas of basic "understanding" and "knowledge" acquisition that the translator must control before the process of translation can proceed apace. To paraphrase Mary

Lydon (1995: 99): as a translator "I already knew that I would need to do a lot of reading" in order properly to translate Cixous.

A simple – and still only partial – list of other "things to check out" noted in my tattered translator's journal will perhaps give some idea of the breadth if not the depth of extratextual knowledge base required for the translation of *La fiancée juive*. Alongside St. Francis we can add the *Confessions of Saint Augustine*, Job, flower imagery (including the significance of roses, daisies, violets, begonias), Milton, Galahad, Tristan, Lancelot, the Sphinx, Satan, temptation and Temptation – in their multiple meanings –, Christopher Columbus, the Torah, the Talmud, Descartes, Venus, Freud, Shekina, Lorenzetti, Dante, St Michael, Joan of Arc, Juliet, and Rosaline – as well as a plethora of animal and insect allusions: an ant (1995: 31), a small rabbit (39), a flock of sheep (52), squirrels (63), the Great White Bull (61), a purple horse (61), Thea the cat (109, 167), a tiger (117), and turtledoves (139), to name but some. Place names and topography are significant as always (Siberia, Moscow, Assisi, Spoleto) as are other languages ("*Non si fa una cadenza, ma s'attaca subito il seguente*", writes the narrator in Italian on page 200). But of course the reason underpinning all this work on building an "understanding" data base for the translation of this text is also at the root of our competence as readers and/or interpreters of Cixous and the necessary pre- and co-requisite as translators.

2.2 Accuracy, Reliability, Loyalty: A Question of Equivalence?

No matter how translators deal with the thorny question of "equivalence", Martin reminds us that this "most problematic concept" (call it accuracy or reliability if you will) is nonetheless very much "a part of everyday translation work. It may be just here that theory and practice meet – or clash uncomfortably" (Martin: 6). As she says,

> [w]hile it is useful for a translator to question the concepts of faithfulness and loyalty (to what, to whom), to deny their importance altogether means going entirely free-range. A state of impulsiveness and ad hoc decisions hardly seems professional, though one can imagine it leading to the occasional brilliant [target language] rendering. Usually however, there is a fact of life to take into account: it is accuracy in representing the [source text] that publishers demand and the public expects – and believes it is getting – when reading published translations. (*id.*)

Here the translator of Cixous must pause to reflect yet again on the questions raised by Robinson in his discussion of Lewis's conception of ab-usive translation. How does the translation of Cixous's French languages ever succeed in conveying the palimpsestic nature of the source text? How does the translator remain "faithful" when the very substance of the reading-translating-reading process centres on that very nearly untranslatable quality of the "always-here-but-elsewhere" quality of Cixous's writing?

"That liberties can and must be taken is obvious; that liberty is all there is is harder to accept. What makes translating so exciting to me is the challenge of being free within strict limits, of making a camel go through the needle's eye and come out alive and kicking" (Martin: 7). This is a key aspect of equivalence as an objective when translating Cixous. The challenge – the fun, the pure joy, and yes, the utter and absolute frustration as well – involves the translator in a work of exploration and discovery, involves the translator in a process that is both exciting and energizing. As Cixous herself has said, "I believe that in order to read – to translate – well, we have to undertake the journey ourselves. We have to go to the country of the text and bring back the earth of which the language is made. – Everything begins with love. If we work on a text we don't love, we are automatically at the wrong distance" (Cixous 1997 [1988]: 227). Just as Martin suggests,

> [w]hat can be seen as the many limitations a translator has to work with are another facet of the various loyalties involved: loyalty to the [source text], author, to the source culture, to the [source text] itself, to the receiving community and the target culture, to the quality of the [target language], to the translator's self. All of these are important, and I would not say that being more loyal to readers means there is a need to be less so to the author. There is no *less*; there is only *more*. (Martin: 7)

Herein, of course, lies the crux of the translator's work, and this is certainly true of the translation of *La fiancée juive*. As two small examples of the kind of "equivalence" problem encountered in Cixous translation, consider the following:

Example 1: *la Penderie*

> *D'un côté une petite table de l'autre l'énorme Penderie. Et moi devant la porte. Dans mon dos le machin du diable. Et le mot aussi. Penderie c'est un mot très banal en apparence. Mais agité. D'ailleurs Penderie s'écrit parfois avec un b. Moi-même j'aurais dit armoire ou placard, c'est selon. "Penderie" c'est le Diable qui le prononce. Et il le bourre (le mot), cela saute aux yeux: les pendus, les pendules, les vêtements-qui-après-nous-vivez, les fantômes accrochés par le collet, les manteaux et menteries que plus personne ne vient réclamer. Penderie s'écrit parfois avec un m et un t. Toujours on reconnaît. Cela a la versatilité de son nom. Cela change de forme comme de pantalon. Le mot lui-même est un lieu pour les moqueries.* (Cixous 1995: 38)

> On one side there was a small table, on the other the enormous wardrobe called a *Penderie*. And me in front of the door. At my back the devil's thing. And the word, too. "*Penderie*" is in appearance a very banal word. But a restless one. Besides *Penderie* is sometimes written with a *b*. As for myself, I never use it. I would have said "armoire" or "closet", depending. "*Penderie*" is the Devil's own word. And he's cramming everything into it, it's cryingly obvious: hanged men, pendulums, the clothes-that-live-after-us, ghosts hanging by the neck, coats and untruths that no one

ever comes to reclaim. *Penderie* is written sometime with an ***m*** and a ***t***. Yet you can always recognize it. It changes its form the way you change your pants. The very word is a site of mockeries.

Our first and most obvious concern is of course with the capitalized word "*Penderie*". We begin with a simple answer: a '*penderie*' is literally a 'hanging place', a piece of furniture generally referred to as a 'wardrobe' or an '*armoire*' (words the narrator would have chosen!). There are thus "equivalents" available in English. (And the translator may perhaps sigh in agreement with the narrator who announces that the word itself is actually "banal" in appearance.) Yet quite quickly we meet the first if not the last complication. "*Penderie*", says the narrator, is sometimes written with a 'b'. Which in French would give us '*benderie*'/'*banderie*' – with the reference to the French '*bander*', itself a marvellously interesting word for Cixous in that its first meaning is either 'to bandage or to blindfold' and its second meaning is 'to strain, stretch or tense', or as a third possibility used as an intransitive verb 'to have a hard-on'. So the "*penderie*" could also be the '*banderie*' (in several senses – as soon as one realizes that the "tempter", the incubus, is also hidden within the room and that the room itself can be seen as the site of sexual temptation for the lovers). The narrator throws out various forms of the '*pendre*' root – "*les pendus*" ['the hanged men', 'the hanging clothes'], "*les pendules*" ['the clocks or the pendulums'] – and reminds us that it is the Devil who chose the word "*penderie*" in the first place.

Yet a second complication arises even before any kind of translational solution can be found for the first one ('*penderie*' → '*banderie*') when the narrator refers to a third possibility for writing "*penderie*", this time with an 'm' and a 't', which gives us now "*menterie*" and sends us running to forms of '*mentir*' ['to lie or deceive']. And the translator writes in her translation journal: "March 15: the Ides of March and *penderie, banderie, menterie* – I'll never find a way out of this!".

Indeed my first translation of this single paragraph (quite a small paragraph in a very long text!), which I have included above, is still very much 'hanging fire', as we say in English. There is always the possibility of leaving the French "*penderie*" (given that 'wardrobe' can be added in apposition) and of adding a translator's note referring to the '*banderie*' and the "*menterie*" including some of my comments from the preceding paragraph. This is not, however, an example of a felicitous solution to an equivalence problem – nor does it demonstrate any possibilities for creative ab-usive translation as described by Derrida or Lewis. The process, however, does serve to illustrate the Cixousian text's recurring demands on both its readers and its translators.

Example 2: *Appellele*

Si mon bien-aimé m'a dit je te donne mon numéro de téléphone mais surtout ne t'en sers pas car je risque de n'être pas là... sauf en cas de mourance, l'incube le sait et aussitôt il m'envoie le rayon monotone appelé Appellele. Non, dis-je. Appellele. Non. Vas-y objurgue le psittacide cuit et sans un son. Vas-y, vas-y appellele, tu sais bien que tu iras, non je ne sais pas bien nié-je. (Cixous 1995: 40)

If my beloved told me I'll give you my phone number but for heaven's sake don't use it because I might not be there... except in a case of life or death, the incubus knows this and immediately sends me the monotonous ray named Callhim. No, I say. Callhim. No. Go on exhorts the drunken psittac and without a sound. Go on, go on callhim, you know very well you're going to, no I certainly do not know, I say, denying.

This second example relating to equivalency or "fidelity" again involves a repeated expression that on the surface at least appears not to offer enormous difficulty to the translator familiar with Cixous's penchant for word play. The telephone (everywhere in Cixous) and the telephone number serve as the jumping off point for the narrator's temptation by the incubus, the monotonous flash of "*appellele*", a typical Cixousian logjamming of two words ('*appelle*' + '*le*') ['call him' (or 'call it – the number')]; but within the "*appelle*" one also sees the feminine subject pronoun '*elle*' as well as the 'apple' of temptation (an actual *gain* in terms of translation to English). Thus the surface simplicity of "callhim" shows a complex loss and gain.

These are only very rather basic examples of the kind of "normative" work involved in translation of a text by Hélène Cixous, normative work in the best sense of the word, in that the translator remains committed to a principle Cixous often reiterates in her own writing: fidelity. Yet the fidelity we look for here is never a blind or rigid adherence to some kind of grammatical or philosophical *rule* but rather "extreme fidelity" to the writing itself. Reliability in terms of some kind of base level accuracy for a Cixous text in translation is almost always within reach; it is the stretch to cover the breadth or depth of the texts' textures and multiple layerings that becomes the sticking point for the translator.

2.3 Target Language Quality

Martin identifies target language quality with the ability of the translator to be as good a writer as possible. The translator needs to use the full resources of the target language and to avoid (in my case) poor English. As Martin points out, choices of the type described here "seldom get noticed, but when consistently made and added up, they have a huge effect on the style. They often concern quite simple and recurring phenomena, so the solutions may become automatic. Finding good answers to recurring problems is of course easily worth the trouble" (Martin: 10).

Obviously one of the principal difficulties in translating Cixous into English rests on the incredible number of losses one must recognize simply because of the rich possibilities French offers for punning and word play (especially relating to gender) that are simply lacking, or at least much rarer, in English. Regarding the work of theorists of *écriture féminine* and its relationship to translation theory and practice, Luise von Flutow has eloquently expressed the role of experimental feminist writing (of which I would argue Cixous's writing is emblematic):

> Most importantly, [experimental feminist writing] has foregrounded the issue of gender in language and caused translators to respond to the resulting technical and theoretical challenges. When confronted with textures full of wordplay and fragmented syntax, translators have had to develop creative methods similar to those of the source-text writers; they have had to go beyond translation to supplement their work, making up for the differences between various patriarchal languages by employing wordplay, grammatical dislocations and syntactic subversion in other places in their texts. [...] The practical work of translating experimental feminist writing has thus politicized numerous translators. Much of the theoretical discussion on gender and translation has been initiated by women translators first faced with these texts. (Flutow 1997: 24)

The question of target language quality remains, of course, one of those highly subjective areas of translation work. A grammatical dislocation or syntactic subversion totally acceptable, indeed praiseworthy perhaps, to some readers may be deemed faulty or even fail completely to carry the source text adequately in the eyes of others. The elusive qualities of "feel" and "rightness" are always hovering in the background as the Cixous translator goes about the work of translating.

2.4 Rhythm

When we consider any kind of translation guideposts, whether in a classroom setting or in the actual work of translation, the maintenance of an "equivalent rhythm" seems to be the one most often taken for granted – and one that is at the same time difficult to pin down. For Martin,

> [r]hythm is a factor some translators consider the most important of all. It is pervasive, appearing at every rank of language, from within the word to the scope of the paragraph and even further. What is not so clear is whether the important thing is to preserve the [source text] rhythms or produce effective [target text] ones. (Martin: 10)

When translating Cixous, just as in reading Cixous, one is always keenly aware of the text's rhythm, the undulating flow of long stream-of-consciousness sentences carrying their ambiguously gendered references, often punctuated by staccato repetitions of words, sounds within words, or the echoes of words or phrases from other parts of the text, or indeed from other Cixousian texts. Here is but one example of Cixousian rhythm:

> Ces mots sont des puits de tant de mots des puits de temps de mots depuis le temps. (1995: 193)
>
> These words are the wellspring of so many words from the wells of time of words ever since the beginning of time.

The repetitions of "*puits*", "*mots*", "*temps*" – along with the "*de*" + "*puits*" and "*depuis*" doublings does not work quite as well in English as in French, but given the existence of the English "wellspring" the rhythm is maintained as well as the general sense of flow.

Although the telephone is perhaps a strange object to choose to further illustrate the quality of "rhythm" in Cixous translation, I choose it because of its graphic *look* in French – "*téléphone*" – complete with two acute accents and its visual rhythmic impact. It is a word that *stands out* on the page and is indeed a recurring motif in Cixous's fictions, where lovers are often connected – or disconnected – by means of the telephone (or "*téléfaune*", a neologism combining two Cixousian favourites, telephones and animals). Finding an equivalence then is not the problem; the challenge is rather to find ways to visually show the rhythmic punctuation of the telephone's appearance within the text. *La fiancée juive* provides, like many previous Cixous texts, ample opportunity for the translator to play with telephone imagery, and it is important (for the translator, the reader, the interpreter, the artist) to remain sensitive to the telephone's various appearances. See, for example, "*ô téléphone, ô téléphone...*" (1995: 46) ["o, telephone, o, telephone..."], "*Et tout cela au téléphone?*" (*ibid.*: 58) ["And all this on the phone?"], "*Un télégramme téléphoné*" (67) ["A telephoned telegram"], "*Ouf! J'entre dans la téléaphonie*" (87) ["Whew! I'm entering teleaphony"], "*le téléphone chinois*" (125) ["the Chinese telephone"], or "*Je crois bien reconnaître la voix du téléphone, chantant 'je t'appelle' dans toutes les langues*" (126) ["I think I can hear the telephone's voice, singing 'I'mcallingyou' in every language"].

2.5 Harmony Between Translation and Illustration

In her own translation work, Martin translates children's books containing illustrations that of course become important elements in the translation process. However, as she points out, "[e]ven when a book is not illustrated, there may be relevant pictorial material to consider" (Martin: 13). Nowhere is this idea more critical than when one is working with the texts of Hélène

Cixous. The *absent* illustration is nevertheless always *present* within the text. It is gestured to, modulated, turned upside-down, displaced, or dreamed, but in some way it must be *translated* into the target language.

Within the title of *La fiancée juive de la tentation* is the obvious reference to the famous Rembrandt painting, commonly rendered in English as "The Jewish Bride". Much critical work, of course, has been done on the interrelationship of various Cixousian texts to their *real life* counterparts in the world of the visual arts (see, for example, the work of Milena Santoro, Verena Conley, Mireille Calle-Gruber, Martine Motard-Noar, Deborah Jenson, or Kathryn Crecilius and Christian Picard). But the real problem here, of course, is that the title of Cixous's text is not simply "The Jewish Bride". (And the problematic ambiguities presented by the abyss that opens up so easily between the concept of "*fiancée*" in French and "bride" in English should certainly be noted.) Given that Cixous's "Jewish bride" is modified by "*de la tentation*", there is also the thorny question of "temptation" to be considered; thus the allusion is not simply an extratextual gesturing towards Rembrandt's painting. And yet the painting is not only critical to the reader's experience of the text but interestingly enough the painting – the "illustration" – actually mirrors in a way the very process of translation itself.

According to most art historians who have discussed "The Jewish Bride", the name of the painting refers to the "long-held view that the picture portrayed the Jewish father of a bride bidding farewell to his daughter" (Bockemühl 2000: 79). The painting is also known as "Isaac and Rebecca", thanks to the existence of a pen and bistre drawing by Rembrandt from 1655-56:

> The picture shows no external actions –not as movement. However, the posture of quiet duration involves a union in the embracing, touching gesture, a continuing activeness in the feeling of giving and receiving, in the growing awareness of a sense of togetherness. This activeness cannot contradict the quiet and static nature of the picture. Rather, quiet is the important condition here for experiencing the kind of incident revealed in this scene. (Bockemühl 2000: 79)

In a strange but intriguing way, Bockemühl's description of the Rembrandt painting resonates as well when one considers the Cixous text. Indeed, the words "a continuing activeness in the feeling of giving and receiving" could easily be applied to Cixous's writing in general.

It is also extremely interesting to note the art historian's description of the way in which the viewer of the Rembrandt painting is visually "directed". Bockemühl notes that when we view "The Jewish Bride" our gaze is controlled "not by individual lines, but rather by the broad, bright surface lengths of the couple's arms and hands" (*ibid.*: 83). We are also drawn to the bright ovals of their two faces, so much so that we may even notice a faint resistance if we try to look at some other element in the painting or to follow the "lengths" of arm and hand. Bockemühl also points out that the observer of the painting is really only able to concentrate on one face at a time, since "the forms lie too closely together for the one to be seen apart from the other" (*id.*). He describes this back-and-forth movement, the observer's gaze being attracted first to the man's face, then to the woman's, as a kind of "twinkling of an eye –in the truest sense of the word", and compares this kind of viewing to listening to a particular musical interval: "if one attempts to listen to one of the tones more clearly, then the other pervades the consciousness all the more" (*ibid.*: 84). The quality of the musical interval, according to Bockemühl, lies between the two tones; it is inaudible yet in some way audible at the same time. And the same is true of "The Jewish Bride": the relationship between the two bright ovals [of the couple's faces], perceived differentially in this way, lies in the quality of the movement between them – simultaneously visible and invisible" (*id.*).

I have taken the liberty of quoting Bockemühl at length because I find his description of "viewing" "The Jewish Bride" (obviously only one way among many possibilities) to be almost totally congruent with my own general reading habits and my own translation practice when dealing with the work of Hélène Cixous. In reading, in translating, in reading again, we are still working with the "in-between", with the space "*entre*", with the simultaneously visible and invisible, here and there, the 'both-and' concept rather than the 'either-or'. It is that sense of looking at a hologram and attempting somehow to capture the very moment of transformation between here and elsewhere, self and other, attempting to find the mystical membrane in the process of textual osmosis.

Bockemühl continues with his analysis of the portrait of Rebecca and Isaac and notes that the brightness observed in the faces of the couple are also linked to other bright forms below them on the canvas. If each face is then taken as both a starting point and an end point of what Bockemühl calls a "movement of observation, one which –seen from left to right– leads over Isaac's shoulder and arm to Rebecca's breast and the bright neckline, upwards to her head", the form inscribed by the viewer's gaze is actually that of a nearly circular form, yet a circular form that does not close above the couple's head. Rather once the gaze reaches the point above the couple's heads, it retraces its path, yet differently this time, "climbing over Rebecca's hand, thereafter gliding back down to the hands again along her right sleeve; from here, following this direction, it continues over the breast border until Isaac's right shoulder is reached, from whence the gaze flows back along the band of his cloak-fastening onto the length of his arm" (*ibid.*: 84). The direction of the viewer's gaze, following Bockemühl's intricate description, could thus be described as inscribing a "reclining figure-eight" in the air (*id.*).

Bockemühl's attention to the reclining figure eight (∞), the loop of eternity, in relation to Rembrandt's "Jewish Bride" echoes what I believe is the underlying figure for the entire process of reading and translating Hélène Cixous –the spiral of infinity itself.

Bockemühl reminds us that through Rembrandt's style of painting, the observer is assigned a constitutive role, one that causes the observer to appreciate the act of revelation instead of merely presenting him with a revealed form at which to look (*ibid.*: 90). The same constitutive role is also required of the translator of Hélène Cixous. "The process of becoming aware of life in the picture, the process of becoming aware of the act of revelation is an encounter with the productive powers of one's own observation. It is in the action of observation that the mystery of the revealed form lies to which we are led by Rembrandt's art" (*id.*).

Of course, dealing with the question of the Jewish bride (and her partner and Rembrandt's painting and its possible and multitudinous resonances within Cixous's text) is only part of the translator's task for even though the words appear in smaller letters on both the cover of the text and the book's title page, Cixous did not call her text *La fiancée juive* but rather *La fiancée juive de la tentation*. Hence, as previously mentioned, the question of temptation is also everywhere implicated within this text as well –just as the question of temptation echoes throughout the Cixousian oeuvre and just as temptation has become a signalling word for her translators. And where does one begin with questions of temptation? Of course, we return to St. Francis of Assisi –and to St. Augustine and his *Confessions*– and to the story of Eve and the apple. And on the story goes, endlessly looping back on itself.

When I began this essay I mentioned that my translation of *La fiancée juive* was "almost –but not quite– finished". Indeed my experience of the "how" of translating this text has felt very much, in a very practical sense, as if I myself have been totally caught up in the "infinite spiral" of my essay's title. Obviously at some point the translator has to say: enough is enough –and off to publication. At which time the translated text joins its colleagues and becomes part of the Cixousian oeuvre. Perhaps then for this essay, too, I should also say, enough is enough, and leave it to readers of Cixous to ponder the intricate web of reading and translating I have rather awkwardly attempted to describe in the preceding pages.

As the French are fond of saying, *en guise de conclusion* (a phrase that has always suggested to me that the writer is donning a kind of costume in order to exit the stage at last after a sometimes long and torturous textual journey), in any case, to conclude this perhaps overly personal but I hope somehow thought provoking account of my journey through reading and translating Cixous, I can only reiterate that this is a process leading inevitably to an infinite (the figure eight lying on its side, just as we saw in Rembrandt's portrait of the young couple) process of reading and translating cultures (in the plural). And to extend the metaphor of translation as the ultimate form of reader response, I simply return to the quotation from Cixous that serves as an epigraph to this essay.

The questions that "cross the horizon" of the translator of Hélène Cixous are eternal questions of "the ethical, politico-cultural, aesthetic, destinal" sort, questions relating in the most intimate way to the writing selves we intuit when we read her texts. Questions of the "usefulness, the strangeness of forever being here and elsewhere, ever here as elsewhere, elsewhere as here" are as important and vital, I would say, to the Cixous translator as they are to the writer herself. The work of translating Cixous involves the translator in the same type of never-ending process as can be found in Cixous's own writing, writing that stretches out existence, enlivens it, troubles it, surprises it. Translating Cixous is a creatively innovative and infinitely productive spiral process, one that invites its participants into the world of Hélène Cixous's writing in a most immediate way.

References

Bockemühl, Michael. 2000. *Rembrandt 1606-1669. The Mystery of the Revealed Form*. Köln: Taschen.
Cixous, Hélène. 1995. *La fiancée juive de la tentation*. Paris: des femmes.
—. 1997 [1988]. 'Conversations' in K. M. Newton (ed.) *Twentieth-Century Literary Theory: A Reader*. London: Macmillan. 225-233.
Flutow, Luise von. 1997. *Translation and Gender. Translating in the 'Era of Feminism'*. Manchester and Ottawa: Saint Jerome Publishing and University of Ottawa Press.
Lewis, Philip E. 1985. 'The Measure of Translation Effects' in Joseph F. Graham (ed.) *Difference in Translation*. Ithaca, NY: Cornell University Press. 31-62.
Lydon, Mary. 1995. 'Re-Translating no, Re-Reading no, rather: Rejoycing (with) Hélène Cixous' in Lynn Huffer (ed.) *Another Look, Another Woman, Yale French Studies* 87: 90-102.
Martin, Alice. 'A Translator's View of Translation Norms' (http://www.eng.helsinki.fi/hes/Translation/a_translator.htm).
Nägele, Rainer. 1997. *Echoes of Translation. Reading Between Texts*. Baltimore, MD and London: Johns Hopkins University Press.
Robinson, Douglas. 1991. *The Translator's Turn*. Baltimore, MD and London: Johns Hopkins University Press.
—. 1997. *What Is Translation? Centrifugal Theories, Critical Interventions*. Kent, OH: Kent State University Press.
Sellers, Susan (ed.). 1994. *The Hélène Cixous Reader*. London and New York, NY: Routledge.
—. 1996. *Hélène Cixous. Authorship, Autobiography and Love*. Cambridge: Polity Press.
Venuti, Lawrence. 1994. *The Translator's Invisibility*. London and New York, NY: Routledge.

"Without your breath on my words, there will not be any mimosa". Reflections on Translation

Sissel Lie

Translations must keep not only the meaning, but also the "rhythm" of the original. Therefore the dilemma for the translator would be between a "beautiful and unfaithful" version or a "tedious and faithful" one. The danger of the first is to "lose the memory" in the way between one language to another; the second instead obliterates the literary value of the text. The translator should not try to "master" the text but to "feel" it with her body and senses, and then create a "new literary text" close to the original one.

Key words: rhythm, faithful translation, translation as a creation, compensation, A. Berman.

Rhythm is a concept often repeated in translation theory, but oh, so difficult to define. We can hear the rhythm of the text, we can try to grasp it, it depends on our sensory apparatus and on our reason. It also depends on the words of the text, on the length of the sentences and of the paragraphs, on the time between the commas and the final stop, but also on the voice of the text, the respiration in the text. When does it stop to breathe, when does it speed up and slow down? There is a rhythm of meaning in the cadences. Rhythm comes from the Greek word for 'flow'. Hélène Cixous's texts give me a feeling of flowing. Come dance with me, her texts say, and it becomes urgent to respond with a translation capable of dancing in a corresponding rhythm[1].

Rhythm is connected to hearing and understanding, to our reason and to our subconscious, to movement and sound. All comprehension and knowledge is based on what is effectively a translation process, what we do not know becomes known and integrated through such a process. Translating as such is also a way of reading, of analysing and interpreting a text to another reader. Even though Cixous claims to be a sorceress, she says she can do nothing without the reader. With the readers, however, the words will come alive, we are all capable of sorcery. Now the translator is a very special reader, but a reader nevertheless, who puts her reading into words, creating a new text dependent on new readers. The relationship between the text and its translator is special, because it implies a greater responsibility towards the original text than that of the ordinary reader. A reader may rush through a book, never concentrating enough, never giving it the time necessary to burst into flames and flowers. When Hélène Cixous writes about the reader, however, she gives her the utmost importance, she has confidence in her, as if every reading is a new creation:

> *Je suis la sorcière maladroite de l'invisible: ma sorcellerie est impuissante à évoquer, sans le secours de ta sorcellerie. Tout ce que j'évoque dépend de toi, dépend de ta confiance, de ta foi.*
>   *Je rassemble des mots pour faire un grand feu jaune paille mais si tu n'y mets pas ta propre flamme, mon feu ne prendra pas, mes mots n'éclateront pas en étincelles jaune pâle. Mes mots resteront mots morts. Sans ton souffle sur mes mots, il n'y aura pas de mimosa.* (Cixous 1986: 175)

> I am the awkward sorceress of the invisible: my sorcery lacks power to evoke, without the help of your sorcery. Everything I evoke depends on you, depends on your confidence, on your faith.
>   I gather words to make a great straw-yellow fire but if you do not put in your own flame, my fire will not start, my words will not burst into pale yellow sparks. My words will remain dead words. Without your breath on my words, there will not be any mimosa[2].

To do justice to the richness of Cixous's poetic text, the translation needs to be a creation. Then it is not only a question of understanding rationally and transferring the understanding from the original to the translation, it is a question of creating movement, rhythms, in the new text. If I can capture the rhythm of the original text, it is possible to translate the multiple meanings without ending up with a much poorer version of the original.

1. The Impossibility of Translation

Henri Meschonnic (1999) says that translating is to translate what cannot be translated. So to translate must be impossible, but we do translate all the time. Antoine Berman (1984) shows how the untranslatable can be translatable and puts forward the idea of a complete correspondence between one language and another, this correspondence being virtual. Berman stresses that it is not a question of making the text more opaque or writing a periphrasis of the text, but of making the untranslatable translatable, which is the task of translation. Translation partakes in the discovery of the kinship between languages, he says. Translation has the techniques to create such a correspondence. Berman speaks of innovation (for example coining a new word, making new structures) – such as when I construct a new word in Norwegian for "*juifemme*" (Cixous 1986: 15) combining the two corresponding Norwegian words: '*jøde*' and '*kvinne*' into '*jødkvinne*'. Berman uses the concept of "compensation" (in the sense of finding a different expression or structure replace the untranslatable original), which is what I do when I have to find a way of transmitting an expression that does not exist in Norwegian. Compensation also makes me think of the rhythm of Norwegian phrases replacing French ones. Berman talks about "transposition": "*décalage*" (Berman 1984: 303) – placing a term or a structure somewhere else than in the original, where it is more easily accepted in the language of the translation. When I translate alliterations, I use different words than the ones I find in Cixous's text. It is not a question of making *good*, normalised Norwegian prose out of Cixous's writing, but of finding a way of making it sound as strange and poetic in Norwegian as it does in French.

But when the original text is rich in allusions, word plays and coinages, as Cixous's texts, a translation sometimes becomes a fight against the words of the new language. How do I translate Cixous's playful expressions "*Du point de vue de l'oeil d'âme. L'oeil dame*" (1986: 12)[3]? I ended up using a footnote as so many of the other translations of "La venue à l'écriture" do, because Norwegian does not have the same sounds in "*âme*" and "*dame*": '*sjel*' and '*dame*'. But even if some of the solutions are not satisfactory, the text as a whole can still transmit the inventiveness and the playfulness of the original.

When in the same text Cixous alludes to the sound of surrealist André Breton's slogan: "*Lâchez tout!*" ["Let go of everything"], saying "*Lâche-toi!*" ["Let yourself go"] (Cixous 1986: 50), I cannot possibly make the Norwegian version of the French words play with the sounds of a text that is not known in Norway, so I make another footnote. But how many footnotes can I make in a poetic text before destroying the poetry? A part of the multiple meanings will inevitably get lost. The possibility of translation is, however, always already there in the original. At times there are no perfect solutions, but solutions do exist! Sometimes a translation uses more words, a translation is expected to be about 10% longer than the original. The greatest danger, I think, is to make a poetic text didactic by explanatory expansions of the text. Deborah Jenson comments on the temptation of expanding Cixous's texts in an English version:

> The explicit presentation of a series of terms in answer to the poetic multiplicity of one term bypasses the relationship between the reader and the French text, in which several meanings may be called into action at once or allowed to lie dormant. (in Cixous 1991a: 4)

Where she does not yield to this temptation, Deborah Jenson regards this as a solution with a "one-to-one relationship of the English terms to the French [...] signposts to other possible readings" (*ibid.*). She thus decides to choose between meanings, to limit the possible connotations of the French words, to conserve what I have called the rhythm of the text.

Literary texts are ambiguous, a word has many possible meanings. How can I transmit the poetic ambiguity in Cixous's texts without giving the reader the feeling that I have not understood what it is all about? It means drawing on all possible resources. I experience the text and I analyse it. I have a rational understanding of the text, and it makes me react and understand with my senses. In this process there is no dichotomy between mind and body. The sensory associations stem from the text and are as objective as my rational explanations, and they are not just a sudden and private experience of the text.

2. Beautiful and Unfaithful, or Tedious and Faithful?

A translating of meaning alone in Cixous's texts would be, of course, ridiculous, their poetic form being part of the meaning. Translated texts, however, may concentrate on the meaning, while the way they are formulated disappears. If we are bent only on retelling the content of a text, the result will not be a literary text, says Henri Meschonnic (1999), but information about the content of the original. He refers to the image of the translator as somebody ferrying a text from one language to another. In Greek mythology, when Charon transported the dead over the river Lethe, they lost their memory. In the same way the translator can wipe out the original, so that the text forgets the travelling from one language to another. In this case, the translation adapts completely to the language of the translation, replacing the original. Thus Cixous would be read as if she wrote in Norwegian. No one would be able to discover the text behind the translation.

In 17th century France the cultural elite talked about "*les belles infidèles*", the beautiful, but faithless translations, where traces of the original had disappeared. This was precisely the way things were done, they abolished the original, appropriating it and veiling the translation process. When the traces of the original disappear, we are in danger of getting a common language of translation making different texts appear anonymous and similar, no matter what the original is like. "*Les fidèles*", the faithful translations, on the other hand, were not beautiful, but tedious and often unreadable. The translation as a window into the original, where the new text is supposed to disappear, is never a satisfying version of the original. The extreme version of this fidelity is the word-for-word translation, which is not, of course, a literary text.

The translation is a text about a text, which means that it is the text of the translator, resulting from a process where the new language and the moment of translation have left their marks. The anchorage in the culture of the translation can give a translation a literary value of its own (like the King James' Version of the Bible). Then the translation will not be transparent or invisible. To make a translation last, it must be a work of art in itself. Otherwise a translation becomes too old very quickly, publishers might say within 10 years.

An example of how the original can become a work of art in the new language is the Norwegian translation of Proust's *À la recherche du temps perdu* by Anne-Lisa Amadou. Proust's long sentences, sometimes over a whole page, were very different from the short sentences common to Norwegian prose. Her translation was criticised when the first tome appeared in the 1970's: 'This is not Norwegian!'. Of course most Norwegian readers did not know then that Proust did not write ordinary French. Happily for my translation of Cixous, we are now used to long passages without full stops. The translation of Proust has participated in creating modern Norwegian, while at the same time it gives us a feeling of the originality of Proust's text. Even so, translating Cixous, I sometimes have to bring in a comma, or a full stop, to ensure that my Norwegian readers accept my version of her text. It still sounds very different from *normal* Norwegian prose, and I hope these texts will make the Norwegian language richer, more *flowing* and less laconic!

If translation is seen as a reformulation of a text where the translator explores the possibilities of the new language, then the translation can be as innovative as the original. Literary texts often transcend standardised language, they cannot be translated with clichés. A translation must have new images just as the original does. This is why the translator needs to know the language of translation even better than that of the original. Of course, the innovation of a translated text depends on the translator's ability to make translation a creative process.

In both cases, in faithful or unfaithful renderings, the reader might get the impression that the translation is the definite version, even if it has very little to do with the original. We can cite cases such as Baudelaire's translation of Edgar Allan Poe, which is supposed to have given the texts an extra dimension. But more often than not the images in a text are dropped or simplified or even rendered with clichés. In the past the translator might even have dropped words, sentences and entire passages if she found the translation too difficult, and that was when she was not cutting out parts of the text to censure it.

We have to be able to trust the translator not to *cheat*. A text is, however, sometimes adapted, through the translation process, to the norms of the country where it is published, often as a result of the censorship of the translator. Alternatively, the translation may have to wait until the translator and the editors consider the readership to be *ready* for such a text, before it can be published. When I translated "La venue à l'écriture", it was impossible to get someone to publish it. It was considered too difficult. Ten years later I was finally able to publish some of Cixous's texts. In between I had translated and published "Le rire de la Méduse" in an anthology of literary criticism. Categorised in this way, the book was addressed to a limited readership that was interested in and could understand *difficult* texts, the difficulties residing both in form and in content. In Norway in the 1980's, for instance, the concepts of psychoanalysis and of modern linguistics were not integrated into the culture as much as in France. The publishers considered too few readers able to understand references in Cixous's texts to these domains. One can only wonder how the texts could have influenced Norwegian readers if they had been published earlier.

Even when the texts were published: how could the Norwegian reader understand "Requième conférence sur l'Infiminité" (Cixous 1986: 45) and its parody of Freud's text? Once again I used a footnote. The Dada manifesto cannot easily be recognised as the background to the Norwegian version of "*détruire, casser; prévoir l'imprévu, projeter*", nor can the Norwegian reader recognize "*Va, vole*" (Cixous 1986: 50) from *Le Cid* by Corneille, a text the French read at school. The transparency of Cixous's references to Medusa, from Greek mythology, when she talks about "*accoucher par la gorge*" (Cixous 1986: 63) ["give birth by my throat"][4], or to the French discussion in the 1960's about *le don*, 'the gift', in philosophy and in anthropology, depends on the knowledge of the reader, whether French or Norwegian. Here both translator and editor must have confidence in the reader's abilities to understand the text. It is not possible for a Norwegian reader to have the same starting point as a French reader. But then again the Cixous original is not read once and for all, it is changing with its readers.

The language of the translation is marked by its situation in time and also by the life and language of the translator. In Norway we have two official languages, one of them has the connotations of *urban* language (*bokmål*), the other of *countryside* (*nynorsk*). Thus a version of Cixous's texts in what is called *nynorsk*, will not be accessed by exactly the same readership as a translation into what is called *bokmål*. The majority of the Norwegians use *bokmål*, which is the form of Norwegian I use. And again, even if the translator is not supposed to add anything about herself in the text, she is present in the text as the one who makes choices of formulations, of vocabulary etc. She is the one who succeeds, more or less, in taking care of the multiple meanings of the literary text. The translator experiences the original text, she reads with her senses, her feelings, her rationality and her subconscious – it is this reading she is supposed to transmit. She depends on her experience and on her curiosity towards the text, to her listening to what is beneath and behind the words to be able to transmit it to us in her own idiom. Or as Henri Meschonnic (1999) writes, translation is about saying what is not said in the original.

3. The Translation Process as Creation

I read Cixous, I listen: the text sings. I want to be in the text, I want the text to be part of me: waves of words flowing in me for a long time. Of course, this is the ideal situation. Most translators have to translate in a hurry to make a living. They have neither the space nor the time to let the text invade them. Luckily, sometimes translation is more than a job. The translator lets the text get under her skin! To make the words burn and pass the fire on to the readers, Cixous recommends that a writer should practise: "*la plus grande passivité*" (1986: 68) ["the greatest passivity" (Cixous 1991a: 57)]. One should never be in a hurry, but wait for the right words to come, listen with one's eyes, one's skin, one's breath.

> *Tu ne cherches pas à maîtriser. À démontrer, expliquer, saisir. Et alors à coffrer. Empocher une part de la richesse du monde. Mais à transmettre: à faire aimer en faisant connaître...* (Cixous 1986: 68)
>
> You don't seek to master. To demonstrate, explain, grasp. And then to lock away in a strongbox. To pocket a part of the riches of the world. But rather to transmit: to make things loved by making them known. (Cixous 1991a: 57)

Listening to the rhythm of the text means being open towards the other in the text and to oneself. For a translator it is worth listening to Cixous's recommendations to the writer. It is not a question of taking possession of a text, but of letting oneself be invaded to be able to give to other readers a text you yourself love and appreciate.

At the beginning of the translating process I stay as close as I can (word-for-word) to the text and then approach what will become the Norwegian version. And into my own language I try to bring something of the French text, letting the reader know this text comes from another language, another culture. I cannot mime the French sounds, Norwegian does not sound like French. But the flow characterising the texts by Cixous can be transmitted. I keep her texts in my mouth, I taste them, I get to know them, I dream about them, I make love to them, I keep them in my body as I am translating them. Does the Norwegian version feel right, taste right? It means listening to my intuition based on years of experience, of knowledge of the languages at play and of literature. Intuition is of course also based on all I have learned, lived through, felt and thought.

The poetic text influences us as bodies (with heads!), calling on our sensory apparatus, on our memories and experiences, on the knowledge we have gathered and on our capacity to understand and to establish new knowledge. When I read Cixous's texts, I think as I have said already: here is a pun that I must not lose, an alliteration to be conserved, a choice of vocabulary, words to be coined in the Norwegian text. But even more important, I want to communicate the feelings of elation evoked in me: yes, it is possible, I can do it; of anger: this is so unjust; of relief: this is how the writing process must be understood; of recognition and identification: this is how it is.

Since openness is important for the process of translation, one should never translate a text one does not like. I once tried to translate a text I detested, it was a hard struggle giving a poor result. Not only must I respect a text I live with, I must also take responsibility for it when it is published. Happiness is when I can translate texts such as Cixous's with thoughts close to what I feel I could have thought myself, or to what I would have liked to have thought and formulated myself, a text permitting me to transcend my own style and knowledge.

My goal is to create a new literary text with a very close relationship to the original on all levels. To be able to do this one has to try to be an artist in the new language, use all resources for feeling, sensing and thinking, one must be a poet, even if one never thought of writing poetry. Translating is something other than writing a new literary text, a translator is not supposed to invent a poetic universe, because she already has this in the original text. Within a more limited space, however, good translations are creations, and they require competence, concentration, application, honesty and creativity from the translator, in order to become good literary texts. Nevertheless, the main interest of the translation is to be a translation of the original text!

---

[1] My translations of Hélène Cixous's texts are published in Cixous (1998), and Cixous (1991b).
[2] The English translation is by Sarah Cornell and Susan Sellers in Sissel Lie (1990: 196).
[3] The English version is "from the point of view of the soul's eye: the eye of the womansoul" with a footnote, in Cixous (1991a: 4).
[4] Cixous (1991a: 52). I wonder why the English translation changes "*la gorge*" to "my throat"?

References

Berman, Antoine. 1984. *L'épreuve de l'étranger*. Paris: Gallimard.
Cixous, Hélène. 1975. 'Le rire de la Méduse' in *L'Arc* 61: 39-54.
—. 1986. 'Le dernier tableau ou le portrait de Dieu' in *Entre l'écriture*. Paris: des femmes.
—. 1991a. '*Coming to Writing*' *and Other Essays* (ed. Deborah Jenson). Cambridge, MA: Harvard University Press.
—. 1991b. 'Medusas latter' (tr. Sissel Lie) in Kittang, Atle et al. (eds) *Moderne litteraturteori. En antologi*. Oslo: Universitetsforlaget.
—. 1998. *Nattspråk* (ed.and tr. Sissel Lie). Oslo: Pax.
Lie, Sissel. 1990. 'Pour une lecture féminine?' in Wilcox, Helen et al. (eds) *The Body and the Text*. New York, NY: Harvester Wheatsheaf.
Meschonnic, Henri. 1999. *Poétique du traduire*. Paris: Verdier.

Desvelo

Mara Negrón

The translator estranges herself from her own language in contact with the original one, which entails a sort of "mourning"; then, there is a "rebirth" in the space of the Other. The author compares the texts by Derrida and Cixous (both in *Veils*) she translated, stating that they both use a "veil effect", which must be preserved in translation. Referring also to the etymological origin of "veil", Negrón concludes that translation means to displace the translator's language, to situate it in an "unstable" place between languages, in order to keep the sense eternally in motion and not to settle it in a solid position.
Key words: otherness, veil, Derrida, *Veils*.

> In the realm of translation, too, the words *En archei en ho logos* [In the beginning was the word] apply.
> (Benjamin 1996: 260)

It starts with a word: *desvelo*.
 Or like in Kafka's dogs words in *Forschungen eines Hundes*: "*Mit jenem Koncert aber begann es*" ["But it began with that concert"] (Kafka 1937: 19). This is a very short German phrase. I would say it is the shortest in Kafka's text. It is a phrase that opens a paragraph. There are not many paragraphs. It is a phrase, which separates and marks a beginning. *Forschungen eines Hundes* has many beginnings. But this beginning is the absolute one: it tells how everything starts. Nevertheless this phrase which tells how we come into being through language, into the law, is not the one pronounced at the beginning of the text. It comes in the middle of the narration, at the end of the story of the encounter of the Dog with the Musician dogs. It was a beautiful morning when the little Dog met the Musician Dogs[1]. The old Dog is now recasting his life as an autobiographical narration and as his first memory he remembers that encounter. What does it start with that concert played by the "seven great musical artists"? We do not know but (it) starts with music. The German phrase remains undetermined; it does not have any subject. This indetermination has to be regarded as an ambivalent rapport with music but also with the law. Those Musician dogs "were violating the law" (Kafka 1937: 14), says Kafka's Dog, the little old

one. The Dog that says 'I' in this story is an ambivalent one too. Sometimes, it is the child who talks in him. He identifies in that encounter with music the beginning, *his* beginning: the experience, which troubles and fascinates him and that puts him apart from the "*Hundeschaft*". Music is an element which "had surrounded me as a perfectly natural and indispensable element of existence ever since I was suckling" (*ibid.*: 9). Music is a kind of language before language and the law².

It ("before") starts with a concert, with a word, with a word which is a concert. I would suggest a translation of Kafka's phrase that starts with the Spanish word: *desvelo*. Kafka's undetermined phrase and *desvelo* play a very similar musical air.

It is a kind of unforgettable moment of reading. I remember. It was late. It was a very beautiful Caribbean night in February. I opened the Book. I opened *Voiles*, "two" texts (maybe more than two, I was/am almost sure more than two, maybe one thousand, like a thousand nights in one night) one by Hélène Cixous, *Savoir*, and another one by Jacques Derrida, *Un ver à soie*. One next to the other, side by side to one another, close to each other, they are just separate by the veil drawings of Ernest Pignon-Ernest. I could not put away the book; seated in my bed I continued to read, falling in reading as falling in love. *I* fell. I could not sleep anymore, and I prefer to say that phrase in Spanish: *Estaba desvelada* [I was sleepless]. I felt *desvelada*. A kind of *dévoilement*, of 'unveiled', happened to me, to my language. The French word '*dévoilement*' does not have the two Spanish meanings ['sleepless' and 'unveiled'] But both languages have almost the same body, it is almost the same word: '*dévoilement*' and '*desvelo*'. I was hearing in that word a confusing music; the experience of translation started through *desvelo*. It says something of my way of playing between French and Spanish, of my way of hearing the Latin language in that text. *Voiles* was translating something for me, translating myself into Spanish-French or French-Spanish which means a sort of not-located place in any language; or a musical place before the law. Besides, the Spanish word '*desvelo*' unveils something of the body's position of the translator. He or she can not sleep; the bodies of her/his languages must keep sleepless, the letters, words, phrases, syntax must be awakened and ready to play between languages.

Spanish is just one of the languages that *Voiles* talks. It speaks many languages, as many as the reader is capable of speaking. And one of the questions in Hélène Cixous's text as in Jacques Derrida's, is the plurality of languages and voices. "How could we translate a text written in several languages at the same time? [...] And if one translates in several languages at the same time, do we say that it is translating?" asks Jacques Derrida (1987: 208). As a form of rebirth, the French was giving me a mother tongue; and let's say it is Spanish, let's say that the language of the translator is Spanish.

As in a sort of allegory, could those stories, Kafka's and mine, evoke something of the experience of translating? And I said as in a sort of allegory. I insist. Since the beginning, I have been telling tales that I pretend can call up more or less the experience of translating. As if I could not define what is translation, or either objectively or theoretically talk about my work on *Voiles*. But I affirm that those allegories are theoretical fictions that place the translation in the realm of experience then of testimony. Every text produces its readings then its metaphors. The translator must be capable of producing a reading in which in some way she or he would write her/his own autobiographical relation with languages and of course with the law. In some way, every translation is an allegory that tells a relationship with the *auto* and the law. Also, when I think and describe the scene of translation as an allegory, I am already implying a theory of reading and writing.

Nevertheless, if it is difficult to answer my question at least we can think the proper as not being *my proper*. Translation is about proper. When I translate it is a double process; *I* am translated. I do not know if I can say that *I am a translator*. I hesitate because I find myself between reading and writing and learning to talk the language of the other in a very passive and anxious, sleepless, way. Translation is like a very particular way of reading; which implies a contract as a "double bind debt" between the original text and the translation (Derrida 1987: 219). I lose my name, *my* idiom, when I get engaged with a text. The translator gets out of himself.

When I translate very generous texts, as those of Hélène Cixous and Jacques Derrida, I feel as if they were giving me a language; as if my own language becomes a stranger to myself. My language becomes *unheimlich*. Both texts give me the possibility of being out. And this is like a concert, it produces rebirth. In every word of *Voiles* I lived a renaissance; I lose, I die (translation too it is a matter of mourning) and then music happens. And music happens after I have been very close to the original text, almost literally touching the words of the original and then just separating enough to dance with, sometimes the translator, like Kafka's Dog, is very old, sometimes he is like a child, sometimes then he becomes masculine, feminine, mineral, vegetal, sometimes he is in front of the statue of Jeanne d'Arc in Greece, or in Algeria or sometimes the translator is just looking at a shoe box with silkworms inside, and all this is the effect of the language of the Other. Translation is like *travelling to the Otherness*.

I can talk to some extent of Hélène Cixous and Jacques Derrida together and make some affirmations about their plurality of languages and about similar voices in both of them. But they are of course very different. If I write about both of them together in this volume about Hélène Cixous's works in translation, it is because they want to be read together in *Voiles*, they want to be read together in one word: "*voiles*". It is a word that puts in question the word as unity of meaning. It is more than that. This is the word that becomes a joint title for dressing *Savoir* and *Un ver à soie* with veils. *Voiles* as a title covers and uncovers those two texts. Let's follow the metaphor. After all, translation is the metaphor of the metaphor of language.

We can say that *Savoir* and *Un ver à soie* have *voiles* in common. They share veils of different kinds, genders and fabrics. But some *veil effect* is shared by both of them: that is what they make together in different ways. And this is what it *has to be* translated, such is my duty, and this is what in translating we can not *totally* translate. In some way, *Voiles* becomes here a proper name of the signatures that the translator has to translate. Between the 'V' and the silent French 'E' of *Voiles* remains something, a secret, that the translator can not unveil, it remains untouched.

I will give different examples of what I call the veil effect. It can be read in the titles. Both of them are singular ones. Even if *Savoir* can contain many *savoirs*. One of them being that of the *voir* and *savoir* in French. How could it be translated that poetic effect produced by homonymy? *Savoir* in Spanish became *Sa(v)er*, instead of '*saber*', which is a neologism made of the verb '*ver*' [to see] and '*saber*' [to know]. In my translation I manipulated Spanish grammar to show the relationship between knowledge and view that the Spanish speaker can hear in the language ('V' and 'B' are pronounced in the same way) but does not see. In Hélène Cixous's works knowledge has to do with different ways of seeing that decentralizes the order of perception such as it has been thought of by the Western philosophical tradition. She tells how to know seeing, and what means to see. In her writing, to see can be to touch and to hear; the reader, as well as the translator, has to readjust his senses.

Derrida's title, *Un ver à soie*, appears too just like one, even if at the end of the text, in the story of the shoebox, there seems to be more than one silkworm. The singular and the plural fold and unfold the questions of the veil as the impossibility of touching the one true thing, the truth. In its plurality and veil effects, what did this title give to the translator and what did it loose? The translator saw and heard in it '*ver*' ['to see' in Spanish] which in French means 'towards', 'verse' and 'glass'. In the word '*soie*', the silent feminine 'E' – French *e muet* –, which suggests the animal, the fabric and the feminine, or like some hypothetical feminine pronoun ('*soi*' does not have any feminine) the translator apparently looses. The right translation for a silkworm in Spanish is '*un gusano de seda*'. But I rediscovered an old Latin word for 'worm': '*verme*'. This old word contains two others words: '*ver*' ['to see'] and the first person of the reflexive pronoun '*me*' ['myself']. *Un verme de seda*, the title in Spanish, keeps and remembers in some way the French '*ver*' but also adds something that is hidden in the silkworm, that only Spanish speaker can hear. *Un verme de seda* is already a kind of strange silkworm in Spanish, already a translation, and because it means also '*a to see myself in silk*'. But still something more: in the word '*seda*' ['silk'], '*se da*' ['to give oneself'] can also be heard. This is part of the multiplicity of veil effects and the music between languages in *Veils*.

Savoir and *Un ver à soie* are in a relationship of reading. They are autobiographical texts. Hélène Cixous describes in *Savoir* the end of her nearsightedness, which becomes possible by a laser operation. *Savoir* relates the last day of her nearsightedness and the first day of her non-blindness. It is a unique day. It happens only once. Jacques Derrida reads Cixous's poem while he is writing *Un ver à soie*, which has the form of a travel journal, kept during a voyage to South America. His text has the form of a travel journal as a shoebox, which instead of shoes contains silkworms. In the same way I do not recognize a certain South America in the text which looks like a journey to this destination. In the first part of *Un ver à soie*, "Towards Buenos Aires, 24 November-29 November 1995", which is also a homage to *Savoir*, Jacques Derrida calls it "a poem of touch"(Cixous and Derrida 2001a: 35). *Savoir* comes to the traveller in *some* Buenos Aires (*Un ver à soie* travels in a flying carpet), it passes into his text, *Savoir* travels within, among its filaments.

Savoir confesses the loss of myopia. There is a *myopic word* in the phrase which opens Cixous's confession. It is *"laisse"*. This word has to be read, heard, touched closely. It says what myopia is as a place of untranslatable tension in the French language. Since the beginning:

> *La myopie était sa faute, sa laisse, son voile natal imperceptible.* (Cixous and Derrida 1998: 11)

> Myopia was her fault, her lead, her imperceptible native veil. (Cixous and Derrida 2001a: 3)

> *La miopía era su falta, su lazo, su velo natal imperceptible.* (Cixous and Derrida 2001b: 23)

And asks Jacques Derrida: "What does *laisse* mean when we're talking about a veil?" (2001a: 34). Or actually about myopia? As an animal the eyes... as animals..., as a dog, they have been kept tight by a lead, by the veil nearsightedness. Some relationship between animality and nearsightedness seems to be folded in that word. *"Laisse"*, in the middle of this phrase tightens the text to its very language, to its body. Some tension occurs here between *'la laisse'* ['the lead'], and *'laisse'* ['leave'], the third person of the French verb *'laisser'*. Then, it is a word with two opposite meanings. *"Laisse"* holds and leaves, it produces just an imperceptible strain impossible to translate in Spanish; it has lost the second blind meaning, to leave, of the word. *"Laisse"* is an event word because it describes how Cixous's text plays, its myopic movement in the moment she is leaving her nearsightedness, in the French language.

"Laisse" is a very funny animal word in *Savoir*, it translates an event of the body that I read from the Spanish as a place of some resistance to translation, and that poetically keeps *Savoir* tied to its languages. And as *desvelo* it tells the allegory of translation but also of writing. Both are confusing, babelian places in a written corpus. *"Laisse"* translates, not what

happens to Hélène Cixous, but the movement of her body, what happens into the body of her language.

Hélène Cixous's fiction is not narrative, does not tell facts; what is at stake are different ways of knowing that happens in the language as a place of perception and implies a position of the ear and of the eyes-hands. She is very aware of the body of the language. It is like a phenomenology, an experience of the world. But what does it mean, the world? Why we can talk of a different reconfiguration of perception? Her texts are *"mouvementés"*. I quote an interview from "These funny horses that are metaphors", in *Rootprints*:

> On the other hand, I write texts that are very much in movement. *Mouvementés*. Eventful. That is what I imagine, at least. There ought then to be a metaphorical grouping, or collection that stems at once from the registers of transport which is our own body. What we are able to do as an exercise in translation with our body or as a translation of our affects in terms of the body is unlimited. I am not saying anything new. The central interchange is the body in metamorphosis. What the dream shows us in its theater is the translation, in the open, of what we cannot see, of what is not visible but can be sensed in reality. (Cixous 1997: 28)

This passage is preceded by an explanation of the process of writing for Cixous. She defines her search in fiction mostly as an exploration of the oneiric. She says: "For me the origin of the metaphor is the unconscious. [...] for a long time I have permitted myself to use the writing of dreams to conduct a certain research in writing" (Cixous 1997: 27). She is describing a kind of involuntary, unconscious act. It is as if the language flows, the writing writes. She lets herself "be carried away on the back of these funny horses that are metaphors" (*ibid.*: 28). The animality in her language has to do with this way of letting the metaphor write. What seems to be active is the language in this process of producing metaphors or translating the unconscious. The English translation of *Photos de Racines* offers to read movement as "eventful": "I write texts that are very much in movement. *Mouvementés*. Eventful". In French, she just says "*mouvementés*": "*Par ailleurs, j'écris des textes très en mouvement. Mouvementés*" (Cixous 1994: 37). How could "eventful" translate as "movement"? Eventful here does not mean facts but movement. The body movement in translation is an event, is eventful. This statement can be understood in two senses: the body produces the metaphors, the body translates, writing is "an exercise in translation with our body" but it is at the same time what has to be translated, "or as a translation of our affects in terms of the body". Also, it implies a way of considering the task of the translator as a position of the body. And the event here is the experience of translating the body with the body, in other words, to produce metaphors. What happens as an event, a movement, is the body of the language – the language *happens*. Hélène Cixous makes something arrive into the French language. So, it happens to the language of the translator because the language of what he is translating happens to him, puts him in movement, I would rather say out of himself.

All this scene of writing as a translation in Cixous is directed by the dream or at least it is the dream that shows us how to proceed which means to make visible what can not be seen, then it is not visible, but is sensible in reality: "What the dream shows us in its theater is the translation, in the open, of what we cannot see, of what is not visible but can be sensed in reality". This is the stuff Hélène Cixous's texts are made of. Between the limits of the dream something is produced that it is not simply visible nor simply real. But it gives to see, the metaphor, in some manner, it translates. In this sense, translation of *Savoir* must give to see, in a myopic way, that is to say, to place in the ear.

But what is the singularity of that event, that movement of translation in *Savoir*? It is an event text in the Hélène Cixous poetical corpus because it is a turning point, the end of the nearsightedness and the entrance into the *visibility*. The myopia or as Derrida calls it "this pre-operatory vigilance [that] is what will have borne an immense poetic corpus" apparently is over (Cixous and Derrida 2001a: 37). She talks in *Rootprints*, about the relationship between writing and myopia before the laser operation: "I owe some of the most fantastical hallucinatory experiences of my childhood to my extreme nearsightedness: vanishing streets, substitutions, metaphorization and metonymization of the world...". The myopia supposes a poetic of the world. The one that she has never known in "the state of a person whose eyes see 'the world-as-it-is-supposed-to-be-seen-by-seeing-human-eyes'" (1997: 89). There is going to be a change from then on but it is not related to a simple way of thinking and writing this visibility.

What happens in Cixous's fiction is the body as place of displacement of senses, thus of what she calls the world. There would be many things to say about the world, its perception, her way of living in it through language and the meaning of that word in her writings. Her texts have to be heard, touched with eyes, because the world is perceived through this displacement or translation that implies a knowledge which does not have to do with visibility but mostly with blindness. The world occurs several times in *Savoir*, a poem where she is coming to see, she is coming to the world, it is a birth. The world is saying yes: "Yes, said the world" (Cixous and Derrida 2001a: 9).

> She was part of that obscure surreptitious race who goes about in confusion before the great picture of the **world**... (*ibid.*: 3)
>
> But at this dawn without subterfuge she had seen the **world** with her own eyes, without intermediary, without the non-contact lenses. The continuity of her flesh and the **world's** flesh, touch then, was love... (*ibid.*: 9)

> I am coming to the **world**, I am climbing day after day the steps of visibility. (*ibid.*: 10)
>
> Do not forget me. Keep forever the **world** suspended, desirable, refused, that enchanted thing I have given you, murmured myopia. (*ibid.*: 13)
>
> What the seers have never seen: presence-before-the-**world**. (*id.*) [my bold]

These quotations lay out the different moments of this sort of ascension to the visible world. But what seems to be joyful in this process is not simply to see but the continuity between the one who is coming to see and the world: "The continuity of her flesh and the world's flesh, touch then [...]" (Cixous and Derrida 2001a: 9). It is not seeing but touching the world, which seems to move the writing. As a matter of fact, when Cixous talks in *Rootprints* and declares that "I have never known the state of a person whose eyes see 'the world-as-it-is-supposed-to-be-seen-by-seeing-human-eyes'" (Cixous and Calle-Gruber 1997: 89), what she is writing in the dashes of this phrase is the continuity. That is what she did not have before the operation. Besides, there is a "*savoir*" which myopia asks her to keep: "the world suspended, desirable, refused [...]" (Cixous and Derrida 2001a: 13). And everything happens in Hélène Cixous's poem as if the body of the language in *Savoir* would be still for the ear-eyes but also for the touch. In this way the translator's language must displace itself, in other words, to think of translation as an unstable, invisible place between languages. The sense must remain in displacement.

Jacques Derrida talks about translation and of its impossibility for both texts, Hélène Cixous's and his. This impossibility is in some extent due to what he calls the "braid of phonemes" which performs out of the view, "is knotted out of sight". I quote *A Silkworm of One's Own*:

> In its received truth, translation bets on a received truth, a truth that is stabilized, firm and reliable (*bebaios*), the truth of a meaning that, unscathed and immune, would be transmitted from one so-called language to another in general, with no veil interposed, without anything essential sticking or being erased, and resisting the passage. Now the braid that here links us to the word *truth*, in the language we inherit, she and I, and whose economy we are here and now putting to work *à contretemps*, this unique braid ties the same word, the true of truth or the veridicity of *veridictum*, not only to the semantic motif of veil [...] but also, *in-dissociably*, to all the formal and phonematic motifs, to all the related vowels and consonants [...] The braid of phonemes is not always invisible, but primarily it gives itself to be heard, it is knotted out of sight, becoming thus a thing of myopia and blindness. More obvious to the blind, it remains forever, like the warp of this text, you must know it, untranslatable. No one will ever export it entire outside the so-called French language, in any case in its economy (so many meanings, so many in so few words) but also outside its corpus, expanding and which cannot get over it. No one, that's the challenge, will extranslate it from the language we inherit – that we inherit even if or precisely because it is not and never will be ours. (Cixous and Derrida 2001a: 55-56)

If "translation bets on a received truth, a truth that is stabilized, firm and reliable (*bebaios*)", if translation just kept tightly to a structure of truth, of one truth, the translator could not leave untouched what it must be. The translator must renounce completeness; the dream of truth. We never finish translating, we never finish reading writing. Every word of *Voiles* turns the process of translation into questions. *Un ver à soie "**tient** un discours"*, talks about the act of translating. Something in *Savoir* and in *Un ver à soie* would resist, would deny itself to translation: "No one, that's the challenge, will extranslate it from the language we inherit" (2001a: 56). Which language are we talking here? He says: *"Personne jamais ne l'exportera hors de la langue soi-disant française tout entière"* ["No one will ever export it entire outside the so-called French language", *id.*]. We are talking of the *soi-disant* French language. Is it French, but not completely French?; that language seems to be – *"la soi-disant"* – a *soi* which says it is supposed to belong to the French. What both Hélène Cixous and Jacques Derrida seem to inherit is their way of transforming, translating, *extranslating* the French, what we call French.

Some music, an unreadable partition, stays inside of *Voiles*, the very word, inside of every word. Translation is about the self and about mourning. What we lose in translation just stays there for the promised reader, for the reader who can feel the music. The translator is a kind of musical mathematician; s/he gives the measures, suggests the times of the notes, and stays at a relative distance from the original text. Let's follow the metaphor, those funny animals. Mine was *desvelo*, the sleepless position of my body, of my language. The translation must operate to leave intervals, to leave some spaces, to keep some distance – never forget the music, the one that came before 'I' was born to the law, nor should we forget Kafka's lesson: *"Mit jenem Koncert aber begann es"*.

---

[1] "I encountered, in short, a little company of dogs, or rather I did not encounter them, they appeared before me. Before that I had been running along in darkness for some time, filled with a premonition of great things – a premonition that may well have been delusive, for I always had it. I had run in darkness for a long time, up and down, blind and deaf to everything, led on by nothing but a vague desire, and now I suddenly came to a stop with the feeling that I was in the right place, and looking up I saw that it was a bright day, only a little hazy, and everywhere a blending and confusion of the most intoxicating smells; I greeted the morning with an uncertain barking, when – as if I had conjured them up-out of some place of darkness, to the accompaniment of terrible sounds such as I had heard before, seven dogs stepped into the light. Had I not distinctly seen that they were dogs and that they themselves brought the sound with them – though I could not recognize how they produced it – I would have run away at once; but as it was I stayed. At that time I still knew hardly anything of the creative gift for music with which the canine race alone is endowed, it had naturally enough escaped my but slowly developing powers of observation; for though music had surrounded me as a perfectly natural and indispensable element of existence ever since I was suckling, an element which nothing impelled me to distinguish from the rest of existence, my elders had drawn my attention to it only by such hints as were suitable for childish understanding; all the more astonishing, then, indeed devastating, were these seven great musical artists to me. They did not speak, they did not sing,

they remained, all of them, silent, almost determinedly silent; but from the empty air they conjured music. Everything was music, the lifting and setting down of their feet, certain turns of the head, their running and their standing..." (Kafka 1937: 8-10; for the German edition: Kafka 1996: 414).

[2] Jean-François Lyotard, talking about the inscription of the law and its machine in the body in Kafka's *Penitentiary Colony*, analyzes the different moments of that mark. When the law does make its *praescripta* in us? He talks about a time in the body before language, before we were there: "*Cet avant, évidemment, on ne le connaît pas, puisqu'il y est avant qu'on y soit. Il est comme la naissance de l'enfance, qui y sont avant qu'on y soit. Le y en question s'appelle corps. Ce n'est pas moi qui nais, qui suis enfanté. Moi, je naîtrai après, avec le langage, en sortant de l'enfance, précisément*" (1991: 39). In *Forschungen eines Hundes* the music says something about that before; *I* was already born but not yet there; "our I" still walking like a steady little dog. In the process of translation, we are in this "I" before the 'I', in some in between place within and before the law.

References

Benjamin, Walter. 1996. *The Task of the Translator*. Cambridge, MA, and London: Harvard University Press.
Berman, Antoine. 1984. *L'épreuve de l'étranger, Culture et traduction dans l'Allemagne romantique*. Paris: Gallimard.
Cixous, Hélène and Jacques Derrida. 1998. *Voiles*. Paris: Galilée.
—. 2001a. *Veils* (tr. Geoffrey Bennington). Stanford, CA: Stanford University Press.
—. 2001b. *Velos* (tr. Mara Negrón). Mexico: Siglo Veintuno.
Cixous, Hélène and Mireille Calle-Gruber. 1994. *Photos de racines*. Paris: des femmes.
—. 1997. *Rootprints. Memory and Life Writing* (tr. Eric Prenowitz). London and New York, NY: Routledge.
Derrida, Jacques. 1985. 'Théologie de la traduction' in *Qu'est-ce que Dieu?*. Brussels: Facultés Universitaires Saint-Louis. 165-206.
—. 1987. 'Des Tours de Babel' in *Psyché: Inventions de l'autre*. Paris: Galilée.
De Man, Paul. 1986. 'Conclusions: Walter Benjamin's *The Task of the Translator*' in *The Resistance to Theory*. Minneapolis, MN: University of Minnesota Press.
Jakobson, Roman. 1959. 'On Linguistic Aspects of Translation' in *On Translation*. Cambridge, MA: Harvard University Press.
Kafka, Franz. 1937. 'Investigations of a Dog' in *The Great Wall of China, Stories and Reflections* (tr. Willa and Edwin Muir). New York, NY: Schocken Books.
—. 1996. *Die Erzählungen Originalfassung*. Frankfurt: Fischer Verlag.
Lyotard, Jean-François. 1991. 'Prescription: Kafka' in *Lectures d'enfance*. Paris: Galilée.

The Betrayal of Textual *Différance* (of the *Voiles*): A Translational Analysis of *Savoir*

Maribel Peñalver Vicea

> The author analyses Mara Negrón's Spanish translation of *Savoir* (in Cixous and Derrida's *Veils*), specifying some linguistic procedures, such as "neologisms", "phonetic losses", translation of metaphors", and "plays on words". She also applies some of the most important images of *Veils* to the activity of translating. Peñalver Vicea argues that translating is the only way to "unveil" some linguistic procedures of Cixous's writing, but it conveys also the risk of "veiling" the ambiguity and so the richness of the original text.
> Key words: linguistics, neologisms, translation of metaphors, ambiguity, *Veils*.

> Translation is the sheer play of difference: it constantly makes allusion to difference, dissimulates difference, but occasionally revealing and often accentuating it, translation becomes the very life of this difference. (Maurice Blanchot)

In this article, my purpose is to describe the translational behaviour of a text by Hélène Cixous entitled *Savoir*[1]. I analyse the translation as a practice of *différance* between signifier and signified which is unveiled in the process of transformation from a language into another. A desired language, for it is foreign, a language that rejects us and attracts us like an impossible love according to Hélène Cixous:

> The supreme statement of love would be: I do not understand you. I do not want to understand you. I love from not understanding you. And love is the explosive, painful tension between not understanding and wanting to understand, between trembling at the very idea of understanding while passionately wanting to be understood and fearing above all any type of comprehension. (Cixous 1990a: 66)

According to J. Derrida, the play of *différance* is erased when translating because one must choose between different signifieds. And *différance*, being itself heterogeneous, chooses neither the one nor the other. Like *Voiles*, two languages (Spanish and French) meet here split by their difference. That is why I have chosen the translation of this text, as a metaphor of the textual and sexual *différance* between languages. Two similar languages attached paradoxically despite their native kinship: the Latin parent language. Like in a love scene, they allied themselves, the one by its beauty, the other by its lack of it, but carried away by their appeal. All that will produce in the translation a painful *étranglement*[2] ['strangling'], which makes the equivalence between the two languages impossible. But translation becomes a Derridean deconstruction that constructs another language, which is, at the same time, the trace of an already existing and hybrid language. When translating a feeling of betrayal arises inside the translator and s/he must be able to cope with it. In return, the pleasure obtained from the penetration into another language leads her/him into this feeling of betrayal. Translation becomes this strange necessity of writing through the language of the other. Conscious of this betrayal, the translator metamorphoses by means of a new writing. As s/he comes into the foreign language, a double bind arises in him/her. It is now when he/she destroys to create the first love scene, arriving through the pain at the pleasure of the transformation:

> the text will be even more virgin after the passage of the translator, and the hymen, sign of virginity, more jealous of itself after the other hymen, the contract signed and the marriage consummated. Symbolic completeness will not have taken place to its very end and yet the compromise of marriage will have come about – and this is the task of the translator, in what makes it very pointed as well as irreplaceable. (Derrida 1985: 192)

I will try to explain the betrayal of *différance*, in translation, by means of the analysis of the following procedures:

1. Neologisms.
2. Phonetic Losses.
3. Translation of Metaphors.
4. Plays on Words:
    4.1. Polyptoton.
    4.2. Paronomasia.

Before starting the analysis of these procedures, I would like to point out that "transcoding"[3] is the first procedure used in the literary translation for two main reasons. Firstly, transcoding, seen with a view for a reformulation of the sense, is never a procedure of automatic passage from one language to another. The thing is a "literal"[4] translation, the closest to its literalness, insofar as the same semantic and morphological equivalencies are kept in order to produce the same effect as in the original text. In this sense, when this procedure can be used, one should not stray from it if the target language allows it. Secondly, Spanish, the target language, shares the same Latin roots as French. This simplifies the task of translating from French into Spanish. On the contrary, the translator whose target language is not a romance one is bound to face a more complete and less rewarding specific work of translation.

I will start by describing how the signifiers play in the two titles *Savoir* and *Voiles*, and their translation into Spanish. The title *Savoir*, metatextual cataphora[5], produces an explosive amphibology and anticipates the *savoir* of this writing. It is a '*voir*' ['to see'] at the beginning of the book, a '*voir*' cut from '*sa*' where two words will fly together over these leaves: '*le voile*' ['veil'] and '*la voile*' ['sail']. The one, perhaps, hidden, the other unveiled to awake the silence of its other. One masculine, the other feminine, but never without being excluded by their *différence*. Here they are joined in plural and in *Voiles*. *Savoir* becomes homophone of:

1. *Sa-voir*, where '*sa*', homophone of the neuter '*ça*', could represent the Latin plural neuter '*sua*', divided in three, like '*illa*'[6]. '*Sa*' plays, likewise, with the feminine possessive determinative '*sa*', but it multiplies itself into the plural '*sa*', through scriptural dissemination. That is how '*sa*' or '*ça-voir*' includes the three genders and, like in a neuter, there is neither the masculine nor the feminine but the two, which make the plurality of this writing.

2. *Savoir* is homophone of '*s'avoir*' where the prosthesis of the *S* provides the first breath to the text and allows the narrator to reveal this textual metaphor which reflects the "non-linear" reading of this writing. In this sense, the Cixousian signifiers spread along the text and reappear by means of the traces they leave.

3. *Savoir* works the weave of the sign because '*SA*' means, for Saussure, the signifier in opposition to the '*SÉ*' ('*signifié*' ['signified']). It is here that the signifiers of *Savoir* arise. '*Sa*' reveals, in this very line, the cut of the word, a word cut with different significations depending on each reader. '*Sa*' designates the *gramme* and becomes a metaphor of the trace of the writing.

4. *Savoir* leads us to know how to see ourselves reflected through the blow of the *SSS* and *VVV* in order to see that it is actually two, veiled and unveiled: the masculine and the feminine. In *Savoir*, "*sa*" is not only the acronym of the "*Savoir Absolu*" ["Absolute Knowledge"] of Hegel but also the homophone of "*ça*" of Freud in "Le moi et le ça"[7] where he talks about the instinct of the personality. In this sense, '*ça (voir)*' is a way of wanting to achieve knowledge.

With regard to the translation of the title into Spanish, *Sa(v)er*, I think it is very successful since it allows us, by homophony, to feel a double sense in Spanish: '*saber*' and '*sa(v)er*'. In this language, the verb '*savoir*' is homophone (but non-homograph) of *saber*. The *B* and the *V* are bilabial consonants at the initial position of a word. But which of the two verbs, '*savoir*' (French) and '*saber*' (Spanish), derived from the Latin word '*sapere*' produces the difference?; is the French language the one which has produced the difference by using the *V*, or is, on the contrary, the Spanish language by using the *B*? Is the parent language to blame for wanting to separate them? This is the play of *différance* in translation since "to translate is to play with similarities and differences [...] in a never ending analysis" (Derrida 1988: 100).

In Spanish, the verb '*sa(v)er*' cannot keep all the senses used by the original text: '*ça voir*', '*sa voir*', '*s'avoir*'. '*Sa*(v)*er*' is neither homophone of '*tenerse*' ['*s'avoir*'] nor of '*eso ver*' (or '*su ver*') ['*ça voir*' in French]. Therefore, the signified cannot be 'un-veiled' as it can in the source language.

With reference to the title, *Voiles*, metaphor of the sexual difference, shows the very play of the *différance*. The word '*voile*' comes from the Latin neuter '*velum*', which is, at the same time, the feminine, '*la voile*' and the masculine, '*le voile*'.

The same word in Arabic means 'what separates two things', and, in the text, '*le voile*' is separated from '*la voile*' by the morphologic gender. They are separated but sectioned in the Cixousian sense, in other words, cut to enjoy joining. However, in Spanish the plural of '*la vela*' ['sail'], '*velas*', and of '*el velo*' ['veil'], '*velos*', is not a homophone. They are separated by gender, masculine or feminine. In French '*voiles*', in plural, is a polysemous word that can be understood doubly: '*voile (la)*' and '*voile (le)*'.

Consequently, the translator had compulsorily to choose one of them: *velos*, in masculine plural. It is there that the play of the *différance* and the exclusion of the translation appear. Translation is a violent act that forces the translator to perform a linguistic castration because of the choice among "two" or several options. Nevertheless, and as mentioned before, *différance*, being itself ambiguous, does not select, does not carve, but it sections by cutting in the Cixousian sense: a cut produced to taste every section. When translating one violates the signified and the play of the polysemy disappears. That is shown in the Spanish translation *Velos*. Translating is to carve. This is a threatening and interlinguistic dilemma in the sense of R. Jakobson:

> There is impurity in every language. This fact would in some way have to threaten every linguistic system's integrity, which is presumed by each of Jakobson's concepts. Each of these three concepts (intralingual translation, interlingual or translation "properly speaking", and intersemiotic translation) presumes the existence of one language and of one translation in the literal sense, that is, as the passage from one language into another. So, if the unity of the linguistic system is not a sure thing, all of this conceptualization around translation (in the so-called proper sense of translation) is threatened. (Derrida 1988: 100)

I will look at the translation of the first paragraph and of other sequences into Spanish, where the transcoding is complete, with the exception of some words that the translator considers appropriate to transform through a partial transcoding:

> *La myopie était sa faute, sa laisse, son voile natal imperceptible. Chose étrange, elle voyait qu'elle ne voyait pas, mais elle ne voyait pas bien. Chaque jour il y avait refus, mais qui pouvait dire d'où partait le refus: qui se refusait, était-ce le monde ou elle? Elle était de cette race obscure subreptice qui va désemparée devant le grand tableau du monde, toute la journée en posture d'aveu: je ne vois pas le nom de la rue, je ne vois pas le visage, je ne vois pas la porte, je ne vois pas venir et c'est moi qui ne vois pas ce que je devrais voir. Elle avait des yeux et elle était aveugle.* (Cixous 1998: 11)

> Myopia was her fault, her lead, her imperceptible native veil. Strange: she could see that she could not see, but she could not see clearly. Every day there was refusal, but who could say where the refusal came from: who was refusing, the world, or she? She was part of that obscure surreptitious race who go about in confusion before the great picture of the world, all day long in a position of avowal: I can't see the name of the street, I can't see the face, I can't see the door, I can't see things coming and I'm one who can't see what I ought to be able to see. She had eyes and she was blind. (Cixous 2001a: 3)

> *La miopía era su falta, su lazo, su velo natal imperceptible. Cosa extraña, ella veía que no veía, pero no veía bien. Cada día había rechazo, pero ¿quién pudiera decir de dónde provenía el rechazo?: ¿quién rechazaba, era el mundo o ella? Ella pertenecía a esa raza oscura subrepticia que, desamparada, pasa frente al gran lienzo del mundo, todo el día en postura de* **confesión***: no veo el nombre de la calle, no veo el* **rostro***, no veo la puerta, no veo venir y soy yo quien no ve lo que debería de ver. Tenía ojos y era* **ciega***.* (2001b: 23) [my bold]

Most of the Spanish words have maintained their semantic content. I will show only a few examples:

The French word "*aveu*" ['confession'], not having the same root as "*confesión*", keeps the same signified in the translation. '*Aveu*', which according to *Le Petit Robert* is the old form of '*avouer*' (from Latin '*advocare*'), is equivalent, from the semantic point of view, to '*confesión*' (from Latin '*confessio*').

"*Visage*" (from '*visum*' (from '*videre*')) and "*rostro*" (from '*rostrum*' (from '*rodere*')) both mean '*figure*' ['face']. In French, the word '*rostre*' exists and designates '*la partie saillante et pointue en avant la tête*'[8] ['the salient pointed front part of the head']. However, the term '*rostro*', in Spanish, came, by metonymy, to designate the face. The two terms which come from '*rodere*' and '*videre*', are, both, a form of tasting, one by means of the mouth, the other by means of sight.

The terms "*aveugle*" (from '*ab oculis*') and "*ciega*" (from '*caecus*' (from '*caecare*')) ('*cegar*' ['to blind']) correspond to each other from the semantic point of view.

With reference to the word '*laisse*', it was translated into "*lazo*", perhaps, in order to maintain the rhythm of the lateral consonant *L*. This consonant supplies the discourse, by iconic instinct, with "*le son du vent des voiles*".

Another example of complete transcoding is showed in the following sequence:

> *Soudain ma myopie, "l'autre" la malvenue, s'est dévoilée: l'autre n'était nulle autre que sa mie, sa modeste compagne née. Son cher secret. Déjà la mystérieuse toundra brumeuse de toujours était effacée. Adieu ma mie ma mère.* (1998: 17)
>
> Suddenly myopia, "the other" the unwelcome, is unveiled: the other was none other than her sweetheart, her modest companion born. Her dear secret. Already the mysterious misty tundra of always was effaced. Farewell my sweetheart my mother. (2001a: 11)

The sequence "*Adieu ma mie ma mère*" refers, by intertextuality, to *Tristan et Iseult*. *Le Petit Robert* says that "*mie*" is the old and tender form of '*amie*' and of '*amie aimée*'. The homophony plays, at the same way, with the amphibology of the word '*mi(e)*', which signifies '*ma mi*' ['my half'], '*ma moitié*'. *Mi* refers not only to the word '*mi*' in the expression '*mi-figue, mi raisin*' but is also an adjective that means 'ambiguous' and 'mixed'.

Although in Spanish this amphibology cannot be maintained, the translation is equivalent. Thus, the transcoding is complete: "*Adiós mi amiga mi madre*" but the signification of the word '*mi*' is lost.

As I said previously, the translation is a trace of the original as it can be seen in the last example. According to W. Benjamin (1970: 139), in translation there are "fragments" since the original is already the translation of other texts, of another "which destabilizes the work of signification, making meaning plural and differential" (Venuti 1991: 7).

I have tried to show that the complete transcoding must be the first procedure chosen by the translator when the target language has the same linguistic equivalences as the source language. As P. Newmark (1992: 37) emphasizes, "the literal translation, if it achieves the referential and pragmatical equivalence with the original, is perfectly valid and there is no reason to avoid it". In this sense, it is advisable that the translator, before resorting to other procedures, performs a transcoding in order to maintain the same sense as in the original text.

1. Neologisms: a Poison or a Potion?

In H. Cixous's writing, neology becomes a requirement of de-construction through the construction of new words. According to A. Goosse:

> Neology is both a good thing and a bad thing. It is a good thing because it shows that language is able to adapt to new conditions, that it is not set rigidly in a kind of perfection which would be the very opposite of life. It is a bad thing because it is

constantly upsetting the balance, which is the foundation of the notion of system. (1975: 69)

It is this double sense, given by A. Goosse, which I use to describe the lexical creativity in H. Cixous. This is an evil, which, used as a weapon to fight the linguistic canons of the academic world, becomes simultaneously the remedy and the antidote of the language. Like a "*pharmakon*"[9], the neology would be at the same time a Cixousian good and evil, poison and potion.

However, what kind of neologisms[10] does H. Cixous use? These are the formal neologisms, which spread their sema along the textual tissue. It is by means of a variety of traces (of other sememes) that Hélène Cixous constructs the following neologisms, whose translation into Spanish I am referring to.

The first neologism is the verb "*mévoir*": "*Le Doute et elle furent toujours inséparables: les choses étaient-elles parties ou bien était-ce elle qui les mévoyait?*" (1998: 14) ["She and Doubt were always inseparable: had things gone away or else was it she who *mis-saw* them?" (2001a: 6)]. It is created from the prefix '*me-*', with a pejorative value, and from the verb '*voir*'. This verb, translated into Spanish by "*malver*" (2001b: 23), reinforces the doubt that is inseparable from the narrator. I say inseparable because "*mévoir*" means, in my opinion, 'to see not clearly' but also to see oneself ('*me(s) voir*') through the neuter "*ce*" which is placed in the sentence before the subject "*qui*"; "*mévoir*" is an ambiguous and reflexive verb.

In Spanish, the French prefix '*me-*' corresponds to the prefix '*des*'[11]. The translator could have created '*desver*' but it is possible that the cacophony had influenced the choice of the translation and so it has been translated by "*malver*". The ambiguity of the sentence sparks the implicit '*voilé*' off by the neuter pronoun "*ce*" that would be included in "*mévoir*", homophone of '*mes voir(s)*': "*ou bien était-ce elle qui les mévoyait?*".

The neologism "*apparitionnement*" is created from the sememe '*apparition*' and the suffix '*-ment*'[12]:

> Ça n'arrêtait pas de venir, d'**apparitionner**. L'**apparitionnement** se poursuivait. C'est ce qui la transportait: le pas de l'Apparition. La venue à Voir. Et qui vient? moi ou toi? (1998: 16)

> It didn't stop coming, apparitioning. Apparitioning carried on. That's what was transporting her: the step of Apparition. Coming to See. And who is coming? You or I? (2001a: 9)

The translation of this term has followed the same morphological steps and "*apparitionnement*" has been translated by "*aparicionamiento*" (2001b: 27). I think that "*apparitionnement*" is created by the need of constructing a new discursive situation. It is precisely here that "*Apparition*" makes "*apparitionner*" but it is "*apparitionnement*" which produces the desire of going on seeing. Cixous creates the verb "*apparitionner*", translated into "*aparicionar*".

Another lexical creation is the past participle "*invu*": "*Quel est l'équivalent d'inouï? **Invu?** Il n'y avait encore jamais eu d'**invu**. C'était une invention. Cela venait de commencer*" (1998: 16) ["What is the equivalent of unheard-of? Unseen? There had never before been any unseen. It was an invention. It had just begun" (2001a: 10)]. The participle "*invu*", translated by "*invisto*" (2001b: 28), is a homophone of '*un vu(e)*' and is presented as a joyful '*invention*' to the '*vue*' because one sees "*à l'oeil-nu*" ['with the naked eye']. "*Invu*" spreads its signified and becomes, by means of the dissemination, masculine '*un vu*' and feminine '*invue*'. In this sense, "*invu*" includes the two genders.

The noun "*étrangèreté*", translated by "*extranjeridad*" ['foreignty'] (*id.*), was preferred instead of the existing one '*étrangeté*' ['strangeness']:

> *Mais si l'on pouvait expulser la myopie, c'est donc qu'elle était une étrangère? Elle l'avait toujours pressenti: sa myopie était sa propre étrangère, son étrangèreté essentielle* (1998: 16)

> But if myopia could be expelled, was it then a foreigner? She had always had the presentiment that her myopia was her own foreigner, her essential foreignness (2001a: 10)

"*Étrangèreté*" is formed with the feminine adjective because it is the gender of strangeness. The writer shows it in feminine because of her own accidental weakness in the writing: the masculine and the feminine.

"*Vissement*" is a another noun invented from the sememe '*visser*' plus the suffix '*-ment*': "*car la myopie a de petites serres, elle tient l'oeil sous un voile serré, **vissements** de paupières, insistances, efforts vains pour passer le voile et voir, front froncé*" (1998: 18) ["for myopia has little claws, it holds the eye under a little tight veil, screwed-down eyelids, insistences, vain efforts to pass through the veil and see: forehead frown" (2001a: 12)]. Translated into Spanish by a formal semantic equivalent, "*atornillamiento*" ['screwment'] (2001b: 29), this new term reinforces, in my opinion, the pressure of "*des serres que la myopie comporte*" and keeps the voiced rhythm of the consonants *V* and *S*. It is not possible to keep the same rhythm in the Spanish translation.

The neologism "*descension*" is created from the sememe of the verb '*descendre*', '*descente*': "*Mais pendant que son âme déliée s'élançait, se formait un élan de **descension**: en s'éloignant de sa 'ma-myopie'*" (1998: 18) ["But while her unbound soul soared, a fall formed: getting away from her 'my-myopia'" (2001a: 12)]. Translated by a noun that exists in Spanish, "*descenso*" ['descent'] (2001b: 29), it could have been transcoded by '*descensión*', since, even though old and little employed, it exists in Spanish. Nevertheless, every translator is free to choose a term or another if the target language allows her/him to do this. In this sense, every translation is different as emphasized by Octavio Paz (1971: 9)[13]:

> Every text is unique and, simultaneously, it is the translation of another text. No text is completely original because the very language, in essence, is already a translation: firstly, of the non-verbal world and, afterwards, because every sign and every sentence is the translation of another sign and of another sentence. Although this reasoning can be inverted without loosing its validity: all the texts are originals because every translation is different. Every translation is, to a certain extent, an invention and so constitutes a text unique.

The neologism "*inarrivée*", was created in the style of "*inespoir*"[14]:

> *l'**inarrivée** du visible à l'aube, le passage par le non-voir, toujours il y a eu un seuil, franchir à la nage le détroit entre le continent aveugle et le continent voyant, entre deux mondes, un pas manqué* (1998: 18)

> the non-arrival of the visible at dawn, the passage through not-seeing, always there has been a threshold, swim across the strait between the blind continent and the seeing continent, between two worlds, a step taken (2001a: 12)

This neologism translated by "*lo inllegado*" (2001b: 29), is formed with the noun '*arrivée*' to which the prefix '*in-*' has been attached. It represents a non-arrival desired and placed between the absence of sight: an arrival within ['*dedans*'] for which it should be necessary to "*franchir à la nage le détroit entre le continent aveugle et le continent voyant, entre deux mondes*".

Another neologism is "*assoiffement*", which is extracted from the verb '*assoiffer*' plus the suffix '*-ment*': "*Ne-pas-voir c'est défaut pénurie* **assoiffement**, *mais ne-pas-se-voir-vue c'est virginité force indépendance*" (1998: 18) ["Not-to-see is defect penury thirst, but not-to-see-oneself-seen is virginity strength independence" (2001a: 12)]. In Spanish this noun was translated as "*sed*" ['thirst'] (2001b: 29), a term that already exists in this language. It could have been transcoded by a neologism in Spanish but the translator perhaps considered it more appropriate not to create a neologism.

The use of neologisms is a recurrent procedure in Hélène Cixous's writing. They become a necessity for Cixous to construct and deconstruct a new writing, and the reflection of a "trace" already existing. The neologisms are created from *grammes*, which disseminated along this writing, chain and weave the discourse. As says J. Derrida, "*le dieu de l'écriture peut devenir le dieu de la parole créatrice*" (1972: 112) ["the god of writing can become the god of the creative word"]. In this way, H. Cixous constructs a discourse always open to multiple chances.

In translation, to obtain equivalent neologisms is not always an easy task. The translator should wonder: what is the feeling facing a transformation seminally unequivalent to that of the source language? The translator becomes a bigamous being bifurcated between the original writing and the translation. However, this powerlessness causes a pleasure that will be satisfied by the writing of the Other. As I said before, it is through this feeling that translation arises like an urgent need of a penetration. It is then that one kills, one penetrates and breaks the hymen according to the words of J. Derrida:

> The hymen, the consummation of differends, the continuity and confusion of the coitus, merges with what it seems to be derived from: the hymen as protective screen, the jewel box of virginity, the vaginal partition, the fine, invisible veil which, in front of the hystera, stands between the inside and the outside of a woman, and consequently between desire and fulfilment. It is neither desire nor pleasure but in between the two. Neither future nor present, but between the two... With all the indecidability of its meaning, the hymen only takes place when it doesn't take place. (1985: 195)

After this quotation, I would like to appropriate one of the metaphors of Hélène Cixous when she writes about the '*connu(e)*'and the "blood":

> *La douleur de n'avoir pas reconnu que l'inconnue ne pouvait être ma mère, la honte de prendre une inconnue pour la connue par excellence, le sang n'a donc pas crié, pas senti?* (1998: 14)

> The pain of not having recognized that the unknown woman could not be my mother, the shame of taking an unknown for the known par excellence, did blood not shout out or feel? (2001a: 6)

Is it therefore the pleasure and the pain of the blood dripping from the hymen? or, is it the pleasure produced by the cutting *di-section* of the hymen? Through the translation, one is linguistically castrated and, though impotent, one needs to transcode due to an attraction that one cannot be separated from. The multiple chances of reading the word '*connu(e)*' ('*con*', '*con nu*', '*con nue*') and the exclusion of the translation prove the pleasure of the betrayal in translation.

2. Phonetic Losses: The Pleasure of the Letter

One of the typical characteristics in the literal translation is the loss of sonority. In Hélène Cixous's writing, the sound of the letter is an essential element that attracts the "ear of the other", the reader. This writing reflects the deconstruction which aims to destabilize the couple *parole*/writing where the sound is already writing and the writing already sound. It can be shown in the following examples:

> *La miopía era su falta [**faute**] [...], su [**son**] velo*[15] *natal imperceptible. Cosa extraña, ella veía [**voyait**] que no veía, pero no veía bien. [...] ¿quién rechazaba, era [**ce**] el mundo o ella? [...] todo el día en postura de confesión [**aveu**]: no veo el nombre de la calle, no veo [**vois**] el rostro [**visage**], no veo la puerta, no veo venir y soy yo quien no ve lo que debería [**devrais**] de ver. Tenía ojos y era ciega [**aveugle**].* (2001b: 23; 1998: 11)

> Myopia was her fault [...], her imperceptible native veil. Strange: she could see that she could not see, but she could not see clearly. [...] who could say where the refusal came from: who was refusing, the world, or she? [...] all day long in a position of avowal: I can't see the name of the street, I can't see the face, I can't see the door, I can't see things coming and I'm one who can't see what I ought to be able to see. She had eyes and she was blind. (2001a: 3)

In spite of the semantic equivalence of the translation, I will show some phonetic losses that are unavoidable in translation.

2.1. The Sexual Bifurcation of the *V*: a Lack of Sound

The sonority of the *V*, which is repeated nineteen times in the first paragraph, blows from its two erotic legs and lags towards the other letters leading to the '*voile*' of the writing. The V is a blown letter since it is fricative (labiodental and voiced). In my opinion, this is an autobiographic letter in Hélène Cixous's writing that one day was blown from the womb of Ève, her Jewish mother, who converted this blown letter into a metaphor of the takeoff, therefore, a metaphor for textual pleasure. This letter also appears in the key words of her writing: "*envol*", "*arrivance*", "*l'envers*", "*rÊve*", "*vélo*", "*ver*", "*voler*", "*Revêries*", "*ravin*". The *V* is a letter that returns and opens itself in two parts and two legs, which leads to the sexual and textual *différance*. But is it "*volée*"[16] ['stolen'/'blown away']? It is an impure and heterogeneous letter. Following J. Derrida:

> *La parole proférée ou inscrite,* la lettre, *est toujours volée. Toujours volée parce que toujours ouverte [...]. Elle n'est jamais propre à son auteur ou à son destinataire et il appartient à sa nature qu'elle ne suive jamais le trajet qui mène d'un sujet propre à un sujet propre.* (1967: 266)

> The uttered word or the written word, *the letter*, is always stolen. It is a stolen letter because it is always *opened* [...]. It never belongs to its author or to its addressee, and for reasons of its own nature it never follows the path from a proper subject to a proper subject.

The *V* is stolen and blown away in *Savoir* and in *Voiles* because it is disseminated and flies from one text to another and from a signifier to another sprinkling the discourse of the narrator: *"sa-voir"*, *"vue"*, *"voyant"*, *"aveugle"*, *"voile"*, *"lever"*, *"livre"*, *"invisible"*, *"voilà"*, *"vissement"*. The story of the *Voiles* could not have been constructed without stealing the veil from the Other; in the same way one cannot deconstruct without being opened doubly. This is why, it is a text doubly robbed and nicked the one from the other: *"points de vue piqués sur l'autre voile"*[17].

The *V* is inside the *F* because it (the *V*) represented, at that time, two different sounds in Latin: [u] vowel and [w] consonant. This was not comfortable for the pronunciation and it was decided to differentiate in the writing by a new sign representing a sound: *digama* but *à l'enVers*, the same letter which is at the origin of *F*. Here we have the metaphor of the difference of the *V*, since the *F*, an *hellène* [Hellenic] importation used in the Greek language for the [w], remained in French as the labiodental consonant [f] [18]. Then the *F* was used for doubling in H. Cixous's writing: *W* is double *V* in French, thus the double of the *V*.

The sonority disappears in the translation since the consonant *V* is not labiodental fricative in Spanish as it is in French, but bilabial, and it can become fricative depending on the position of the lips. That was the case of the sound of the consonant *V* which inaugurates the Spanish word '*velo*' ('*voile*') that is bilabial. Thus, words like *"confesión"* (*"aveu"*), *"ciega"* (*"aveugle"*) completely lose the blown sound and the eroticism of this letter doubled in *two* axes.

The same loss occurs in the translation of the verb '*voir*', which as H. Cixous writes: *"est-il la jouissance suprême?"* or *"est-ce: cesser-de-ne-pas-voir?"*. In this sentence one cannot hear, one cannot read either à l'*"oeil-nu"*. In translation, one always reads and interprets with glasses on but never *à l'oeil nu*.

The sonority of *Voilà* is also lost in translation. Firstly, because the presentative is not so used in Spanish as it is in French. Secondly, the translation can be different: '*éste(a) es*' ['this is'], '*he aquí*'. This presentative is a very important word not only because it is recurrent but also because it is an amphibologic term. The narrator uses this word, not only due to the sonority of the *V*, but also since it includes, by metonymy, '*le voile*' and '*la voile*', both veils included in a plural neuter. *"Voilà"* is also cut in two: '*voi(s)*' and '*là*'. This last word is homophone of '*là*': *la* is cut from '*il(la)*'; '*la*' is also the '*mi*' ['mid'] of '*les*'. It is there that the play of *différance* appears since '*voilà*' implies '*voir là*' and '*voir les*', the two. It is a way of seeing in plural through the play of the '*voiles*'.

In the Spanish language, this play is not possible to translate. When translating, the play of the polysemy is erased, and as long as a sign always refers to another sign, the plurality of signifieds disappears in the process of translating. It is along this line that deconstruction refuses the exclusion where the ambiguity, which is innate to the sign, disappears. In translation the neuter is absent for it should never be translated because it is impure. This is the impurity of languages and all these plays on letters make the *différance* arise in translation.

Similarly, it happens in sequences such as "*le voile dans l'oeil*", "*le voile dans l'âme*", "*elle voyait venir la vue*", "*elle voyait le lever du monde*", "*elle avait déjà vu tout cela sous verre avec lunettes*". The sonority of the *V* is lost in Spanish. It is there that the translator realizes the play on letters and the play of the writing.

2.2. The phonetic and semantic loss of the neuter pronoun '*ce*' is unavoidable in translation: "*était-ce le monde ou elle?*" (1998: 11). The use of neuter pronouns is of the utmost importance in H. Cixous's writing because the neuter is a "*ne-uter*"[19] like '*un(e) phénix(ie)*'. The nest of love is veiled in the uterus and from there the one and the other arise, both, with their other, "*mais ni l'un-ni l'autre*"[20].

In the French language, this neuter placed in the middle of the sequence leaves the statement ambiguous. In translation, there is no ambiguity any more among "*ce*", "*le monde ou elle*", in other words, among "*ce*", "*le*", "*la*", but between "*el mundo o ella?*" (2001b: 23). Is the world or she? or is '*ce elle*'? This pronoun will be also repeated throughout the discourse: "*les choses étaient-elles parties ou bien était-ce elle qui les mévoyait?*" (1998: 14) ["had things gone away or else was it she who missaw them?" (2001a: 6)]. The loss of the neuter is unveiled in the translation by means of the choice: "*o bien era ella quien las malveía?*" (2001b: 23).

2.3. Another sound, whose voiced strength is lost, is the sibilant play of the *S*: "*La trahison du sang du sens ainsi on peut se tromper de mère être trompée jusqu'à la mère?*" (1998: 14) ["Treachery of blood of sense so you can get the wrong mother, be wrong up to and including your mother?" (2001a: 6)]. The blow of the *S* and the feeling of being in trance is erased in the translation: "*¿La traición de la sangre del sentido de tal manera que uno puede equivocarse de madre, y estar equivocado hasta la madre?*" (2001b: 26). This sound is often lost when translating in Spanish.

2.4. The voiced play of "*se tromper*", "*être trompée jusqu'à la mère*", and "*trempée*", paronym of "*tromper*", is lost in Spanish.

2.5. Another phonetic play erases the double sense of the word in the translation. Such is the case of the word "*connue*": "*La douleur de n'avoir pas re***connu*** que l'in***connue*** ne pouvait être ma mère, la honte de prendre une in***connue*** pour la **connue** par excellence, le sang* [...]" (1998: 14) ["The pain of not having recognized that the unknown woman could not be my mother, the shame of taking an unknown for the known par excellence, did blood [...]" (2001a: 6)]. "*Inconnue*" was translated into one of the multiple signifieds: "*desconocida*". The exclusion of the translation veils the other meanings of this word such as "*con*", and "*con nu(e)*".

2.6. The homophonic play of "*elle*" and "*aile*" is also lost in Spanish:

> *le secret de son enfance:* ***elle*** *avait été l'**élue** de la famille, la myope parmi les cygnes [...] une impuissance imméritée qui était **elle**-même et contre laquelle **elle** [...] car cette myopie qui l'**éli**sait et la mettait à part était aussi indétachable d'**elle** que son sang de sa veine, c'était **elle**, **elle** était **elle*** (1998: 17)

> the secret of her childhood was dying: she had been the chosen one of the family, the myope among the swans [...] an unmerited impotence that was herself and against which she [...] for this myopia that had chosen her and placed her apart was as undetachable from her as her blood from her vein, it was she, she was it (2001a: 11)

"*Elle*" becomes, by homophony, the "*aile*"[21] which rebels against itself. In Spanish "*ella*" ['she'] is not homophone of "*aile*" ('*ala*') ['wing']:

> *el secreto de su infancia: había sido la elegida de la familia, la miope entre los cisnes [...] una impotencia inmerecida que era ella misma y contra la cual [...] porque esa miopía que la eligió y la colocó aparte era también tan indespegable de ella como la sangre de sus venas, era ella, ella era ella* (2001b: 28)

The wings symbolize the narrator's takeoff and, by means of their lightness, the power of flying through the writing. With the wings of the veils (and sails), the writer rises into the airs and becomes *ailée* ['winged'] and *hélée*[22] ['hailed'].

The loss of the sonority is unavoidable in translation as it deconstructs the *One*, H. Cixous's language, and opens to *otherness*, the translators' language. It is a necessary destruction but "the destruction is serious [...] It means killing" (Waldrop 1979: 42). However, in spite of the awkwardness and the faults, one needs to transgress through the language of the other.

3. Translation of Metaphors

The problem of the translation of metaphors has always worried, and still worries, translatologists. Most of them state that metaphors are not possible to translate. That is the case of E. Nida (1964) and Vinay and Darbelnet (1958/1960). However, I think that every metaphor is a special case. According to Snell-Hornby (1988), the metaphor is neither impossible to translate nor completely translatable since its translation would depend on the (con)text and on the language where it appears. I think that the closer two languages are, from a semantic and cultural[23] point of view, the less difficult it is to translate the metaphors. This happens to French and Spanish, which are Romance languages. The metaphors I show keep their meaning in the translation. I have only chosen four examples, for reasons of economy, which show that complete transcoding is preferred by all the translators when the target language permits it.

The first metaphor *in absentia* is the locution "*voir à l'oeil nu*", translated by "*ver-a-ojo-desnudo*" (2001b: 27). The narrator plays, in my opinion, with "*à l'oeil nu*" (which can be translated, either literally by '*con-el-ojo-desnudo*' ['with the naked eye'], or by means of a modulation[24]: '*a simple vista*'). In both locutions, what takes priority is the *nudity* of the eye, in other words, it is to be naked like a worm to enjoy not the sight but to see naked. '*Voir à l'oeil nu*' is also a sign of sensuality in the metadiscourse of the narrator because one "separates oneself", in this case, from the "*lunettes*" ['glasses'] to become naked.

In "*Les lunettes sont de faibles fourchettes bonnes tout juste à attraper des petits bouts de réalité*" (1998: 14) ["Spectacles are feeble forks only just good enough to catch little bits of reality" (2001a: 6)], metaphor *in praesentia*, literally translated as "*los anteojos son tenedores flojos apenas buenos para atrapar pequeños trozos de realidad*" (2001b: 23), in Spanish the sense has not changed. The "*lunettes*" become the prosthesis of the sight. The "*lunettes*" are forks with legs. One is separated from the glasses in order to cut what one desires. Translating is a process always done with glasses on, since it is the prosthesis of translator, whose translated words are sent into exile and never return. As H. Cixous emphasizes, "you never become too familiar and you never come to the point when you can hear it speak to you and you think you speak it... Exile as one of the metaphors, one of the structures of depropriation" (1990b: 12).

The following metaphor which I want to underline, "*Les yeux sont les lèvres sur les lèvres de Dieu*" (1998: 16) ["Eyes are lips on the lips of God" (2001a: 9)], is translated literally: "*Los ojos son los labios sobre los labios de Dios*" (2001b: 27). In my opinion, the eyes are the lips because they blink like the lips that move when pronouncing words. Understood from a linguistic point of view and, by iconic instinct, the eyes, which are the lips, see and read the writing. The lips belong to the *parole créatrice* of the narrator, a deconstructor god who destabilizes the logocentric oppositions of the *dedans* and of the *dehors*, of the *parole* and of the *écriture*. "*Être et ne pas être ne s'excluaient jamais*" (1998: 14) ["To be or no to be were never exclusive" (2001a: 7)] and as J. Derrida would say, voice is already writing. "*Les yeux sont les lèvres*" and the hands of writing.

With reference to the word '*myopie*', I think that it is a metaphor of the Other and, being under the skin of the translator, it is what permits betrayal. Myopia makes the writing of the other a betrayal and a mistake. All translators should be myopic. One never finds a translator without glasses. Myopia is a prosthesis from the danger of being naked with (the) other. "*Elle fait régner une éternelle incertitude qu'aucune prothèse ne dissipe*" (1998: 14) ["It opens the reign of an eternal uncertainty that no prosthesis can dissipate" (2001a: 6)]. As in love-making, in translation one makes love with myopia in order not to see what is veiled. Myopia is a "*cligner des yeux*" ['to blink'] and sees its birth separated. Myopia implies seeing oneself and seeing the other born "*mongolien*"[25], dead but present, the other '*mi*(e)' fallible who moves away and returns. Myopia is the *différance* of the other being far away, who is the trace of the same one.

I wanted to show some examples of translated metaphors. Translation becomes a metaphor for our own language, which leads us towards the language of the Other. Translating is a way of writing with (the) other and being born through (the) other.

4. Plays on Words

I will show only a few examples:

4.1. Polyptoton

This procedure uses "different grammatical forms of the same word" (Mazaleyrat and Molinié 1989: 269). In Hélène Cixous's writing, certain words disseminate their sememe to chain the semantism the writer wants to emphasize: "*don*", "*dation*", "*donation*", "*donner*". In translation, these words do not change their sense since the two languages are Romance. Translation permits the intimate relations between languages to be shown. As W. Benjamin would say, languages are not strangers to each other since they keep some similarities in order to say their purpose.

4.2. Paronomasia

Paronomasia is a procedure that consists in approaching two words whose signifieds are different but whose signifiers are similar. It is not usually kept in translation since it plays with sound. That is the case of "*aveuglement*" ['blindness'] which let us understand, at the same time, '*aveuglément*' ['blindly']. I think that one writes blindly, I mean, one writes with the unconscious: "*La myopie ébranlait jusqu'à la propre paix qu'établit l'aveuglement*" (1998: 14) ["Myopia shook up everything including the proper peace that blindness establishes" (2001a: 7)].

Another paronymous play which disappears in the translation concerns certain consonantal combinations. That happens to /TR/ and to the vocalic ones /a/ and /o/. H. Cixous plays with *"tromper"* and *'tremper'*: *"La trahison du sang du sens ainsi on peut se tromper de mère être trompée jusqu'à la mère?"* (1998: 14) ["Treachery of blood of sense so you can get the wrong mother, be wrong up to and including your mother?" (2001a: 6)]. She can get the wrong mother since she can get soaked by the sea and, similarly, she can get soaked by her mother as she has learnt from her mother how to use and merge in her discourse the poetic fluids of life.

5. Conclusion

The aim of this contribution has been to describe, from the standpoint of *différance* between signified and signifier, the way Hélène Cixous's writing is translated, a writing which exceeds the limits of the language. Translation as transformation permits, on the one hand, to unveil certain linguistic procedures which seem unapproachable when reading this kind of discourse. On the other hand, it allows veiling and erasing the amphibology and the plays of language in the source language. Thus the translation of neologisms, homophonic words, metaphors, etc., forces the translator to castrate the language, but a castration which produces a new language. This is why I have emphasized the feeling arising in the translator: a feeling of betrayal itself betrayed by the pleasure that this painful action produces.

I have found a semantic-referential link between the title (which includes the two original texts, *Voiles*) and the fact of translating two languages; in other words this/these title/s, being a metaphor of the sexual *différance*, require(s) and magnetize(s) the translation in order to destabilize the language of the Other. In this sense, to translate this writing involves a deconstruction, which constructs a language already de-constructed.

Translation becomes a semio-linguistic tool, frequently indispensable, for the comprehension of a language, whose textual alchemy cannot be transported "to anywhere". It must be felt like a love scene between languages whose innate infidelity implies "to *strange*". Translating is no more than a strange(r) need of writing through the language of the Other, of smiling by means of the language of the other and of being (with) Other and in (an)Other.

---

[1] In Cixous and Derrida (1998).
[2] According to Hélène Cixous: *"je n'étrangle pas les mots, je les* étrange" ["I don't strangle words, I *strange* them"].
[3] There are two types of transcoding: complete and partial. *"Le transcodage n'est pourtant qu'une composante de la traduction, il n'est pas* la *traduction. Seuls peuvent être transcodés dans les textes ou les discours les éléments, termes ou expressions, dont la signification reste la même, qu'elle soit envisagée au niveau de la langue ou actualisée dans un discours"*

(Seleskovitch and Lederer 1996: 7) ["Transcoding is however only one of translation components, it is not translation itself. The only elements, terms or expressions that can be transcoded in texts or speeches are those which keep the same meaning, whether considered at the language level or actualized in a speech"].

[4] *"Qui est selon la lettre, selon le sens strict des mots [...]. Une traduction littérale (= mot à mot)"* ["Which is in accordance with the letter, in accordance with the words' strict meaning [...]. A literal translation (= word for word)"]. *Lexis de la langue française*, Larousse, 1977, s.v.

[5] *"À l'inverse de l'anaphore, mais traduisant comme elle la même relation d'identité partielle entre deux termes inscrits sur l'axe syntagmatique du discours, la cataphore se caractérise par le fait que le terme repris précède le terme en expansion"* (Greimas and Courtés 1993: 33) ["Although it translates the same relation of partial identity between two terms on the syntagmatic speech axis, the cataphora, contrary to the anaphora, is characterized by the fact that the term which is retaken comes before the term in expansion"].

[6] *Illa* is another title of H. Cixous.

[7] 1923, in *Essais de Psychanalyse*. Paris: Payot, 1979.

[8] *Le Petit Robert*.

[9] *Cf.* Derrida (1972).

[10] The formal neologisms are different from the semantic neologisms. The first ones are the new signifiers affected by the signifieds whereas the second ones are already existing signs, which are affected by a/some new sememe/s.

[11] An example of translation for this prefix can be shown by the verb '*méconnaître*' ['*desconocer*'] or by the noun '*mépris*' ['*desconfianza*'], or by '*méfier*' ['*desconfiar*'].

[12] "The suffixes *-ment* are all based on a verb, a verb from everyday language"(Goose 1995: 2).

[13] My translation.

[14] *Cf.* Cixous (2000b).

[15] I write in boldface the words whose phonetical losses are obvious.

[16] The French polysemic adjective *"volée"* means not only 'stolen' but also 'blown away'.

[17] *Cf.* Cixous and Derrida (1998: 23).

[18] The *digama*, the other way round, for the consonantal sound [W] and the [V] for the vowel [U]. Afterwards the *F* was only used for the F. The V agglutinated other uses when the U appeared.

[19] *Cf.* Cixous (1972).

[20] *Ibid.*

[21] *Cf.* Cixous (2001: 103-113). H. Cixous disseminates the semantism of this signifier in *"le battement des ailes"*, *"battre de l'*aile*"*, *"à tire d'*aile*"*, et *"d'*Élie*"*.

[22] *Cf.* Hélène Cixous: "Les noms d'Oran".

[23] According to R. M. Dagut, "metaphor as governed by a subtle interaction of cultural experience and semantic associations; so that what determines the translatability of a SL metaphor is not its 'boldness' or 'originality', but rather the extent to which the cultural experience and semantic associations on which it draws are shared by speakers of the particular SL" (1976: 28).

[24] *Modulation* is a very common procedure in translation. Vinay and Darbelnet created this term.

[25] *Cf.* Cixous (2000a).

References

Benjamin, Walter. 1970. 'La labor del traductor' in *Angelus novus*. Barcelona: Edhasa.
Cixous, Hélène. 1972. *Neutre*. Paris: Bernard Grasset; Paris: des femmes, 1998.
—. 1990a. *Reading with Clarice Lispector*. Minneapolis, MN: University of Minnesota Press.
—. 1990b. 'Difficult Joys' in Helen Wilcox et al. (eds) *The Body and the Text. Hélène Cixous, Reading and Teaching*. New York, NY, and London: Harvester Wheatsheaf.

—. 2000a. *Le jour où je n'étais pas là.* Paris: Galilée.
—. 2000b. 'Vues sur ma terre' in Mireille Calle-Gruber (ed.) *Hélène Cixous, croisées d'une oeuvre.* Paris: Galilée. 235-254.
—. 2001. 'La peau en plus' in *Portrait de J. Derrida en Jeune Saint Juif.* Paris: Galilée. 103-113.
Cixous, Hélène and Jacques Derrida. 1998. *Voiles.* Paris: Galilée.
—. 2001a. *Veils* (tr. G. Bennington). Stanford, CA: Stanford University Press.
—. 2001b. *Velos* (tr. Mara Negrón). Mexico-Buenos Aires: Siglo XXI.
Dagut, M. B. (1976), 'Can Metaphor be Translated?' in *BABEL* 22(1): 21-33.
Derrida, Jacques. 1967. 'La parole soufflée' in *L'écriture et la différance.* Paris: Seuil.
—. 1972. 'La pharmacie de Platon' in *La dissémination.* Paris: Seuil.
—. 1985. 'Des Tours de Babel' in Joseph Graham (ed.) *Différance in Translation.* Ithaca, NY and London: Cornell University Press. 165-207.
—. 1987. 'Shibboleth' in A.D. Colin (ed.) *Argumentum e silentio, International Paul Celan Symposion.* Berlin and New York, NY: W. de Gruyter.
—. 1988. 'Roundtable on Translation' in *The Ear of the Other. Otobiography, Transference, Translation. Texts and Discussions with Jacques Derrida.* Lincoln, NB and London: University of Nebraska Press.
—. 1989. 'Yo – el psicoanálisis' in *Jacques Derrida*: '*¿Cómo no hablar?*' *y otros textos*, Barcelona: Suplementos Anthropos. 36-41.
Díaz-Diocaretz, Myriam. 1985. *Translating Poetic Discourse.* Amsterdam: John Benjamins.
Goosse, André. 1975. *La néologie française aujourd'hui. Observations et réflexions.* Paris: Conseil international de la langue française.
Greimas, Algirdas Julien and Joseph Courtés. 1993. *Dictionnaire raisonné de la théorie du langage. Sémiotique.* Paris: Hachette.
Kristeva, Julia. 1988. *Étrangers à nous-mêmes.* Paris: Fayard.
Mazaleyrat, Jean and Georges Molinié. 1989. *Vocabulaire de la Stylistique.* Paris: Presses Universitaires de France.
Newmark, Peter. 1992. *Manual de traducción.* Madrid: Cátedra.
Paz, Octavio. 1971. *Traducción: literatura y literalidad.* Barcelona: Tusquets.
Seleskovitch, Danica and Marianne Lederer. 1996. *Interpréter pour traduire.* Paris: Didier.
Venuti, Lawrence. 1992. 'Introduction' in Lawrence Venuti (ed.) *Rethinking Translation: Discourse, Subjectivity, Ideology.* London and New York, NY: Routledge.
Waldrop, Rosemarie. 1984. 'The Joy of the Demiurge' in William Frawley (ed.) *Translation. Literary, Linguistic, and Philosophical Perspectives.* Cranbury: Associated University Press.

PART III: Translating Sexual Difference

Transreadings*

Nadia Setti

The author states the importance of "writing the sexual difference" in the work of Cixous. This is not a question of changing the grammatical structures of French but a "complex strategy", involving also syntax, rhythm, sound and sense. The translator must be aware of the "indecision" of Cixous's idiom in order not to reduce the original text's strangeness in its own language(s). Cixous definitely operates in various languages, but the intrusion of other languages into French is not here a violent disruption. It is more likely an unconscious and poetic reference to this "m'other" language, made of rhythm, music, and breath.
Key words: sexual difference, rhythm, multiplicity of languages.

> *L'échangeabilité, l'aller à l'autre, le se tenir-ouvert devant l'autre, le (tenter-de-) se-mettre-à-la-place de l'autre est en fonction de leur générosité à chacun. Mais il y a aussi une part qui est inéchangeable – ce qui ne veut pas dire qu'elle est imperceptible: une part de toi qui reste à jamais promise, seulement promise, heureusement seulement promise.* (Cixous 1994a: 68)

> Exchangeability, the going to the other, the holding-open of oneself in front of the other, the (attempt to) put oneself in the place of the other is a function of one's generosity towards the other. But there is also a part that is not exchangeable – that doesn't mean that it's imperceptible: a part of you that stays promised forever, only promised, happily only promised. (tr. David Williams)

The starting point of this series of remarks will be a rather evident but indeed necessary reflection: translation questions are above all questions of reading. As a translator I draw on what the reader in me has learnt. And the reader apprenticeship is continuous, it begins again with every new book. It is similar to learning a foreign language that is so inventive and rich in transformations that even were you to learn it by heart, it would always amaze you. Through my experience as reader, translator and teacher, I see Hélène Cixous's works as coming out of several languages, because her writing is an open questioning of language as singular and definitive.

La langue is the pronominal and personal subject of many of Cixous's texts. In particular, I would cite "La venue à l'écriture" ["Coming to Writing"], *Illa, With ou l'Art de l'Innocence* in which *la langue* as *l'écriture* usually are interchangeable and connote each other through the personal feminine pronoun '*elle*'. For Cixous, the writing of sexual difference is more than a grammatically gendered feminine language: it is not only a theme or argument, but an essential part of a linguistic and writing project. It is less a feminisation of language (as for example, the word feminisation) but a much larger and complex strategy investing syntactic, rhythmic, semantic structures. What is announced and in many ways signified, exposed, developed, is already performed, acted, executed by the text in the meantime. It is this performing which precedes the thematic development that should interest us as translator, as transreaders, that is readers from the other side, towards the other side, at the crossroads of language.

Language identifies me and you, so that we can understand each other. But there is a part of me or you that will always be out of understanding, evaded, changing out of exchange. I can't translate you in my terms completely, term by term, word after word. It is like a portrait (of you in me), and it is incomplete: the most difficult thing, I believe, is to reproduce the other in his/her terms, without me.

Translating a poem or a text in another language, without submitting it to my language, means letting it be different in its own way. The danger during translation is to try to assimilate the otherness of the text, to reduce or suppress it. As in the loving relation between two people, one risks incorporation, domination or submission to a unique model or image. On the one hand, I cannot claim to achieve a bare identical reproduction of text, according to a fantasy of fidelity. I observe that some works are especially resistant to what language should be because they escape the rules and laws which condemn writing to immobility. Translation has to detect the marks of clandestine language. Secondly, while it would be easier to think that I translate from one language to another, from the language of this text to another, say *my* language, the question is what is really mine and what is not? What is really (fully) foreign and what isn't? This is difficult to answer. One would have to make a preliminary decision between one's own language and the foreign language in Cixous's works. And can we say how many languages a text by Cixous proffers? Through the French language, other undeclared languages may show here and there, the German of the author's mother, but also the textual languages of the author's favourite writers and poets. *Language* has necessarily a larger meaning, not identified with a particular *foreign language*.

We might compare this language born by foreign languages to Joyce's Babel, *Finnegans Wake*, the kind of work which forbids translation because it foresees every other language, it contains all languages, it engenders all the other possible or impossible languages. Any translation has to choose only one language and eliminate the others (*cf.* Derrida 1987).

Yet I don't really think that Cixous's writing has anything to do with the hypersophisticated Joycean textual machine. I don't think it is her scope. Even if her works come from "*le plus puissant calcul d'écriture*" together with "*le plus spontané du vocable*" (Derrida 2000: 22), her other languages don't come into her writing to disrupt it, to "babelise" it, to make war, but rather to give voice, in terms of orality/aurality, ear and vision writing. The languages which inhabit her language come from an intimate and at the same time far-off memory, a musical one, unconscious, inter-textual and multi-poetical. It is less a question of words, of mixing together words belonging to different languages than an intimate, deep translation of the other's poetic language. It is pre-linguistic, pre-textual.

The written language has nothing to do with a national language; it is rather made out of voice: "I had this luck, to be the daughter of the voice. Blessing: my writing stems from two languages, at least. In my tongue 'foreign' languages are my sources, my agitations. 'Foreign': the music in me from elsewhere"[1]. I like very much this declaration of kinship, which, without naming father and mother, gives to foreign languages no specific boundaries. So French may also be a foreign language and be blessed in the same way. We may ask ourselves what is translation, when the writing source is already a blending of different languages, translating each other continually? The text is the result of a series of translations: all these languages are happily "other" and related to the "m'other language".

But of course these other languages don't blend in the work in the same way. The "music from elsewhere" is first the *Hochdeutsch* of the mother's voice. This first music for the ears gives some touch of m'other country. All that is rhythm, breath, punctuation, musical composition in her writing belongs to this m'other language, more voice than grammar; what resists laws and grammatical rules comes from this mixture, this foreign musical language married to the French language. Cixous herself names her mother's *Hochdeutsch* "savage language". Nonetheless French and German have both their vocal characteristics; they compose an accord in a chasm before confounding their fluids in the writing river:

> *beau Hochdeutsch, chaleur rauque du Nord dans le frais parler du Sud. L'allemand maternel est le corps qui nage dans le courant, entre mes bords de langue, l'âmant maternel, la langue sauvage qui donne forme aux plus anciennes aux plus jeunes passions, qui fait nuit lactée dans le jour du français.* (Cixous 1976, 1986: 31)
>
> beautiful *Hochdeutsch*, throaty warmth from the north in the cool speech of the south. Mother German in the body that swims in the current, between my tongue's borders, the maternal lovesoul, the wild tongue that gives form to the oldest the youngest of

passions, that makes milky night in the French day. (tr. Deborah Jenson, with modifications by Ann Liddle and Susan Sellers in Cixous 1991: 21)

As we see in the images Cixous employs, "Mother German is the body who swims in the current, between my tongue's borders". This meeting puts together North and South, warmth and freshness, but also sounds peculiar to the way of speaking these languages as we can hear by alliteration: the R in *"chaleur"*, *"rauque"*, *"Nord"*, *"frais"*. But we may think: this insistence on sounds functions differently with each reader, because it depends on each person's particular pronunciation. That is exactly the point: while reading the text we have to turn or return to the oral language, and we become conscious of differences, vocal differences, tones, accents. This vocal substance escapes rules because it doesn't belong to grammar, it has no syntactic structure, it is what each reader may receive or bring to the text without any fixed or previous listening experience. Even were I to transpose this series of phonetic figures into other languages, the effect would be the same. The text would attract the reader towards the sound of words, awaken acoustic memory. Moreover, this stress on foreign languages and voices as *savage* as well as most familiar is undoubtedly associated with pleasure. Textual vocal arrangement is sensual and even erotic, and has a considerable part in the text's semantic development.

When we speak of the difficulty or impossibility of translation we usually mean the way textual language exhibits its multiplicity, shows its particular way of signifying. I will give an example to illustrate this idea. I have already suggested that French may play with homophones in a very interesting way. The point is that the similarity or identity of pronunciation produces meaning; it isn't just musical play. So if we want to transport both we are obliged to make a choice or to introduce other meanings. It is even more difficult to transport the entire series of phonemes and syllables dispersed throughout the text and constituting its very phonetic texture. What this means is that we have to abandon the idea of word to word translation, and aim for a textual translation faithful to a sense of repetition and variation.

We should think of this poetics of dissemination as phonetic weaving, a meaningful display of linguistic possibilities. Should translation avoid what language offers as possibilities? This would mean that no equivalent is possible, no passing, but also no transgression, repetition, or insistence. We have to pay attention (perhaps a distracted attention) to signifier displacing through the text: something which doesn't maintain an assigned position but may present itself in various compositions, and many possible meanings, all of them coming to mean together. Because dispersion is not a definitive status, it points to a meaningful bunch of signifiers.

Instead of quoting large text sections, I'll stick for the moment to quoting some syllables: (pro)nominal title *Illa*, a fiction of 1980, an echo of another one, *La* (1976). Is this a common word or possibly a full name? We have first to decide its grammatical status. We may refer to our knowledge of another language, Latin, a *dead* language: in Latin '*illa*' means the third feminine person, that person, she. As we see we are already translating, we are already between at least two languages. But of course we can pursue another avenue and consider that "*illa*" is the composed word '*il* + *la*', masculine pronoun + feminine article, 'he and the (she)'. Masculine and feminine are associated, the feminine adds to the initial masculine and modifies it, as a supplement and a promise. This second hypothesis may seem quite surprising but we can find its echoes in the general plan of this book that is itself like a voyage from a situation rooted in the ancient world dominated by masculine paternal divinities, to another one created by feminine affections and forces.

If we choose to translate the composed word we lose the ambiguity between old and new language, we lose Latin, a certain root for the neo-Latin languages. *Illa* is also a questioning about origins, uprooting, genealogies and links.

Of course I am interpreting here: I am suggesting what a French reader might hear in the title and eventually find later, if the reader is a thoughtful and cultivated reader. The title is full of suggestions, some of which will resonate in other languages, some of which will not. The words and meaning we can translate are reserved, that is still open to translation.

The second title I mentioned, *La*, so short, so apparently laconic, is at the heart of gender determination: the definite article is what allows us to establish, in some occurrences, the gender of a noun. But it is unusual to find it alone, it should be followed by another word, it aspires to continuation, it calls for a feminine word, which isn't yet there. So it isn't only a mark of feminine (absolute feminine) but also of expectation about the possible forms this person would take. If we make explicit the womanly being of this person we take away what this word gives: the announcement of the feminine whatever she will be. But here it comes out, becomes visible, rich of meaning: it becomes a title, something important, promising. When translated into English we lose the gender mark, 'The'; to recuperate it, we may add another word 'The (feminine)'[2] or renounce the feminine accent and leave the ambiguity of gender, a possibility of the English language but not of French.

In Cixous's fiction *Ou l'art de l'innocence* (1981), language is the subject object of a poetic reflection about enjoying language out of repression. The text is divided among different voices or figures: their description concerns above all the emergence of their names. They usher in a linguistic narrative weaving phonetic suggestions. The very first name is "*Aura*". We can pronounce it as a diphtongue, like '*aurore*', or as a hiatus, like the Latin word '*āura*'. Wherever "*Aura*" appears she is like a fairy who makes words turn on themselves so as to produce an "auroral text". What is the equivalent of this oral text in other languages?: "*AURA – Gémeaux, j'aime eau, gemme mot etc...*" (Cixous 1981: 62).

A series of homophones with changeable meanings of course constrain every translation to renounce either meaning or homophony, or to find a series of sounds similar to play with which is clearly suggested by the text, more like "*un jeu de mot*". In fact both pronunciations of "*Aura*" are effective: it depends on rhyme, on another word which is associated with "*Aura*", for example '*Paura*', or "*Auram expelles furcam*" (*ibid.*: 67). The character/voice Tinouk offers a sort of explication of this game, explaining that it is a kind of lesson about how to read:

> *Tinouk a pensé avec ses oreilles: "Aura du verbe avoir. Aura c'est le futur."* A *entendu. Il y a o, il y a au, avec tous les o possibles, il y a eau haut et au. Et il y a ra au moins deux, ras de chose, râ le soleil, ra la bête. Il y a l'or. Ça vient de la. L'or vient de Aura. Il manque un je pour faire éclater l'aura-je. Il ne manque pas: aura aurage en je.*
> *Il y a t'aura, en continuant, il y a thora.* (*ibid.*: 90)[3]

If Tinouk thinks with his ears, I imagine the reader has to do the same thing. Do we think with our ears? Do we realise how we think? I imagine that a poet may think with ears, and write while listening. Tinouk proposes the series of equivalents corresponding to the same sound in the preposition "*au*", the name "*eau*" ['water'], the adjective "*haut*" ['tall', 'high'], and even in the word "*or*" ['gold/or']. The name "*aura*" is a name and a verb, the future of '*avoir*' ['to have']. This thinking by ear also has its grammatical and lexical notions. The text itself proposes all the different translations of the parts of this word when decomposed. We realise that the smaller part may always be richer in meaning: it is up to us to do the work of association, as for example with "*ras de chose*" which is the generic expression for "*à ras de terre*", "*au ras des eaux*", "*au ras du sol*". The reader has to complete the word when it lacks a letter, for example, "*ra la bête*" for '*rat la bête*'. We may also reverse the sentence direction so as to hear through "*Il y a l'or*" '*l'ora, Laura...*'.

How can a translator make a reader of another language play this word game when we know that there is no equivalent except in the play itself? We may keep the game's rules but we have to change the words. Of course, the example is extreme and not all the pages of *With ou l'art de l'innocence* are like this one, but even if it is a playful lesson, it presents us with a network of words, a work of association and of recollection where each word calls for another one, the next one, the previous one. Once we have understood the game we can continue to play it with other ears. I imagine multilingual ears, suggesting perhaps to the foreigner some hints of French phonetics[4].

If we want to keep the play on homophones, which we can't do in all languages, we are obliged to recall the function of the sign, the dissociation between signifier and signified, an association which is not still nor stable.

> *Qui a l'oreille sublime entend nettement ces paroles sans voix.* (Cixous 1988a: 22)
>
> Whoever has a sublime ear hears plainly these voiceless words. (Cixous 1994b)

How can we put borders between sounds, texts, genders and poems? In the book *Manne, aux Mandelas aux Mandelstam* many different borders are crossed over, beginning by those among different poetic texts and languages. We know that in this text, through this text, two histories and two couples meet: the Russian Ossip and Nadejda Mandelstam, and the South-African Nelson and Winnie Mandela. Nothing apparently permits any comparison or communication between them. Historically they never meet, but poetry engenders another land and time where they can touch each other. To be clear, I am not suggesting any kind of direct imitation or mimesis of their languages, either of Mandelstam's poetry or Mandela's political discourse, but I wonder about the function of these *foreign* languages in the creative fiction: they are perhaps definitely not at all strange to the author but intimately familiar. Cixous herself reminds in her interview with Françoise van Rossum-Guyon about *Manne* (in van Rossum-Guyon and Díaz-Diocaretz 1990) that she came out of three or four languages, and she has en ear for languages coming from the poetical abroad. She needs to be poetically, humanly stricken, she needs to receive a stroke to begin to work, on the unconscious and then conscious level. A poem may be that strike.

We do not find the Russian words of Mandelstam's poems in the text, but rather Dante's lines in Italian, the language Mandelstam learnt reading the *Divine Comedy*. The migration from one language to another, from one poetical country to the other has already begun. Then the text passes here and there to the poetic form, so that silence and space arise around words and lines. The poetry's call forces textual arrangement to change in the middle of the narration when the tone changes and the tale necessarily becomes a prayer or lamentation. If the author calls Dante "my grandmother" it is because she recognises through this story a tone familiar to her.

In a very interesting way Cixous approaches and puts side by side different poetic displays: poems may be vertical or horizontal. They cross Dante and Mandelstam's texts in the manner of birds, up and down, by earth and by air, in every possible plane and direction, space or time. When we read Dante's verses[5], we find them in OM language and time, at the beginning of the text mixed with the narrative poet's voice. Poetic time brings together voices and texts.

> À Voronèje, aux quatre hivers, vivait son dernier hiver OM reste d'un grand poète chassé de terre, chassé comme l'étourneau par la rafale, jeté de ça, de là, en bas, non, plus d'en bas, en haut, en hors, nul espoir, nul repos, nulle compagne, nulle compassion, le monde est un éboulement mauvais,
> Vivait de riens, de restes de mémoire, de restes d'ongles de tissu terrestre, de restes de langue jadis nombreuse et orgueilleuse, aujourd'hui ruinée, un homme au nom usé, au cœur rongé par les froids, l'exilant ouragan, les rageuses pensées (Cixous 1988a: 7)
>
> In Voronezh of the four winters, OM was living his last winter, remains of a great poet chased from the earth, chased like the starling by the storm, cast here, there, below, no, no, more below, above, beyond, no hope, no rest, no companion no compassion, the world is a bad caving in,
> Living on nothing, on the remains of memories, on the remains of fingernails, the remains of terrestrial tissue, on the remains of language once numerous and proud, today laid waste, a man with a worn-out name, with a heart consumed by the cold, the banishing hurricane, raging thoughts (Cixous 1994b)

This language is no imitation of Dante's or Mandelstam's poetry, no counterfeiting: it is inhabited by hints, voices, silences. It may be considered a result of previous translations, of reading each through another. As Cixous says, she finally read Mandelstam through Tsvetaeva. It is not at all an interpretation nor a real translation, but a transwriting, a result of passing through these works and giving echoes of them.

Another very important aspect of this vocal structure is rhythm and punctuation, which define text tempos, paragraph dimensions, sentence and pause length, continuity and interruption. While the poem usually operates as intensity, concentration on words as if time were limited, Cixous's poetical narratives propose large rhythmical units where interruption plays inside continuous paragraphs, sometimes developing over several pages. The sentences continue until the limit of breathlessness and then breath returns. This has nothing to do with what ordinary or narrative language performs, it plays rather against narrative structure. I would suggest that the poetic narrative of Cixous doesn't renounce vocal, polyphonic narration. The stating (*énonciation*) becomes more important than the statement (*énoncé*). In the uninterrupted development of Cixous's narrative, semantic and syntactic focuses are regulated by an almost non-existent punctuation, as if the reader should take up the narrative composition as part of the work of reading.

I think that when we read a Cixous text we are at first startled or caught by a certain rhythmical figure commanding the text, different for each text, as if every story or emotion or theme needed its own particular tempo. I'll give a few examples but of course one should consider larger extracts of many texts.

Tout le temps où je vivais en Algérie je rêvais d'arriver un jour en Algérie, j'aurais fait n'importe quoi pour y arriver, *avais-je écrit*, je ne me suis jamais trouvée en Algérie, il faut maintenant précisément que je m'en explique, comment je voulais que la porte s'ouvre, maintenant et pas plus tard, *avais-je noté très vite*, dans la fièvre de la nuit de juillet, car c'est maintenant, et probablement pour des dizaines ou des centaines de raisons, qu'une porte vient de s'entrebâiller dans la galerie Oubli de ma mémoire, et pour la première fois, voici que j'ai la possibilité de retourner en Algérie, donc l'obligation... (Cixous 2000b: 9)

The whole time that I lived in Algeria I dreamed of one day going to Algeria. I would have done anything to get there, I had written, *I never found myself in Algeria, now is precisely the time when I must explain myself, how I wanted the door to open, now and not later,* I had jotted down quickly, *in the fever of a July night, because now is the time, and probably for tens or hundreds of reasons, that a door has cracked open on the Forgetful Porch of my memory, and for the first time, I now have a chance to go back to Algeria, and therefore a duty...* (tr. David Williams)

Through the punctuation, we apprehend that this is only one paragraph without a real end because it finishes with suspension points. The length of this paragraph is fixed by quotation marks but also by italics: we perceive immediately that this beginning is isolated from the rest of the text, as if there were two different beginnings. This is the very first signal of interruption, even before we enter the narrative itself. Then we may observe that in the interior of this paragraph several commas separate sentences – asyndeton form is neatly preferred – but in fact sentences have a rather parallel structure and they are intertwined about each other. The most evident effect of juxtaposition are the sentences of the narrative voice, the *author's statement* concerning the writing act: e.g., "I had written", "I had jotted down quickly". The past perfect of these verbs stands out in a narrative where the imperfect tense is dominant, nonetheless we feel a strong effect or sentiment of general temporal displacement: what should be recent (the time of narration) is past, what belongs to the distant past joins the present time. All the sentences are at the same level, the co-ordinate structure permits us to connect past to present, to install continuity between past desire and thoughts and present ones, the 'I' she was, with the 'I' who writes. But are these apparently identical subjects truly identical? Does the contiguity of subjects and sentences mean a true continuum?

The real subject, we guess, of this paragraph is "All the time", time as a whole, supposed as indivisible, where cuts can nevertheless happen, as for example the beginnings and the ends, the arrivals and the departures. This paragraph cut out on the border of the narrative contains all the themes and questions of the text. What is the relation between the "now" at that time and the "now" in the actual moment, if the word "*maintenant*" is exactly the same?

We should not conclude too quickly that the continuum prevails because in fact the narrative voice takes place in other voices, other narrators whose narratives interfere with the first one. It's a curious and original form of anacoluthon[6] because in this case it is another stating subject who interrupts the main narrative voice. The short sentence "*dit ma mère*" ["my mother says"] appearing in the middle of the narrative warns us of the change in subject. This introduces another form of oral narrative:

> *Nous n'avons pas souffert à l'école. Une fois j'ai été invitée à un anniversaire et je suis allée. Et on allait à Norderney, tous les juifs sont allés à Norderney sur la Nordsee. Dans le Ostsee il y avait des plages où tous les juifs ne sont pas allés, à Helgoland il n'y avait pas mais à Norderney il y avait beaucoup – rien que des Juifs? Demandai-je – tout le monde dit ma mère, jamais je ne vais chez les Juifs dit ma mère j'étais encore très allemande ensuite les gens commençaient à être sionistes ce que je n'ai jamais été, chaque fois qu'il y a un nationalisme je ne vais pas, j'ai toujours été internationale.* (Cixous 2000b: 107)

> We didn't suffer at school. Once I was invited to a birthday party and I went. And we would go to Norderney, all the Jews went to Norderney on the Nordsee. On the Ostsee there were beaches where the Jews didn't go, there were none in Helgoland but in Norderney there were many – just Jews ? I asked – everyone said my mother, I never go where the Jews go said my mother I was still quite German and then people began to be Zionists which I never was, every time there's a nationalism I stay away, I have always been international. (tr. David Williams)

As in the previous example we should read here a kind of story, since "my mother" is remembering her past, in Germany. Here the supposed continuum is expressed by a very frequent expression "*tout le monde*", 'all': it should be a whole without separation or differences but is in fact crossed by all sorts of distinctions which can eventually become real barriers. What first catches our attention is the narrative rhythm: what commands the succession of sentences is mainly breath, it's not the syntactic rule. This is most evident when commas are absent so that one passes from one idea or subject to another without any halt. The sentence should stop but the narrating person can't stop her narration, she has to go on, elsewhere. She cannot stop there, before passing the limit, the border.

We can see that in this case the deep signification of this recording tale is related directly to the rhythmic score more than the syntactic construction. Besides, the semantic syntax is open, not fixed nor finished: it is up to us to give it an ultimatum, to impose the connections and conjunctions. The tale is rather rough without the conjunctions which allow one to pass from one side to another ('because', 'then', 'so that', etc.).

In Cixous's works we may find many examples of a tale which further develops all the possible sides, meanings or forms of a narrative spring. Translation should not precipitate those choices introducing, for example, subordinate forms. This point is very important and, like the preceding ones, is connected with sexual difference. How can we stand this indecision, this accumulation of sentences, this parallel semantic construction?

We often have the feeling when we read Cixous that all that usually is kept aside, or cancelled, comes out here and is displayed. A non-selective choice offers and gives us many chances to see hidden thoughts. We must be patient and wait for all the different meanings to emerge, it may take some time. It is a sort of continuous translating, writing what is continuously changing. That's what I call a living language, or a language that is tempted by life, tuning with life's sounds. Cixous's language is a living one because she writes French as a foreign language, "*langue vivante*": she succeeds in preserving it from sclerosis, from every form of rigidity, straightness, imprisonment.

I think that all that is living in language, in writing, is the *true* mother language (*langue maternelle*): the language which preserves life and otherness, the lively foreigner in our language. It is perhaps to this "m'otherness" that Derrida refers when he remarks the "*intraductible*", the impossible translation of many Cixous's texts. What resists translation is also what attracts and draws translation. We cannot sum it up or reduce it, we just have to find a creative language for it.

So when we begin to translate, we should know that we must abandon every idea of identity, identical, anything that has to do with copy. How to copy a living text? Remember Poe's tale, the famous *Oval Portrait*, the tragedy of the unique, live or die, one or the another, only one Life is authorized, the young woman's or her portrait's, truer than the living one. Let's take this tale as an allegory, and think that something of this working with the living material of the text is part of the translation's work.

Every text, every new experience may change our way of reading, our appreciation of language, our language. I do not pretend to produce some sort of theory out of this experience, I can just try to think about what happens in this experience of journey through languages. As Henri Meschonnic remarks theory as well as experience are unfinished:

> *J'ai rassemblé quelques éléments pour une poétique de la traduction, et une expérience. La théorie n'en est que l'accompagnement réflexif. Toutes deux, inachevables. L'expérience est première.* (Meschonnic 1999: 9)

> I put together some elements for a poetics of translation, and an experience. Theory is only what accompanies reflection. Both unfinishing. Experience comes first. [my translation]

I agree, experience comes first, because it has something to do with the first time, with the pleasure of discovering words, to come as nearly as possible to the linguistic work of the text. It is the experience of language becoming poetry, coming to poetry, turning to poetry. A language that only in part confirms our knowledge of language, but in fact turns to another one, during our reading, makes us discover other possibilities.

Because of this 'being-not-one' or perhaps anyone, you cannot hold down language, catch it, make it your own or possess it. Now, is translation a mean of appropriation, since one can reduce what is deviating, escaping oneness? Of course these questions are the same ones we ask of the poem and of poetry, which means that our experience of translation is an exercise of poetic language. The different ways of modifying grammar forms or syntactic constructions keep the reader's attention on language itself, on textual performance. One becomes conscious of the text as something alive, making itself before us, with and without us. Above all, it asks the reader, anyone, the other one, to stay there, to accomplish something, perhaps just to wait for the writing performance.

This is probably what Meschonnic calls the subjectivity or historicity of the text, orality and writing. It is what inserts the book and the text into a space where we find time, subjects, history. It is not only a text functioning by its own rules and structures, but being modified by reading and changing our approach to reading. So translation reveals what language is doing, what the text is performing. We may then understand that translating isn't simply to pass from one language to another, but to make perceptible these different changes, first of all of the language itself.

Je réserve la traduction (Arthur Rimbaud)[7]

Translation detects what is exposed to ambiguity, what is susceptible to loss when translated. The translation economy is constituted of gains and losses: it means to accept leaving some parts of the text out of translation, in a sort of reserve not translated. But it is also true that the forms of subversion and invention in the text open the way to research and the discovery process. This fatal mourning is also what make us think about the language work in the text, what the text holds in store for us, we are stimulated into looking for deeper resources of language. There is something still waiting on the other side, like a promised land, out of reach.

That's why I don't want to call these examples of Cixous's writing translation problems. They are that, but above all they are open questions to our reception of language and particularly of poetical language. Every example I have given points to the differentiation process, to what makes gender difference perceptible: nouns and adjectives are usually more visible than articles, adverbs, preposition. This part of the language function above all as links, they connect the different parts together. We don't see them, but they are there.

Through the translation work (that is a rereading through the other language) we could detect the capillary work of echo and recall like a sort of internal rhyme. I will give another series of examples taken from "Tancredi continues" (Cixous 1983). Since this text has been translated into different languages, let's try to make a comparison between these translations, not to establish which is 'the best' but to analyse how each language answers in its own way to the poetical and textual work. Let's see how this text begins:

> *Je lis la* Jérusalem Délivrée, *à corps perdus, à corps troublés, à corps délimités.* (Cixous 1983, 1986: 141)
>
> I read *Jerusalem Delivered*, rushing headlong into the fray, merging with other impetuous bodies, troubled bodies, delimited bodies. (Cixous 1988b: 37)
>
> *Leggo la* Gerusalemme Liberata *a corpi persi, a corpi mescolati, a corpi delimitati.* (Cixous 2000a: 57)[8]

The very first surprise for the attentive reader comes from one letter, 's', the plural of *"corps"* which is an invariable word in French, *"perdus"* plural indicates that many bodies take part in the reading act just like in the act of loving. At the same time we acknowledge that we are really reading a text because the plural ending is a graphic and grammatical mark, but not an aural one. We are not supposed to hear it, just to see it.

On the contrary, in the Italian translation this plural is much more evident, and repeated. There is even an effect of alliteration, of rhyme, of agreement, of concordance between noun and adjective, between the three nominal groups. But we haven't yet finished with the alliteration phenomenon which inscribes a supplementary meaning, and an essential one for the comprehension of this text. Because of the repetition we may hear the word *"accord"* as homophone of *"à corps"*: this is a musical way to introduce the music of differences, the leitmotiv of this Rossinian Cixous's text. Bodies tuning, on common chord, search for a gender agreement, through endings and internal rhymes.

In the process of reading there are many bodies, the text is also a body, her name may be a feminine one, "Jerusalem Delivered": there is a trouble and an exchange between the physical bodies and figural textual body. What could permit us to detect signals of difference, marks, signs in this musical and textual trouble?

We have already pointed to endings (plurals or gender endings) but we can see that they are extremely changing. Just another example:

> *Mais les autres, les débordants, Tancrède, Clorinde, les amants de la franchise, ces deux créatures singulières, plus fortes qu'elles-mêmes, oui capables l'une et l'autre*

> d'aller, [...] jusqu'à l'autre – le plus lointain, le plus proche. [...] Je ne sais plus si je dois dire ils ou elles. (141)

> But the Others, the irrepressible ones, Tancredi, Clorinda, the lovers of freedom, these two singular creatures, stronger than themselves, yes, the one and the other capable of going, at the price of life, for the love of truth, for love, beyond their own forces, all the way to the other – the farthest, the nearest. [...] I no longer know if my "they" is masculine or feminine. (37)

> *Ma gli altri, gli straripanti, Tancredi, Clorinda, gli amanti della franchezza, queste due creature singolari, più forti di se stesse, sì, capaci, l'una e l'altra di andare, a costo della vita, per l'amore della verità, per l'amore, al di là delle proprie forze fino all'altro – il più lontano, il più vicino. [...] Non so più se devo dire essi o esse.* (57)

This long sentence unwinds a series of appositions that are not really fixed on the names of Tancredi and Clorinda, because at each turn of the phrase new qualifications are thrown and gender changes. So in the first series there are nominal groups (masculine nouns) "*les débordants*", "*les amants de la franchise*" referring to Tancrède, Clorinde; in the second series all the appositions are feminine and refer to "*ces deux créatures*", which command the following feminine determinants until the final "*l'une et l'autre*".

If we follow the logic of this sentence Tancredi as Clorinda are concerned by many gender changes. In particular, the other is potentially both: that's why the English translation allows the ambiguity to continue longer than, for example, in the Italian where each change is precisely indicated.

The reader like the translator has to be continuously awake since from one sentence to another the subject may change sex, from "*je les ai vues*" to "*je les ai vus*" ["I have seen them"] (who?):

> *Je les ai vues glisser, l'une toute en blanc, l'autre toute en bleus sombres, [...] Pour en revenir à mes deux précieux apparus, pour tout dire, dès que je les ai vus glissant l'un vers l'autre [...] Glisser, oui, toute en blancs, l'une brillant à la rencontre de l'autre toute luisante de bleus profonds.* (150)

> I saw them slip in, one all in white, the other all in dark blues [...]
> To return to my two precious apparitions, to tell the truth, as soon as I saw them, gliding toward one another [...] Gliding, yes, all in whites, one shining forth to meet the other all shimmering in deep blues (42, 43)

> *Le ho viste scivolare, l'una tutta in bianco, l'altra tutta in blu scuri [...] Per ritornare ai miei due preziosi apparsi, a dir la verità, appena li ho visti scivolare l'uno verso l'altro, [...] scivolare, sì tutta in bianchi, splendente l'una incontro all'altra tutta di blu profondi rilucente.* (64)

We may observe that all the possibilities of "concordance" are exploited, stressed, employed, underlined. But except for the quick passage to masculine ("*apparus*"), the entire passage is turned to feminine, the question itself is feminine but the gender of the other is "a mystery".

We can maintain the continuous variation of mystery in Italian, and even add supplementary marks of gender, "*l'altra*". In each case, at each decision, language makes difference sound with a different tune; what comes out is how we hear difference, what may sound strange or doesn't sound at all.

With my Italian ear I am much more sensitive to all the occurrences of endings and their agreements, but in French some changes are just visual, so I see them when reading but not when I read them aloud. We may now interpret this repetition of sentences referring to vision, as an invitation to pay attention to the sliding from vision to hearing: "gliding", this is the verb which returns frequently, it is the movement between these two figures, or mysteries, or beings, but it is also the way we apprehend writing, gliding from what we see to what we hear.

I consider that I can't speak or reason about meaning without analysing these forms of phonetic and grammatical tunes or out of tunes like:

> *Il était le plus beau d'une femme, il était la plus majestueuse des femmes*
> *[...]*
> *Et plus belle qu'un jeune homme, plus beau qu'un chevalier de la foi, elle était noble de la puissance d'un héros.* (153)

> He was the most beautiful of a woman, he was the most majestic of women
> [...]
> And more beautiful than a young man, more beautiful than a knight of faith, she was noble with the power of a hero. (44)

> *Egli era il più bello di una donna, era la più maestosa delle donne*
> *[...]*
> *E più bella di un giovane uomo, più bello di un cavaliere della fede, ella aveva la nobiltà della potenza di un eroe.* (66)

The comparison is utilised here as a way to trouble identity, to give feminine attributes to the masculine subject, even in a superlative way. We do not have an ordinary and usual comparison between feminine and masculine qualities, or directly between man and woman. The comparative structure is displaced or crossed, and indeed we don't know exactly what is the resolution of this comparison: how can we rightly represent a man being the most beautiful of a woman? which kind of beauty is it? To come to figure it we have to pass through a feminine majestic beauty. And finally we haven't already, immediately, an image of it, we have to look for it, to compose after comparison, what is beyond comparison.

The importance of comparison as a figurative structure compels the use of personal pronouns that could be otherwise suppressed, in Italian, in which they are not obligatory. I could eliminate them, but in that case one wouldn't appreciate the swaying of gender attributes in the terms of the comparison. What is really out of tune is equally out of comparison, we hear it, we understand it but can we imagine it? Not yet, perhaps at the end of this text we shall be able to know who is or may possibly be Tancredi according to Hélène Cixous.

This seems to me very near what I'd call an intimate habitation of the other voice, even if this voice is born in fiction. In a similar way Tancredi is inhabited by a feminine voice since a mezzo sings Tancredi in Rossini's opera. But we can also say that Cixous's text is haunted by voices. What is named as a mystery may also be considered a metaphor of what is being performed by the text: we listen to what we actually don't hear or see unless we have "a sublime ear which hears plainly the voiceless words". Intimate voice or oniric words are not immediately audible, nonetheless Cixous's text drives continually towards an oral execution, or a musical one which is a composition with multiple voices.

In "Tancredi continues" we perceive very clearly the moment of vocal intensity which corresponds to a libretto-like composition; some of the verses are echoes of Tasso's *Jerusalem Delivered*[9], as well as Baudelaire's poem "Invitation au voyage".

But this reference doesn't mean a real quote, rather a kind of intertextuality or interweaving of verses coming from those texts. Nonetheless the author doesn't borrow the classical forms of epic versification (like octaves in *Jerusalem Delivered*). The length of each 'verse' is different, so that it is really the spatial disposition on the page which transforms the text perception into the vision of an aria-poem. Then, even if the meter is rather free and various there is still a metrical and rhythmical construction which translation has to keep in mind and in time. There is a real tempo that we can rather easily detect and mark.

Tu n'est plus ma sœur	Non schivar, non parar, non ritirarsi
Je ne suis plus ton enfant[10]	voglion costor, né qui destrezza ha parte.
La colère et l'obscurité ne sont ni feints ni mésurés	Non danno i colpi or finti, or pieni or scarsi;
Leurs pieds sont immobiles, leurs âmes au contraire	toglie l'ombra e il furor l'uso dell'arte. Odi le spade orribilment urtarsi
s'agitent, et s'excitent, les glaives retombent, soit de taille soit de pointe	a mezzo il ferro ; il pié d'orma non parte: sempre è il piè fermo, e la man sempre in
Que fuis-tu mon amour? Debout flanc à flanc. Ne se voient pas...	moto; né scende taglio in van, né punta a voto.
Rien ne les sépare	[...]
Qu'est-ce qui le sépare? L'obscure méchanceté de l'Histoire	Tre volte il cavalier la donna stringe con le robuste braccia; ed altrettante
Le combat devient de plus en plus serré, Déjà ils ne peuvent plus se servir de la pointe, C'est avec les regards qu'ils s'aveuglent	da que' nodi tenaci ella si scinge[12].

| Trois fois Aménaide reçoit le regard de Tancrède |
| Trois fois elle se dégage de cette attirance qu'elle redoute |
| Te croire plutôt mourir |
| Mais de toute ma vie malgré moi je te crois |
| Tu n'es plus mon enfant |
| Je ne suis plus ta soeur[11] |

I think it rather useful to put Cixous's lines side by side with Tasso's verses: we can better appreciate the textual work on rhythm and meaning as well as their connection. The Italian poet uses the typical epic form: a *stanza* [octave] of eight verses, each one being an hendecasyllable with prevalent dactyl feet, alliteration (R), anaphor (*"non"*, *"no"*, *"né"*, all words stressing negation) and asyndeton. All these metric and phonic figures contribute to the dramatic narrative, the deadly fight between Tancredi and Clorinda.

Cixous's lines are visibly not constrained in any metrical form. On the contrary the sentences are longer, they continue farther by enjambment, pauses are more important: verses don't run towards their ending but extend towards an unending. Narration and direct discourse alternate, as the various voices of characters and narration. The entire construction slows down the result. In fact this vertical arrangement of the text seems to add time, to create longer pauses and suggest another *epic* where fight is in fact union, attraction, slow approach.

The problem for the translator of Cixous's texts is that (s)he has the function of an interpreter and a reader of a palimpsest, continuously reading writing itself. Translating becomes an extremely receptive moving construction, working in an internal/external way on duality, relation, intimate dialogue. A text is at any moment *à l'écoute de*, listening to what one may call *voices*, the writing itself which emerges between me and *you* in/out of me. Even when this dialogic form isn't explicit, it is yet effective, active. That's why I have spoken of continuous and intimate translations. This sort of auto-reflection is in no way narcissistic, autistic, but on the contrary turned towards exchange between interior and exterior. It moves further by degrees, by successive and successful approaches, the limits of exchange, or in linguistic terms, of permutation. The translation should succeed in maintaining movement, organising displacements, finding the numerous connections between levels, vertical ones (phonetic, semantic, syntax) and horizontal ones (narrative and textual development). The aim is to maintain as long as possible the polyphonic orchestration of this writing which is rhythmic construction where signifiers work much more than narrative representations. These texts don't ask us to dismiss signified or semantic levels, but to take care of the "auroral" language, made out of breath, voice, song, body rhythms announcing the unexpected word or country, the next already here-and-now sentence or page.

All that I can hope for as a translator is to offer to my mother language (Italian) the m'other language that Cixous's texts teach us, to enrich it with a *savage language*, a *primary* polyphonic voice, which has not been previewed, pre-scribed, but awakened and vividly, deeply sent for, inspired, aroused. I hope that what in these texts is free and infinitely calculated will liberate in a similar way literary language from its cages and barriers.

We care more often about the losses which translation is supposed to provoke than the enrichment of the other language: Cixous's works come from so large a textual generosity that their overflowing economy can only benefit the foreign language. That is what I'd call the gain of translation beyond the economy of lack: to exceed my/other language, on each side.

---

* Special thanks to Karen Badt and Stephanie Genty who accepted to read and correct my English, to Catherine McGillivray for sending me her translations of *Manna*, to Marguerite Sandré for finding and sending me the translated quotes of *Coming to writing*, to David Williams for his several translations of *Les rêveries de la femme sauvage*, *With ou l'art de l'innocence*, *Contes de la différence sexuelle*, to Susan Sellers for supervising them.

[1] So she writes in *Coming to writing* ["La venue à l'écriture"]. See next quote.

[2] Susan Sellers in her *Hélène Cixous Reader* (1994) has chosen for example the French and English forms "*La*" – "The (feminine)".

[3] Two approaches follow for this text:
1) Tinouk thought with his ears: "Will have from the verb to have. To have is in the figure tense". Has heard. There's o, there's au, with all possible o's, there is water high and to. And there is ra at least two, full of stuff, râ the sun, rat the animal. There's gold. It comes from there. Gold comes from Will Have. Just an I is missing to make "I'll have" burst out. What's not missing: will have storm in I.
There's will have you, and moving on, there's thora.
2) Tinouk thought with his ears: "Will have from the verb to have. To have is in the future tense". Has heard. There's will, there's wheel, with all the possible wills, there is well while and wheel. And there is have at least two, have got, have not, half as much. There's gold. It comes from there. Gold comes from Will Have. Just an I is missing to make. "I'll have" burst out. What's not missing : will have "Isle of" I.
There's will have you, and moving on, there's a will haf you (tr. David Williams).

[4] This is what I have begun to do. It is certainly not finished: "*Tinouk ha pensato aura con le sue orecchie: 'Aura, avrà dal verbo avere. Aura è il futuro'. Ha sentito: C'è o, c'è au, con tutte le o possibili, eau haut e au (aria, ria, ira) (ara, ora, urrà). Avrà almeno due rà, tavola rasa, râ il sole, ratto – l'animale. C'è l'aureo. L'auro viene d'Aura. Con un io in più si fa l'ore-cchio. Non ci manca niente: Aura temporale in io. / C'è l'avrai, continuando, c'è thora*".

[5] I wish to cite here the Dante's terzina which precedes as an exergue the beginning of the text:

> *E come augelli surti di rivera*
> *quasi congratulando a lor pasture,*
> *fanno di sé or tonda or altra schiera,*
> *sì dentro ai lumi sante creature*
> *volitando cantavano e faciensi*
> *or D or I, or L in sue figure.*
> (Dante, *Paradiso*, Canto XVIII)

> And as birds, risen from the shore, as if rejoicing together at their pasture, make of themselves now a round flock, now some other shape, so within the lights holy creatures were singing as they flew, and in their figures made of themselves now D, now I, now L. (Dante 1975)

[6] According to Lausberg, anacoluthon is an unbalance, an asymmetrical form typical of spoken language. See Dupriez 1984: 43.

[7] I propose: "I store aside translation".

[8] For the following notes I'll just put the page number of each edition at the end of the quote.

[9] I remember that the famous madrigale by Monteverdi *Il combattimento di Tancredi e Clorinda* is based on Tasso's original text.

[10] Cf. the beginning of Baudelaire's poem "L'invitation au voyage" in *Les fleurs du mal*: "*Mon enfant, ma sœur / Songe à la douceur / D'aller là-bas vivre ensemble*".

[11]
> You are no longer my sister
> I am no longer your child
> The anger and darkness are neither feigned nor measured
> Their feet are immobile, but their souls are restless, excited, the swords come down, broadside, or point first,
> What are you fleeing my love? Standing together. Do not see each other...
> Nothing separates them,
> What separates them? The dark malice of History
> The struggle forces them closer and closer,
> Already they can't use the point anymore,
> They blind one another with looks
> Three times Amenaîde receives Tancredi look
> Three times she breaks free from this attraction she fears
> Believe you I'd rather die
> But with my whole life in spite of myself I believe you
> You are no longer my child
> I am no longer your sister. (Cixous 1988b: 46)

[12] Tasso 1969: Canto XII, vv. 433-440, p. 234.

> LV
> They neither shrunk, nor vantage sought of ground,
> They traverse not, nor skipped from part to part,
> Their blows were neither false not feigned found,
> The night, their rage would let them use no art,
> Their swords together clash with dreadful sound,
> Their feet stand fast, and neither stir nor start,
> They move their hands, steadfast their feet remain,
> Nor blow nor loin they struck, or thrust in vain.
> [...]
> Thrice his strong arms he folds about her waist,
> And thrice was forced to let the virgin go,
> For she disdained to be so embraced

From *Jerusalem Delivered* by Torquato Tasso (1544-1595) published 1591 in Parma, Italy. Translated by Edward Fairfax (1556-1635), translation first published in London, 1600.

References

Cixous, Hélène. 1976a. 'La venue à l'écriture' in *Entre l'écriture*. Paris: des femmes, 1986.
—. 1976b. *La*. Paris: Gallimard; Paris: des femmes, 1979.
—. 1980. *Illa*. Paris: des femmes.
—. 1981. *With ou l'art de l'innocence*. Paris: des femmes.
—. 1983. 'Tancrède continue' in *Entre l'écriture*. Paris: des femmes, 1986.
—. 1988a. *Manne aux Mandelstam aux Mandela*. Paris: des femmes.
—. 1988b. 'Tancredi continues' (tr. Ann Liddle and Susan Sellers) in Susan Sellers (ed.) *Writing Differences*. London: Open University Press.
—. 1991. *Coming to Writing and Other Essays* (tr. S. Cornell, D. Jenson, A. Liddle, and S. Sellers). Cambridge, MA: Harvard University Press.
—. 1994a. 'Contes de la différence sexuelle' in Negrón, Mara (ed.) *Lectures de la différence sexuelle*. Paris: des femmes.
—. 1994b. *Manna for the Mandelstams for the Mandelas* (tr. Catherine A. F. MacGillivray). Minneapolis, MN: University of Minnesota Press.
—. 2000a. ' Tancredi continua' (tr. Nadia Setti) in Paola Bono (ed.) *Scritture del corpo, Hélène Cixous variazioni su un tema*. Rome: Luca Sossella.
—. 2000b. *Les rêveries de la femme sauvage. Scènes primitives*. Paris: Galilée.
Dante. 1975. *The Divine Comedy* (tr. Charles S. Singleton). Princeton, N.J.: Princeton University Press.
Derrida, Jacques. 1987. *Ulysse gramophone, Deux mots pour Joyce*. Paris: Galilée.
—. 2000. 'H.C. pour la vie, c'est à dire...' in Calle-Gruber, Mireille (ed.) *Hélène Cixous, croisées d'une œuvre*. Paris: Galilée.
Dupriez, Bernard. 1984. *Gradus. Les procédés littéraires*. Paris: 10/18.
Meschonnic, Henri. 1999. *Poétique du traduire*. Lagrasse: Verdier.
Sellers, Susan (ed.). 1994. *The Hélène Cixous Reader*. London and New York, NY: Routledge.
Tasso, Torquato. 1969. *La Gerusalemme Liberata*. Milan: Principato editore.
Van Rossum-Guyon, Françoise and Myriam Díaz-Diocaretz (eds). 1990. *Hélène Cixous, chemins d'une écriture*. Amsterdam-Paris: Rodopi-PUV.

Problems in Translating Hélène Cixous into Japanese Feminine Language

Isako Matsumoto

Japanese people distinguish between a "masculine" and a "feminine" language. Women's language tends to be polite and respectful to the other, showing the traditional submissiveness of women in Japan. The feminine "I" in "The Laugh of the Medusa", translated into Japanese by Matsumoto, is not that of the passive and subordinated woman, but the "I" of a new and assertive feminine subject. The translator could not then use the traditional Japanese women's language, but a new "unconventional" one, not too "mannish" but not too "feminine" either, because the latter would mean adhering to the usual sexism in Japanese society.
Key words: sexual difference in language, Japanese, women's language.

"The Laugh of the Medusa" begins with the word "I": "I will talk about feminine writing". When the Japanese say 'I', it is not a firm statement as it would be for a European or an American speaker. In the Western world, 'I' signals an independent existence that is clearly distinguished from the other. By contrast, the 'I' in Japanese always exists in relation to the others. In other words, it is nothing but a being captured in human relationships. The kind of person expressed by 'I' is prescribed and confirmed for the first time in its relationships with 'you', 'he' or 'she'. Instantly and unconsciously the Japanese measure relationships between themselves and others, as psychological and social distances – depending on whether the relevant social status is a close or a distant one; this means that they choose the first or second person pronoun that best suits them. In fact, in the Japanese language there are many first and second person pronouns. For example, the English 'I' can be translated in several ways: '*Watashi*' is the most popular form and can be used by both men and women. '*Watakushi*' is slightly more polite than the former. '*Boku*' can be used only by male speakers, usually by both adults and children. '*Ore*' is also used as often as '*Boku*' by men, but gives a rather stronger, rough impression. Therefore, when a little boy uses this word, it may sound a bit comic and, as a consequence, we may find the boy cute as he asserts his *masculinity*. The "I" of *I Am a Cat*, by Soseki Natsume, corresponds to '*Wagahai*' in Japanese. This word is almost not used anymore, as it gives the impression of haughtiness. That is why when a cat says "*Wagahai*" it has a humorous effect. Unfortunately, when translated into a simple 'I' – in English – or '*je*' – in French – the humour is lost. '*Washi*' is a men's word too, and not a very polite way to say 'I'. At the same time, however, old women in the countryside, and recently even young girls sometimes, say '*Washi*' to protest against the restraints affecting women. As to the first person pronouns for women, there are several, including: '*Atashi*', '*Atakushi*', '*Atai*', '*Uchi*'. Currently there are over twenty different expressions for the first and second person pronouns.

One of the most characteristic examples in Japanese of how personal pronouns show human relationships is found in the realm of the family. In Japanese, members of a family are called according to the relationships amongst its members, and from the standpoint of the youngest. For instance, a mother says to her son: "Elder brother, bring water to Hanako and mum". Here, the elder brother is a brother of Hanako's, daughter of the mother speaking, and "mum" refers to herself. The mother does not say 'I' or 'me'. I will provide another example: "Mum is going out now". Here, again "Mum" refers to the speaker herself and not to her mother. In Japanese, it is not rare that nouns indicating the third person are used instead of first and second person pronouns. At the same time, we use first person pronouns as a substitute for second person pronouns. For instance, instead of asking a little boy, "What is your name?" we say "*Boku no namae wa?*" ["What is the name of I?"]. In the same way, in a restaurant we may ask Mr. Yamada, "What will Mr. Yamada eat?" instead of saying "What will you eat?".

Just as there are many ways of articulating the equivalent of the English 'I' taken in relation to the 'you', as shown above, there are many ways to say 'you': '*Omae*', '*Anata*', '*Anatasama*', '*Kimi*', '*Anta*', '*Onushi*', '*Temee*', '*Kisama*', '*Onore*', etc. A great number of variants exist for the English 'you', from 'you' with respect and politeness, to 'you' forms expressing contempt, or 'you' used with anger in a quarrel.

Furthermore, in Japanese we have a great number of personal pronouns having nuances of respect, politeness or modesty, and the sexual difference in their uses is also clear. However, in spite of the existence of many first person pronouns in Japanese, we always try to avoid them. As long as the word 'I' is recognised as such in a context, it is often more natural to omit it in Japanese. But even when the subject 'I' may be omitted, it is not implicit, as in Italian, in a conjugated verb. Japanese verbs do not conjugate by subjects. So when we try to translate a Japanese sentence into Indo-European languages, it happens sometimes that even the Japanese do not know if its subject is 'I', 'we' or something else. For example, the opening sentence of *Snow Country* by Yasunari Kawabata is as follows:

> *Tonnele wo nukeruto soko wa yukiguni deatta.*

[*Tonnele* = 'tunnel', *wo* = particle which shows that the noun preceding this word is an object, *nukeruto* = 'passed', *soko* = 'there', *wa* = particle which shows the noun preceding this word is a subject, *yukiguni* = 'snow country', *deatta* = 'was'.]

> Passed the tunnel, there was a snow country.

Who passed the tunnel? The hero? The train? The speaker? The Japanese sentence does not indicate it. The Japanese do not care if subjects are not expressed. With the influences of Buddhism and Zen, the consciousness of building up a subject is very weak for the Japanese speaker, and it is also the case from the point of view of the language.

One day in my class I took one Japanese sentence as example and asked my students to translate it into English. Then the questions emerged: who is hungry and whether the subject is singular or plural.

> *Harahetta naa, meshi kuini ikouka.*

[*Harahetta* = 'hungry', *naa* = particle for the emphasis, *meshi* = 'meal', *kuini* = 'eat', *ikouka* = 'shall we go?']

> Hungry, shall we go to eat meal?

In one class of about forty students, most answered that the sentence might have a singular subject, but three or four answered that it might have a plural subject. In another class, one third of the students answered "plural" and the rest "singular". This is because both subjects are possible; it is perhaps better to say that the subject is something highly ambiguous, resisting definitions one way or another. (My son said the subject was "I and you". The native speakers of English may say that if so, 'we' is enough as the subject. However, this Japanese sentence has really something to suggest that the subject is 'I and we'.) We should also pay attention to how I asked this question in each classroom. In the first class, I first let students raise their hands if they thought the subject was singular. In the next class, I first let students raise their hands if they thought it was plural. When several of them raised their hands, the rest, tempted by the first ones, were very likely to raise theirs, too: the self-assurance of the Japanese in this context is not so strong.

In spite of the fact that first and second person pronouns are often omitted, the Japanese language has many ways of expressing pronouns. Another complexity is that verbs and adjectives do not change according to person or gender. However, unlike Indo-European languages, the difference between men and women in Japanese is quite obvious. For instance, in French we can distinguish whether or not it is a woman's language, through the adjectives in the feminine form. Nevertheless, the femininity is only in the grammatical rule, which does not give by itself a feminine mood to the language. By contrast, Japanese grammar does not have any gender difference. Nevertheless, we can discern the sexual difference in the pronouns, (ad)verbs, and particles that close the sentences. If we want, we can also construct a sexually neutral language. When reading texts, we can understand if they are men's or women's words. In this sense, Japanese is quite a peculiar language.

One of the differences between Japanese and Indo-European languages is syntax. In Japanese, (ad)verbs come at the end of a phrase. And among these (ad)verbs which show if a sentence is positive or negative, there are those used by women, by men or by both. For example, the adverb *'Da'* is, "[i]n writing, a neutral style, but in speech, it is not as polite as *Desu · Masu*"[1]. The adverb *'Desu'* shows "a polite feeling of the speaker to the listener, and is as polite as *Masu*". *'Masu'* is "used mainly in speeches. In writing, it is used mainly in letters, but outside of letters, it is often used deliberately to move the readers emotionally. The level of politeness is almost the same as in *Desu*, and the style using these two (*Desu · Masu*) is opposed to the *Da* style, which is a neutral style regarding its level of politeness. This shows the polite feelings of the speaker to the listener".

Furthermore, in Japanese it is possible to put a particle after these adverbs *'Da'*, *'Desu'* or *'Masu'*. What is a particle? This is a characteristic Japanese short sound and is explained as follows in the dictionary:

> A postpositional word which does not conjugate. It is always used attached to an independent word or to an independent word followed by a particle or an adverb, and shows a relation between a word and another word, or adds a meaning.

There are a number of particles called ending-particles, which come at the end of phrases. For instance, the ending-particle *'Wa'*, when used by men, "can be used to emphasize impressions, and to describe vividly the scene with astonishment". When it is used by women, however, "[i]t shows an impression as a conviction, and is used to supplement a curt way of objective description of the phrase by an impressive intonation, and makes soft the expression as well as expresses the assertion or determination of the speaker in the impressive, significant tone". Another particle, *'No'*, is also used mainly by women and children to soften decisive or interrogative sentences[2]. As a consequence, for example, while the phrase 'I am a woman' is translatable only as *'Je suis une femme'* in French and *'Ich bin eine Frau'* in German, in Japanese it can be translated in many ways. If we line up several translations from a strong, decisive and maybe even mannish tone, through a neutral tone, and to feminine, polite tones, they may be as follows:

1. *Watashi wa onna de aru.* [*Watashi* = 'I', *wa* = particle indicating the preceding word is a subject, *onna* = 'woman', *de* = particle preceding *aru*, *aru* = adverb indicating an affirmative.]
2. *Watashi wa onna da.* [*da* = adverb indicating an affirmative.]
3. *Watashi wa onna desu.*
4. *Watashi wa onna desu yo.* [*yo* = ending-particle to force one's opinion on others.]
5. *Watashi wa onna desu wa.* [*wa* = ending-particle used by women showing a light assertion or determination.]
6. *Watashi wa onna desu no.* [*no* = ending-particle used by women and children to soften a tone of voice.]
7. *Watashi wa onna de gozaimasu.* [*gozaimasu* = polite expression of *aru*.]

All these translations are, of course, translations of the same English sentence 'I am a woman'. But each translation has a different nuance in Japanese. For example, sentence 1 is a little stronger in tone. Sentence 2 is neutral but the expression in this sentence is more mannish than in sentence 3. This is because sentence 3 is quite neutral. Sentence 4 is quite feminine because of "*yo*", which is used only by women. Sentences 5 and 6 are additional versions of sentence 4. Sentence 7 is also feminine and the most polite. Other expressions are also possible, and of course we can change "*Watashi*" into '*Watakushi*', '*Atashi*', etc. Whereas in English we have only one word for 'give', for instance, in Japanese we usually have an honorific word used to show respect to the person addressed, a modest word to show modesty, and a polite word, and we have to change these words to suit the occasion. Generally speaking, women's language is said to be polite, using words or mood with politeness. So it becomes a serious problem, when we translate foreign languages into Japanese: how much the translator adopts words of respect and how to translate the first and the second person pronouns. If the translator adopts an extremely polite level of speaking or writing, it will be evident that it is a woman's language, but it will show at the same time that the translator accepts the traditional image of women. The translator's image of women and his/her practice of feminism from a lexical point of view must also be scrutinized.

When H. Cixous says "I" in "The Laugh of the Medusa", it is the 'I' of a new woman – not 'I' as a woman subordinated to men, trapped in a classic image suitable to men. In Japanese society and culture, women, captured in classic and traditional concepts, do not enter public society, but manage the domestic budget well, care for the family, and sacrifice themselves for the family. In short, they are the classical women that Cixous has described in "The Laugh of the Medusa" as women to be overcome. So when Cixous's "I" as a new woman is translated into traditional Japanese women's language, there is the risk of not conveying her real intention. That is to say, the style and the tone of language in translation must be those of a "new woman" too. To translate the "I" of Cixous into Japanese, the translator must therefore take care to adapt a tone that expresses clearly that this "I" is a "new woman".

Cixous emphasizes motherhood as another characteristic of this new woman. In Japan, motherhood is strongly respected, encouraged and stimulated. However, the motherhood imagined by the Japanese means the self-sacrificing mother who holds others gently and sympathizes with others. And as far as sympathy is concerned, the Japanese have developed an understanding of it. Nevertheless, as I mentioned previously, in Japan, not only women but also men lack the Western linguistic sense of self-assurance.

The motherhood that Cixous argues for is the same from the point of view of sympathy, but on the other hand, it is not a motherhood based on self-sacrifice: Cixous's motherhood is one which caters for the self as well as others, and is a quality to be appropriated not only by women but also by men. While femininity in Japanese is part of the binomial opposition between men and women, Cixous persuades readers to overcome this opposition and to change society. These ideas are opposite. If I translate Cixous's femininity into Japanese women's language, a gap will be formed: the problem is how to overcome the differences of social contexts, how to show, in a language, a different image of motherhood from the one the Japanese usually imagine, and at the same time, how to show an 'I' based on clear self-assurance. Into what kind of language should we translate an abstract and ideal not-yet-existing woman as proposed by Cixous? We must search for an unconventional woman's language. Thus, the Japanese translator must overcome the difficulties imposed by the task of translating Hélène Cixous; in addition to his, there is a continuous trial and error because of these Japanese characteristics.

In this difficult situation of the Japanese translation of Cixous, there was a division between my co-translator and me in the interpretation of *The Conquest of the School at Madhubai*. As I am also a university professor, I tend to translate the text precisely, not neglecting even a word. It is not possible, however, to use that kind of translation for the scenario of a play. The language used on a stage must be vivid, spoken language, and should not sound like a translation. Besides, particularly in spoken languages the distinction between men's language and women's is very clear, and the neutral language does not exist except in lectures for conferences. The editor, having read my translation – which should have sounded to her like a translation –, decided to show it to a playwright, since she had hoped to publish it as a dramatic scenario, and so she proposed Koharu Kisaragi, a playwright and theatre director, as co-translator. I agreed. She rewrote my translation into the language of a play. As a consequence, Sakundeva of Kisaragi has become an Edo dialect-speaking Sakundeva. What is Edo dialect? Edo is an old name for Tokyo, and so Edo dialect is a dialect of Tokyo, known for its vividness of 'downtown' expressions: in other words, it's very macho. Kisaragi has focused mainly on the masculine side – a bandit, a killer – of Sakundeva. After reading her translation I complained saying that Sakundeva should speak a more refined language. Kisaragi said that the refined bandit was impossible. Fearing to emphasize the subordinated position of women in Japan by giving her a woman's language, she must have been repelled by the idea of giving a feminine language to Sakundeva, who can put her own strong will into practice. Therefore, her Sakundeva has become someone who speaks with a strong masculine tone. There is no spoken Japanese language that is neither masculine nor feminine. But I think that Cixous focuses not on the past life of Sakundeva, but rather on the motherhood of Sakundeva and her aunt. They certainly have both phallic and mothering aspects capable of bringing up others. If so, isn't a too mannish language out of character? At my request, Kisaragi rewrote the play completely, still using man's language, although it was no longer Edo-dialect. Thinking, for example, that the communication between Sakundeva and the Minister was better in man's language than in the strong woman's language I had thought of at first, I left everything to Kisaragi.

Now, let's go back to the problems of "The Laugh of the Medusa". This beautiful essay was a manifesto of "feminine writing", and Cixous expressly stated in it a farewell to classical women. Besides, it is an essay. So I thought that the translation should not be mannish, but not too feminine either, because the essay also protests against the subordinated place women occupy in society. If I translate it into extremely feminine words, readers may take for granted the sexism that is quite strong in Japan. So I began the translation neither in man's language nor woman's, but in a neutral one. In other words, I adopted the neutral *Da*-style. This style gives a stronger impression than the polite *Desu·Masu*-styles. Nevertheless, as the pages went by, Cixous began to express her concepts of the "new woman", motherhood, "Other Love", etc., and then this neutral style could not show the sexual difference and femininity. Shouldn't we emphasize femininity? So I began my translation once again from the beginning with a woman's language. But then there were traps and I fell down: it became – because of the usual habit? – so feminine that eventually I became fed up with it. I returned again to neutral language – I had to repeat over and over, going back and forth between a woman's language and a neutral[3] language. A Japanese text with two co-existing styles is not considered to be good. And in the end, I began to translate as if I was talking to another woman, for Cixous was praising, as women's features, the mother as speaking-subject and the mother's child (and even adults)-rearing voice. Moreover, this essay begins really with "I will talk about...". So, by translating as if I was talking, I avoided the neutral style and tone suitable for an academic article lacking sentiments. However, I didn't use the ending-particles like '*No*' or '*Wa*', because these give sentences a too feminine, too weak or too gentle impression: being a manifesto of a feminine writing and of a newly born woman capable of changing this world ruled by men into a new world ruled by love and an economy of gift, the translation must not only be that of women's language, but also powerful.

> *Anata wa kossorito deha are, sukosi wa kaite mimasita ne.*
>
> Besides you have written a little, but in secret. (Cixous 1975: 40)

This tone is as polite as a professor talking to a student. To a stranger, he may say more politely, '*Okakini narimasita ne*', instead of "*kaite mimasita ne*". This most polite way of saying may be good when we speak, but in writing it is too polite and a little bit verbose. Therefore, I avoided excessive femininity, and translated it into rather gentle, polite, spoken but vigorous Japanese. I wanted to try to reveal a gentle but resolute woman's image.

I translated "I" into "*Watashi*", because usually all women say so. And to solve the most difficult problem – how to realize in my translation a self-directed 'I' capable of creating relationships, using the Japanese 'I' which is usually buried under relationships – I dared to use the subject 'I' often omitted in Japanese. However, if I write this subject every time, it must be an eyesore and sound too noisy for most Japanese, but when it is necessary to make readers feel the strong will of the speaker of the text, I dared to write 'I' and 'we'. Let me show you an example:

> I didn't open **my** mouth, I didn't repaint **my** half of the world. **I** was ashamed. **I** was afraid, and **I** swallowed **my** shame and **my** fear. (Cixous 1975: 40)

The underlined "I"'s and "my"'s may be usually omitted when translated into Japanese, but by repeating them, I tried to create the self-awareness of a present 'I' reflecting a past 'I'. Let's take another example.

> **Our** glances go by, **our** smiles flew by, the laughs of all **our** mouths, our blood flows and **we** extend ourselves without being exhausted, **we** do not hold **our** thoughts, **our** signs, **our** writings, [...] (Cixous 1975: 41)

By repeating "our", I emphasized women's existence and consciousness.

"The Laugh of the Medusa" was my first translation of Hélène Cixous, and since then, this spoken-tone writing that preserves femininity while asserting resolutely the self and maintaining always self-assurance, has become the basis of my translations of Hélène Cixous.

[1] Kindaichi and Ikeda (1979). All the quotations about Japanese grammar are from this dictionary.
[2] It may be evident that the short poems of Haiku are only possible thanks to the functions of these particles. It is the ending-particles that give subtle colors to the world of Haiku.
[3] However, it is the same in the East as in the West that we must be careful with this word "neutral". When I write an article, I often feel ill at ease in adopting this Japanese 'neutral' style.

References

Cixous, Hélène. 1975. 'Le rire de la Méduse' in *L'Arc* 61: 39-54.
Kindaichi, Haruhiko and Yasaburo Ikeda (eds). 1979. *Grand Japanese Dictionary of Gakken*. Gakusyu-Kenkyu-Sha.

PART IV: Translating Other's Culture, or Translating Words into Bodies

"Translating HC/ Writing the Self"
(*L'Indiade* and the Replication of an Elusive Dream)

Anu Aneja

From her own experience of translating *L'Indiade* into Hindustani, the author elaborates the metaphors of the erotics of translation, and of the translator as a mother: translating means yielding to the seduction of the other's text; and to combine the other (text or language) and the "flesh of your own words" implies becoming "the M/other". Aneja also stresses the violence that translation always carries, especially when it consists in rendering a postcolonial text into a European language. This essay blends personal memories, political reflections, and images of the sculptural work of the author related to the issues discussed in it.
Key words: Maternity, India, history, myths, postcolonialism.

To translate the other's text is first to permit the other's seduction, to allow yourself to be charmed, always, and bedazzled, sometimes, to immerse yourself slowly in the ocean of the other's words, and then, in this unique coming together, to conceive of the other, to become full of the other's meanings, and finally, to give birth, to re-produce the other's scent of meanings in the flesh of your own words. To become the M/other. But to translate a French work about India's independence, into Hindustani, in the post-colonial moment, is also to carry the burden of an ancestral memory of European colonization, and to be aware of the seduction of Europe for post-colonial India.

> *Like the lover's body, the French text invites me to savour its difference. French is not my mother tongue; to speak it, to read its sinuous, sloping-forward words is to glide recklessly on the silk of the other's body. The flesh of the French text emanates a strange foreign scent, its sentences rise up in a cadence all around me, like the contours of hills beyond which lies a foreign country. I have never quite been able to fathom the difference between reading the French text, and translating it, for I am unable to read French without being challenged by its unfathomable strangeness, without being aware, at every moment, of its difference from my mother tongue, from the tongue of my mother. But we are sure to fall in love with just that which sets itself apart, which promises the adventure of difference. So it was that*

the French language, to which I was drawn at the age of sixteen, often became confused with the seductions of teenage romances. Like them, it sauntered just ahead of me, full of promise, seething with desire, but never quite completely visible. Following at its heels, I faltered often in the mist of its foreignness, falling, rising, and falling again, but always pulled onwards by its seductive charm.

Strange elusive sentences from my Mauger Bleu, the bible of the Alliance Française in the seventies, float before me as I write these words. 'Cette jeune fille, qui est-elle? Mais, elle est Mireille! Mireille habite au... rue Montmartre'. *Reading aloud fragments of Mireille's life, I felt as if I was transported to another world on the wings of a new music, a world that smelled of the perfumes of Paris, where sentences often sounded like questions, and pleasure was full of uncertainty. But no matter how familiar I grew with Mireille's life, the street that she lived on, her mind, her heart, the colour of her eyes and her hair, her sweet and gentle mannerisms, there were always obscure spaces in Mireille's reality that would remain just beyond my reach, at the point of the* au-delà...

During my first examen oral, *the French tutor, Monsieur C, cool and crisp in his pale blue starched shirt, looked up from behind his wooden desk and pierced my anxiety with his angel-blue eyes. Then he spoke those never to be forgotten words* – 'Avez-vous confiance, Mlle?' *My heart pounded madly in my chest, as my mind quickly flipped through the illustrated pages of the Mauger Bleu, speed reading its phrases and images, desperately searching for that lost word,* confiance. *What was this new unfamiliarity, this* confiance? *I stared back in desperation, as though the clue might be concealed in his gaze, but all I saw was the crispness of a starched collar, and in my ears the humming of his distant, mocking tone, as he repeated the question.* Confiance, confiance, confiance, *my mind whirred madly around this obscure word, just beyond my reach. What was it? A book, a garment, jam, a pen,* un stylo, une craie? *What do I have/not have, so that I am approved in my foreignness, deemed worthy of knowing French, of being a future translator? Looking down at my empty hands, I tried to conjure up this mysterious object, but I possessed nothing that could be of value to the French man. I had nothing to call my own, to offer him in the guise of compensation for my non-knowledge of a European word.* 'Non, Monsieur', *I said diffidently,* 'je ne l'ai pas', *trying at least to influence him with the well-placed* objet direct. *A veil of contentment seemed to cover his eyes. He smiled, a smug, arrogant smile.* 'Merci beaucoup, Mlle, c'est tout'.

I was sent away, out into the babel of the world to look for my elusive confiance. *I had failed the exam, naturally. The keeper of the French language had decided, based on my lack of one word, that the test was finished. I had been unable to find the correlative of one significant word in either one of the two other languages that I spoke, unable, in other words, to perform the act of naming, the taxonomy of cross-cultural translation. I* determined never to admit to anyone again, je ne l'ai pas. *I made up my mind not to be locked out of the other's language, that dance of sounds and intonations that I fell in love with, that familiar pattern of interrogation at the end of an affirmative sentence, those strange sentences that slid about, climbing up and then down,* vous avez la confiance... n'est-ce pas?

That unique way that French has of turning certainty into question, of mettre en question, all solidly held declarations, that willingness to accept any answer, to open itself up to surprise, of expecting the unacceptable, of being generous to possibility... It stirred me up, it spoke to me. Just as Urdu and Persian wrap themselves around my tongue like tiny, white fragrant blossoms strung on silken threads, the French language surrounds me like the scented vapours rising out of a flacon of perfume, attar to the senses. At sixteen, French was the body of the lover I desired to open myself to, despite persisting anxieties about an elusive confiance. But at sixteen foreign languages are nothing more than invitations into uncharted, foreign territories, as well as a refusal to recognize the dangers of submitting to those who wield authority.

To come to HC's work, many years later, in the guise of the reader and then the translator, meant a revival of this initial ambivalence towards the foreign tongue, the language of European elegance, as well as of European hegemony over some parts of the third world. So I came in not through the main door, but slyly, through a side entrance, one that was more familiar, the cover of a book I half-recognized already, a story not about France, but about India. Translating *L'Indiade* was to translate not only a French woman's otherness for myself, but to translate my self and the other simultaneously, to mis-recognize our differences.

Here was a work that was not only French, but French and Indian, that had already made that courageous leap over difference that I dreamt about, that whispered to me, confidentially, between the rustle of its pages, it is possible, don't be afraid, it can be done, you can do it, tu as la confiance, n'est-ce pas? Je la désire, *I responded, I desire it, to know your text/body, to explore myself with you. In the story of Inanna, the Sumerian princess, Inanna, enters the underworld naked, stripped of her royal garments at each of seven gates, bent humble and low before her nether self, her sister, Ereshkigal. Inanna must die so that Ereshkigal can give birth to her again. When she sees her sister in the belly of the seventh cave, Inanna has no idea that what lies in the darkness is her own shadow, a darker shade of her self. Transported into the nether world by her desires, Inanna is translated into her own reflection that lies on the other side of the mirror, seduced by an image of herself. In translating you, I end up translating myself.*

1. "Translation"

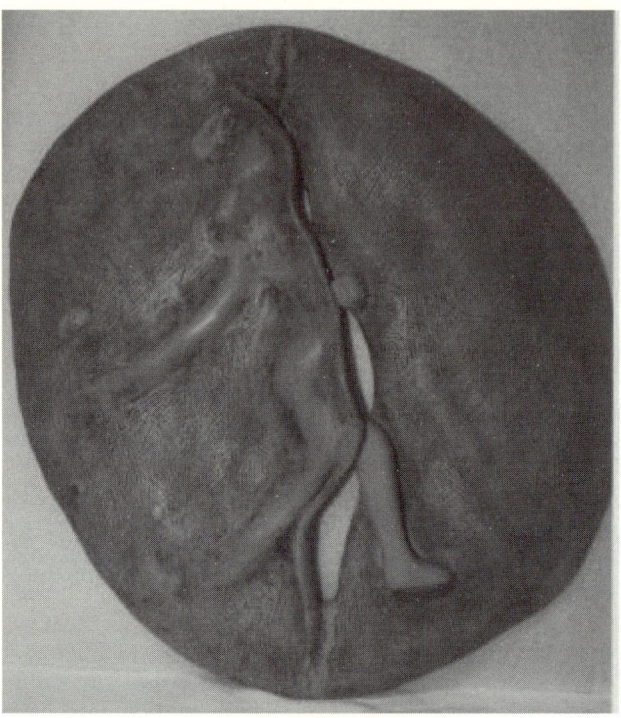

Translating HC is to translate HC's dream of an eternal feminine, not an essential feminine frozen within a patriarchal framework, but a femininity that slips in and out of the gender divide, wide-eyed and open to all possibilities. Much more than a relationship of language to language, and beyond the conventional task of the translator, the rapport between the writer and the translator must here become *une liaison amoureuse*, an exchange of fluid currents between textual bodies. Over the four years that it took me to complete this translation, I carried the two texts within me – the dream of the original French text as I imagined it, and the potential text of my mother tongue, like a woman who was expecting twins but reluctant to give birth, coaxing the French words to find their Hindustani counterparts, turning the foreign tongue towards my mother tongue, making it over into my familiar.

I was overcome by the desire to create, to labour over sonorous words that spoke of my own nostalgia for a lost, secular India. Yes, to receive French words on my fertile tongue, and to watch them dance, transforming themselves into new shapes, forms, sounds, transmogrified into words only my mother would speak, word made flesh, the miracle of birthing.

What resulted was a child, a text that I look at with the anxiety of a mother, and an aunt. Translation teaches you what the mother already knows – that mothers do not believe in the perfection of their creations, that they worry about their imperfections, their bumps, and bruises. But most of all, the labour of the translator/mother is the outcome of the desire to create a thing of beauty, that will carry the mother on the wings of new words beyond the limits of signification.

Translating *L'Indiade*, I discovered, was not a difficult task, it was a task that required a passion made possible only by opening oneself up to the possibility of becoming the translator-writer, a giant leap over that cliff that keeps one divided from the latent rhythms of the unconscious. But to be a woman-translator-writer is to know already what a huge risk that is, for women, especially, are expected to know and not-know creation – to know it as a giving of a gift to the other, but to keep unrecognizable that part of the self that wants to be born every time a woman creates. For centuries women have kept that passion of the self at bay, but it has always taken hold of them, has swept them up in its undeniable force like an oceanic wave that curls up, over and about the female body, that washes out the grains of sand cleaving to your skin to leave it feeling stripped, exfoliated, re-born.

Years later, I gave birth to my only child, a boy I have named Kabeer, in memory of that mysterious Sufi poet whose body turned into blood-red rose petals the morning after his death. Kabeer, born a Hindu, raised by Muslim parents, belonged to a family of yarn-spinners. At first his love of spinning took the shape of spools of coloured thread, and later, pushed him to compose philosophical poems like pearls of brevity which he offered to a world as though he was a hakim, *doling out small doses of medicine to people dying of the inability to love, the malady of death, as another French author has called it. In his defiance of borders and boundaries, in his refusal to accept the division of his own body, Kabeer created daily doses of poems, and flung them out to the world, where they would be scattered and disseminated. When Kabeer died, Hindus and Muslims fought over his dead body, wanting to cremate him, or bury him, to claim the right of religious ownership of flesh already turning to dust. So Kabeer turned his body into rose petals, and the petals were distributed amongst all those who loved him, who hated him, who worshipped him, who were terrorized by his call to love. In the poems of Kabeer, I smell the deathly perfume of the deep, sweet scent of roses, and I hear the murmur of a faint voice calling us to drink from the cup of Jamshed, to become intoxicated by difference. The Persian Jamshed, who is the same as the Hindu Yama, the god of death. Yama, transmuted into Jama, when the Sanskrit 'Y' elided with* the Persian 'J', and Jamshed became the king who is taught mysterious languages by the demons, and who drinks from their goblet of desires.

So I dream that you, my son, conceived by the ocean in the shadow of the half-moon, water-child, moon-child, you too will have the courage to carry forth a dream as tender and perfect as your ancestor's, that you will translate my dreams into the world, just as your body translates mine into a new form, that this translation will link us in that eternal chain of immortality, where the desire to give birth finds its source, and I worry then of the weight of this legacy that I have placed on your tiny shoulders.

2. "Expecting"

Two primal desires – that of being mothered, and of mothering – are intercepted by translation, which sits at the crossroads between them. To translate HC has meant learning to live both at once, to be child to the French, mother to the Hindustani, to experience the moment of parturition between being mothered and mothering. The translator's work, secondary, imperfect, flawed by its very obligations of copying, of mimicking, is still touched by the perfect, for what it tries to replicate is the vision that the writer has seen, a vision as perfect as the fragrance of dying roses. *Oui, je dis, avec confiance, oui, je l'ai.*

Like Kabeer, the Gandhi of Indian history also spun yarn. In fact, the spinning wheel, or *charkha*, became such an integral part of his life that it is difficult to imagine the Mahatma without his *charkha*. In a silent political battle that he fought against the colonizers, spinning became an act of rebellion, Gandhi whirling out spools of home-spun in the face of a giant British power that had carried out an exploitative cotton trade in India for more than a century. At first he must have seemed crazed or foolish, sitting with his spinning wheel outside his humble cottage, one man attempting to undo an entire colonial industry. But the word spread and soon hundreds and thousands of spinning wheels began springing up all over the country, in cities, towns and villages, and a million hands spun the magical handloom, *khadi*, that would for many future generations become the garb of patriots and politicians alike. In the India of his dreams, Gandhi imagines a nation of adept spinners, whose hands move rhythmically to the spiritual "music of the spinning wheel". "I believe that where there is pure and active love for the poor there is God also, I see God in every thread that I draw on the spinning wheel" (Gandhi 1947: 113). *Khadi*, the fabric of a cottage industry that soon sprouted up all over the country, became the dreamtent under which Gandhi regrouped his soldiers, and with whose help he continued to fight the war against colonial oppression.

Kabeer and Gandhi, linked by the spinning wheel, as well as their love for the other, their common desire to move beyond the divisions between names, such as Islam, and Hinduism. Spinning lends me a perfect metaphor for the art of translation. The writer translates the other's story, spinning it into the yarn of the familiar self. The translator re-inscribes that story, unraveling the thread of the plot, dyeing it in new colours, and winding it around a new spool.

But Gandhi's *charkha* puts another spin on the history being re-told in *L'Indiade*, because while it points to the historical Gandhi's vision of economic independence, it also reveals his perspective on the role of Indian women. Gandhi, who fought for equal rights for women, also often described women as being examples of patience, sacrifice, passivity and chastity. Women, he believed, were naturally suited for the work of spinning:

> The restoration of spinning to its central place in India's peaceful campaign for deliverance from the imperial yoke gives her women a special status. In spinning they have a natural advantage over men... Spinning is essentially a slow and comparatively silent process. Woman is the embodiment of sacrifice and therefore, non-violence. (Kishwar 1986: 14)

In her capacity of patience, resignation, non-violence, and sacrifice, the Sita of the *Ramayana* becomes Gandhi's favoured Indian heroine, the ideal he would want all Indian women to emulate: "Take the case of Sita. Physically she was a weakling before Ravana, but her purity was more than a match even for his giant might" (Gandhi 1947: 229). The ideal Sita, the image of Sita as it has been translated by Indian patriarchy, including Gandhi, has no desires of her own. She desires nothing more than to preserve her chastity, her absence of desire.

There is a famous episode in the Ramayana. *One day, Sita, the wife of the exiled prince Ram, is walking in the forest. All of a sudden, like a dream or an apparition, a deer of singular beauty, his skin flecked with gold and silver lights, runs out of the trees, a few feet away from her, and then vanishes in the blink of an eye. Unable to forget that ephemeral dream, tempted by its haunting beauty, she learns the meaning of desire. Sita insists that her husband go out and capture the deer for her. Swayed by the power of her keen desire, Ram, and then his younger brother, Lakshman, go out to perform the male duty, to hunt, and to provide. Before he leaves, Lakshman draws a line in the dust, the Lakshman-Rekha, marking a magical circle around the forest hut. The marking of the line is meant to protect Sita against all dangers. She is left with clear and strict instructions – do not cross that line, within its boundary you are safe. If you cross it, you incur great danger and shame to yourself, and to us. It seems to me we have heard that same story so many times before, that we almost believe that we have dreamt it. That familiar plot which recurs in the stories of Persephone and Eve, Red Riding Hood and Snow White. Don't cross, Don't cross, Don't cross that path. For you never know what lies on the other side of the invisible line.*

Difference is embodied as danger. Women know this because they have heard it a million times, but they never really believe it. We know this because we continue to dream of it, this tempting difference, this crossing over erasable lines in the sand. Hélène Cixous's Gandhi has this dream often – a dream of a nation without religious borders. The miraculous thing about him is that, unlike most of us, he remembers the dream every time he wakes up from sleep, and carries it forward into the daylight to let the world gaze and wonder at its delicate beauty.

Gandhi is the translator par excellence, translating his dreams from night into the day, sitting across gender lines, nations, and religions. In *L'Indiade*, Cixous's Gandhi slips deftly through various nets, traversing the borders between the feminine and the masculine, India and Pakistan, Hinduism and Islam, Christianity and Judaism, Father and Mother, and gradually brings to our awareness the fact that borders are made so that the notion of crossing becomes possible, that borders exist in order to be crossed, that they are imaginary lines in the sand, not to be reduced to insurmountable boundary walls.

In re-visioning Gandhi, Hélène Cixous further translates the historical Gandhi across time, and in this sense, exemplifies the traditional Indian view of translation. The Hindi for translation is *anuvad*, and as Harish Trivedi reminds us, its original Sanskrit connotations adhere much more closely to a movement across time than one across space: "The underlying metaphor in the word *anuvad* is temporal – to say *after*, to repeat – rather than spatial as in the English/Latin word translation – to carry *across*" (Bassnett and Trivedi 1999: 9). The chronological shift in *L'Indiade* gives the reader a telescopic perspective on India's past, enabling the shift from history into metaphor. It also reveals an often neglected aspect of translation – its ability to recreate, over and over again, that which has already been said, and bring about an erasure between author and subsequent translators.

But I do not forget that the word anuvad *contains my name,* anu, *as a prefix. The dictionary offers me several choices for the prefix* anu, *which include: 'after', 'similar', 'resembling', 'again' and 'along'. In its use as a prefix,* anu *often implies likeness, verisimilitude, the repeatable. But when* anu *appears on its own, and is written with a hard 'n', an untranslatable phoneme, then it becomes a small particle, the indivisible atom, the individual. So the word maps out the gap between the similar and the unique. In my mother tongue, translation, or* anuvad, *carries me over the difference between being unique and being cloned. In the trace of that difference, it reveals to me the path of the translator, who repeats to create a simulacrum, but ends up writing herself in a new, different space.*

So what happens to Sita, the pure woman, in the absence of her male benefactors? In every good story there is a villain. The evil one, Ravan of the ten heads, appears at the boundary line, disguised as a mendicant, a holy beggar of alms, wearing the mask of sameness, concealing, like the golden deer, temptation. He is a well-prepared actor, who has furnished himself with the right props for the scene. With his slippery voice, his sly words, his accomplished mannerisms, he convinces Sita to step closer and closer, to approach him at the magical line which he cannot cross, for he knows it will burn him to cinders. Sita is persuaded by his mask, compelled by his words. She extends her hand over the line to offer him alms for his bowl. She transgresses. What follows is the inevitable. Sita is kidnapped, seduced and captured by his otherness, carried away in a flying chariot, hijacked into the sky and transported to the evil kingdom of Lanka, where she will spend many months imprisoned in a beautiful but corrupt palace. The rest is his-story. Ram and Lakshman must now pay for her mistake, fight the long and strenuous battle of good over evil. Victory is assured from the beginning, but Sita, the chaste, will never be the same again. No matter how many times she goes through the test of fire, she will always be suspect, forever perceived as the woman who is capable of being tempted by difference, always threatened by the fear of abandonment. As woman, she has shown evidence that she is one, that she is always capable of crossing the line, pushing the circumference, tasting the pomegranate, devouring otherness, of being captivated by the scintillating gold of the deer disappearing into the dense foliage of her forest.

The Indian woman learns early the significance of the Lakshman-Rekha, and no matter how often or in how many ways she tries to live outside its definitions, to voice her opposition to its very existence, the line in the sand keeps appearing in her dreams as a reminder of the daily losses she must sustain to keep her courage alive.

L'Indiade, a defiance of borders and boundaries, a protest against the injunction that teaches us not to love difference, not to be seduced by its otherness, is in this sense, a work about the desire to translate despite the taboos set against it. For the translator, like the writer, must write over and beyond that initial fear of the division between the conscious and the unconscious. But beyond that, *L'Indiade* is also, in many ways, a *translating* work that takes historical entities and re-clothes them in new costumes, new disguises, showing us the path of the translator to be one of dissimulation. Hélène Cixous's *L'Indiade* transports Pre- and Post-Independence Indian history onto the contemporary stage in a variety of ways. At a linguistic level, its French text has already absorbed some of the intonations, expressions of Hindi so that the French text, especially as it was first staged under Ariane Mnouchkine's direction in 1987, had a distinctly 'ethnic' flavour. The text itself uses Hindi words, translations of Indian songs and poems, and Indian mannerisms to convey a foreignness that the French has made its own. Additionally, at a literary level, the text transforms history into myth, turning the historical figure of Mahatma Gandhi into a literary metaphor of androgyny and a celebration of love beyond difference. How then does one translate a palimpsest that re-covers meanings in every layer of its folds, a literary text which has consumed the history of a nation to re-present it as drama?

If cannibalism implies a devouring of the other and an organic absorption of its flesh into one's own body, both of these connotations of translation are already present in the writing of *L'Indiade*. For the historical Gandhi has been engulfed into the larger than life legend of Gandhi that is created in the context of the drama. Cixous insists that her Gandhi is human (Cixous 1987: 15) susceptible to errors, and fallible, but one has only to compare the Gandhi of *L'Indiade* to the one who appears in the cultural criticism of contemporary feminists, to be struck by the gap between metaphor and history (see Kishwar 1986). The story of India's independence, told here with exceeding love and attention to detail, is simultaneously a history turned into theatre, the dream of a utopia which serves the French writer in deliberating on her vision of femininity, of *écriture féminine*, of love and of difference, through the characters projected onto the screen of her/our imaginations. The history of the postcolonial nation's struggle for independence is employed to recover a story of the self. Is there an irony then in this form of passionate devouring of the other? Does the spiritualism projected onto the postcolonial other once more become the repository of the West's desires for what it lacks, an image not of the other, but a desired reflection of the self? A neo-colonial spin on the same old story of exploration? Or are these unreal fears born of our own postcolonial anxieties? How then do I, a postcolonial translator of a French text about India, even begin to undertake this effort which threatens to reduce me to my history? In translating *L'Indiade*, I translate all of my own anxieties, all of my fears.

Several critics and writers have recently pointed to the violence that is inherent in translation. Hélène Cixous, in her postscript to the play, "Écrits sur le théâtre" tells us that what she has tried to do in *L'Indiade* is nothing other than an extremely faithful translation of passions: "*Ma traduction des passions doit être d'une extrême fidélité*" (Cixous 1987: 262) ["My translation of passions must be born of an extreme fidelity"]. At the same time, however, she draws our attention to the violence implicit in translation: "*Traduire: retrouver la simple violence du rêve*" (*ibid.*) ["Translate: to recover the simple violence of the dream"].

In the postcolonial context, this inherent violence of translation is imbued with an additional (violent) connotation, especially when it refers to the translation of postcolonial texts into European languages. In their introduction to *Post-Colonial Translation*, Susan Bassnett and Harish Trivedi emphasize this violent relationship between translation and colonization, especially as it relates to the ferrying over of certain third world texts into European languages: "Moreover, the role played by translation in facilitating colonization is also now in evidence. And the metaphor of the colony *as* a translation, a copy of an original located elsewhere on the map, has been recognized" (Bassnett and Trivedi 1999: 5).

Another translator, Gérard Macé, describes his work as a combined activity of reading and writing, of reading with a pencil in one's hand, in order to write between the lines of the original text: "*Traduire, c'est lire avec un peu plus de patience que d'habitude, et même avec un crayon à la main pour écrire entre les lignes*" (Macé 1997: 32) ["Translating is reading with a little more patience than usual, and even with a pencil in hand so that one can write between the lines"]. Translating *L'Indiade*, I write notes in the margins of this play, and attempt to ferret out that which the author is seeing, so that I too can see that barely translucent image. But the play also begins to unfold another drama in my mind, that political one where I am positioned as the other of this history, and I am caught between what I read and what I translate. A careful reading/translation of the play must reveal the various intentionalities latent in the body of the text. While the translation I undertook in bringing the French text into the folds of the Hindustani does not participate in the violence described by Trivedi and Bassnett – that is, the selective transportation of indigenous third world literatures into European languages – there still remains the question of the violence that is present in the original translation of Indian history into French literature, and the translator's (my) subsequent role in unquestioningly carrying this violence back to its homeground. How then does the postcolonial translator, taking this story about India back to the original cultural environment of the play, avoid a certain violence that is inherent in such a translation? Clearly, it is not a question of the evasion of violence, but of its containment to the connotation indicated by Hélène Cixous. The only way to do this, is for the Hindustani translation to remind the reader, as does the original French, that the heroic and non-heroic characters of this play are exaggerated mythic versions of their historical counterparts. In Cixous's play, the historical Gandhi is made over into both angel and beast, finding a reflection in the bear who loses her senses when faced with the horror of human violence. The bear, like the deer in the *Ramayana*, takes us in the direction of dreams. As a translator of Cixous's work, the bear reminds me that my translation must retain this mythic aspect of the French play, so that we never forget that the Gandhi of the text is a dream, as well as a dreamer of dreams, a golden deer who tempts us to cross the borders between awareness and the unconscious. At the same time, as a reader and an Indian woman, I cannot let go of that other Gandhi, whose patriarchal views towards Indian women were part of the fabric of his complex historicity. The translator must dance at that fine line between reading and the imagination.

3. "Reading at the Edge"

What such a reading reveals is that poetry can become the nectar of history, and that while as reader I am surrounded by various possible readings, as translator, I need only drink from the manna of the poem that is *L'Indiade*. Gandhi, along with Jinnah, Nehru, Sarojini and all the other characters of the play, are masked actors driven by the force of the imagination and love of a passionate writer. I leave history behind, resting in its silent tombstone that was witness to a century of imperialist violence, and move towards the metaphor of the literary work, always aware of a certain violence in that departure from my nation's burdened past.

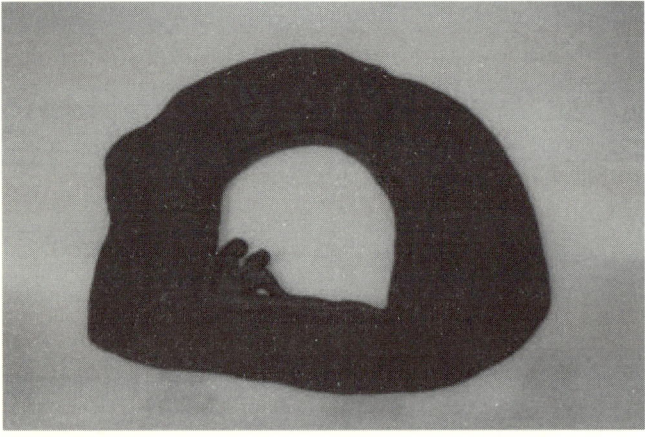

Reading L'Indiade *in Hindustani, my mother, my first reader, wept when she came to the section where Hindu and Muslim lovers separated from one another, when Muslims and Hindus were forced to flee from their homes on either side of the border, when scores of people died in the exodus. She remembered, she said, her own home in Pakistan, relatives who had died in the carnage, a childhood left behind forever, the loss of innocence in the killing of the bear. Translating from French into my mother tongue, I had unwittingly linked myself to my mother's memories, my mother's tears.*

L'Indiade translates the broken fragment of an Indian dream into French, mimicking an India by calling forth Indian sounds, smells, colours and streets. H. Cixous's text transports her imaginary India of 1947 onto the French stage, unveiling the author's vision onto the screen of the symbolic. The translator, in soft pursuit of the secret imagination, must follow not just the trace of the words on the page, but the trace of the dream embodied in the flesh of each word, imagining a vision that simulates, but is never identical to, the dream of the writer. Seduced by the writer's imagination, the translator births a text that carries forth two dreams together into life.

Blindly, I mold clay with my hands to make it conform to the veiled secret that my unconscious alone sees. My hands pursue the outlines of the image reluctantly, unnerved by its invisibility. There is a low noise in my head that holds the vision submerged just below the surface of the dream that I cannot remember. I breathe slowly, like a pregnant woman whose time has not yet come, and let the quiet surround the walls of my mind like a calm lake whose waters must not be stirred. In the rest of the moment that follows, an image begins to reflect itself on the watery mirror. My hands see the shape and follow it in stealth, my eyes hear the sound of the falling tide, leaving in its wake a seascape of oysters, pearls, sandcastles, and mermaids who walk on sand as easily as they swim in the ocean, and scampering among them all, a deer speckled with stars of gold. I look down into my womb and see the egg that turns into a flower, that turns into a book. Finally the infant that I have dreamt of begins to emerge, tender, quivering with life, marked by curious imperfections, but inspired by the invisible deer in the lush forest. I sculpt my dream into clay, I re-inscribe its contours into the hieroglyphics of wet, erasable mud.

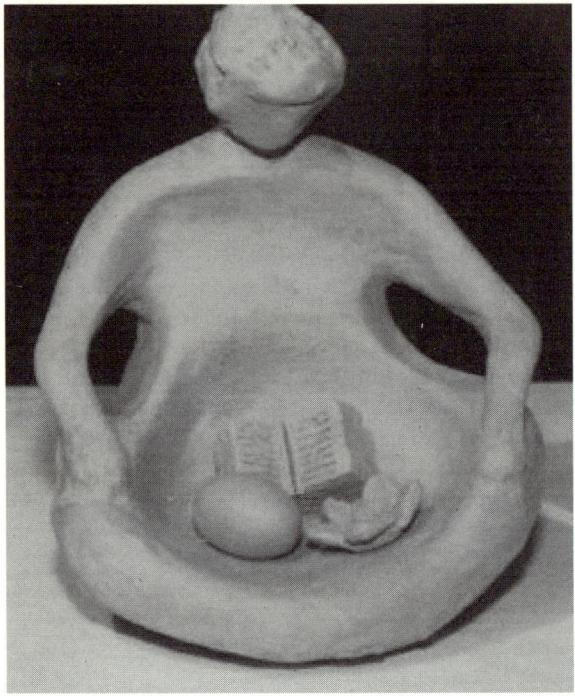

4. "Wombdreams"

Sculpting clay to resemble dreams that I have, I come to the realization that the visual arts set themselves apart from literature in their untranslatability.

Writing allows us to carry the tracing of its marks from one sheet of paper to another, between language systems, through a re-inscription of signs. The Persian word '*varaq*' takes me back to the link between reading and eating. *Varaq*, originally the leaf of a book, or a sheet of paper, became, over time, the thin silver or gold leaf that is used to cover Indian sweets, in other words, became edible. *Varaq bikharna* still implies, in Hindustani, to be scattered, as in the coming apart of the leaves of a book, or the loss of one's self-possession (Fallon 1984: 1185). As reader, I eat up the meanings of the words that my eyes graze over, foraging them for familiarity, cannibalizing them like sweetmeats. As translator, I learn to lose my self-possession, to be like the crazed bear of *L'Indiade*, to be captivated by the dream of the writer. Both the writer and the translator scour lines into paper, marking out the trace of a vanishing, unforgettable dream, the sighting of a mythical deer. The visual artist is both fortunate and unfortunate in this sense. Her work will be unique, inimitable, but also inedible, never to be loved/eaten up, by another translator in the way that the translator bestows love upon the writer's text.

What the narrators of the Ramayan *always forget to mention is the tender miraculous beauty of the nimble-footed deer, the power of something seen fleetingly, but believed in. Does the deer exist? Or is it a figment of a hysterical woman's imagination who has lived in patriarchal exile for years on end? Certainly, it is not Ram but Sita who notices the deer, not Ram but Sita who desires it beyond all other desires.*

The story of the female imagination captured by the deer repeats itself in classical Indian literature. In Kalidasa's Abhigyana Shakuntalam, *an urban King wandering about in another Indian forest, catches sight of Shakuntala, a forest nymph, and immediately falls in love with her image. They are secretly married, and the king returns to the city leaving her with a ring, and a handful of promises. But some time later Shakuntala loses her ring, and destiny erases the image of the beloved from the King's mind. In her time of separation in the penance-forest, Shakuntala's constant companion is a young fawn, an animal that Shakuntala nurtures like a mother, and someone whose unfailing devotion plays a foil to the King's short-lived memory. Pregnant with memories, and unable to wait any longer for her lover-husband, Shankuntala decides to follow her dreams. But the price she pays is the abandonment of the beast-child she has nurtured. Shakuntala must now give up her (m)other love and go in search of a perfect love that exists only in her dreams.*

L'Indiade confronts us with this question: does one always have to kill in order to be born? The act of translating asks the same question in another way: does the move from the mother tongue into another language always involve a form of murder? Julia Kristeva reminds us about the price the foreigner/writer must pay: "*Il y a du matricide dans l'abandon d'une langue natale*" (Kristeva 1998: 388) ["There is an element of matricide in the relinquishing of the mother tongue"]. At the same time, we are reminded by critics writing about translation from the other side of the colonial/postcolonial divide, in their reference to the vision of Brazilian translator Haroldo de Campos, that translation may also be a killing of the father: "a form of patricide, a refusal to repeat that which has already been presented as the original" (Bassnett and Trivedi 1999: 15). If we are to believe both of these perspectives, we must conclude that the translator does away with both parental figures. Orphan to memory, orphan to the law of repetition, the foreigner-translator seems to have been set adrift on a rudderless boat.

But is there another way to look at the shift away from the mother tongue? Isn't translating/writing also about remembering? Hélène Cixous tells us: "*Il faut ne pas oublier. L'écriture ce n'est au fond qu'un anti-oubli*" (Cixous 1990: 22) ["One must not forget. At bottom, writing is nothing but an un-forgetting"]. And Abdelkebir Khatibi, that "professional foreigner" who writes in the crevices between languages, who is perpetually translating himself into French, remembers that as writer-translator, he is also a scribe who works on memory: "*Je suis alors scribe, 'scribe enquêteur': j'enquête sur ma mémoire, la mémoire des langues, une mémoire active, en devenir, qui s'acharne sur l'effacement des traces et leur transformation, leur métamorphose*" (Khatibi 1997: 140) ["I am, then, a scribe, an investigator-scribe: I investigate my memory, the memory of languages, an active memory in the process of becoming, a memory which is intent on the effacement of traces and on their transformation, their metamorphosis"]. Perhaps what these writer/translators successfully reveal to us is that the acts of writing and translating, in their distanciation from the mother tongue, attempt to recover the mother elsewhere, avoiding a certain matricide, and repeat the passion of the original dream, avoiding a certain patricide. Translation need not be only about what is lost, it may also be about a supplementary wandering love that ultimately finds its home in the translated text.

The stories of female remembrance of a perfect love, a perfect other, proliferate in classical Indian literature, and serve as indicators of women who escape patriarchal boundaries in search of their dreams. At the same time, they remind us of the main task of the translator, who must awaken to the dream of the writer, acknowledge her seduction, and be willing to pursue the deer in the forest.

Gandhi's relevance, like that of Hélène Cixous's *L'Indiade*, is revived over and over again by history, and translated for us by the writer, like a recurring dream that yearns to be deciphered. On the day that I write this, in Gandhi's Gujarat, Hindus and Muslims burn each other to death, Muslim and Hindu men rape the daughters of those they claim to have loved. A bloodbath is being staged once again in the name of religion. A half century after the death of Gandhi, Ahmedabad makes its way back onto the map of the world, reminding us that in Gandhi's hometown, the utopic dream of a singular man continues to be smashed into unrecognizable shards on a daily basis. While history repeats itself, it becomes the task of the writer/translator to unravel its patterns and spin the yarn of history into stories of mythic proportions, so that we do not forget either the violence or the love of which we are capable.

References

Bassnett, Susan and Harish Trivedi. 1999. 'Introduction' in Bassnett, Susan and Harish Trivedi (eds) *Post-colonial Translation*. London and New York, NY: Routledge. 1-18.
Cixous, Hélène. 1987. *L'Indiade ou l'Inde de leurs rêves*. Paris: Théâtre du Soleil.
—. 1990. 'De la scène de l'Inconscient à la scène de l'Histoire: Chemin d'une écriture' in van Rossum-Guyon, Françoise and Myriam Díaz-Diocaretz (eds) *Hélène Cixous, Chemins d'une écriture*. Amsterdam-Paris: Rodopi-PUV. 15-34.
Fallon, S.W. 1984. *Hindustani-English Dictionary*. Allahabad: Bharti Bhandar.
Gandhi, M. K. 1947. *India of my Dreams*. Ahmedabad: Navajivan Publishing House.
Khatibi, Abdelkebir. 1997. 'Un étranger professionnel' in *Textuel* 32: 139-141.
Kishwar, Madhu. 1986. *Gandhi and Women*. New Delhi: Manushi Prakashan.

Kristeva, Julia. 1998. 'L'autre langue ou traduire le sensible' in *French Studies* 52(4): 385-396.
Macé, Gérard. 1997. 'Vita Nova ou Vita Nuova' in *Textuel* 32: 23-33.

Translating Hélène Cixous's *Tambours sur la digue*: the Ineffable on Stage

Judith G. Miller

> The author recognises the influence of her activity as an American stage director in her translation of *Tambours sur la digue*. It made her transform its puppets into "characters", by ascribing to them a colloquial language that gave the puppets a more human presence. She examines several passages of her first translation and compares them to the second version, written with Brian Mallet. Miller concludes that, in her case, and perhaps due to the "incompatibility" of Cixous's and her own theatrical language, the only way to respect the force of the original text has been working together with another translator.
> Key words: theater, Mnouchkine, puppets, translator's ego.

Life tenders experiences of such horror that even the most audacious of theater people recoil from attempts to represent them. Even outside of theater, such occurrences (and I think particularly of genocide and its sickening frequency in our times) belie the ability to communicate, for they are situated outside of language, beyond the structuring devices which give form. Sometimes we learn more from the way the person who has known this horror holds her body, stumbles over words, or clutches her hands than from what she says. We grasp intimations of shapeless dread, suffering and unbelief. We read the body: it is the theater of her pain. But when we try to bring this "theater" to the theater, we risk containing the experience in such a way that it becomes less than what it was – because through representation, the experience (and perhaps "experience" is too comforting a concept) becomes bearable.

      Hélène Cixous's theater does not give form to the unbearable, although much about which she speaks is heartbreaking and condemnable – her theater making us look hard at power and power's compromises or raw ambitions, thus forcing us to confront what is most heinous about the human condition. The unbearable, however, haunts Cixous's work: meaningless deaths, hatred beyond all understanding. Yet her theater operates to redeem the sacrifices, to stop the hostility, to convey a metaphor and reinforce a myth of possibility, of transformation, and of hope. Thus she navigates through the unbearable to the ineffable. Expressing the ineffable in *likenesses* of reality, her theater communicates what might come or what has yet to be named, the in-between, the more than two, the tremulous.

When I speak this way of the theater of Cixous, I am inspired by a work in three dimensions, for I see it this way both with my own director's eyes and as incarnated, shaped, and given rhythm by Simone Benmussa, Claude Régy, Daniel Mesguich, and, especially Ariane Mnouchkine, the French *metteurs en scène* who have staged Cixous. The luminosity of Mnouchkine's productions, in particular, their generosity and exquisite physical beauty, seem to marry perfectly the startling images of Cixous's poetic prose and the quirky sensibilities of her characters[1]. Moreover, the extraordinary energy of a Mnouchkine performance, the balletic discipline of the choreography, and the haunting percussive underscoring of the dialogue all contribute to realizing Cixous's unearthly vision.

The boldness which characterizes Mnouchkine's stage work had, nevertheless, an unexpected effect on me as translator when working on a first English-language version of Cixous's 1999 piece, *Tambours sur la Digue: Sous forme de pièce ancienne pour marionnettes jouée par des acteurs* (which Brian J. Mallet and I eventually translated as *Drums on the Dam: In The Form of an Ancient Puppet Play Perfumed by Actors*). In allowing myself to be inhabited by Mnouchkine's pungent and tightly controlled *mise-en-scène*, which I had seen a number of times, I tended in translating to reign in the floating and often enigmatic language which characterizes the play. My first version of *Drums* disappointed Cixous. A second version, in collaboration with Mallet, a respected and much-loved translator[2], produced an English-language text more attuned to her creative imagination, as well as a lesson in how the felt materiality of theater can skew the translation of a dramatic text, in this case purloining the work's purposeful "otherness"[3].

That I should have erred in such a way is ironic, considering my own objections to a New York staging (June 1998) of my and Christiane Makward's translation of Cixous's *Le Nom d'Oedipe: Chant du corps interdit* [*The Name of Oedipus: Song of the Forbidden Body*]. In what was otherwise a fearless operatic production of Cixous's reworking of the Oedipus myth by an engaging feminist company, Voices and Vision – with an original score by Ruth Schonthal –, the director chose, by staging Jocasta's dying and then isolating Oedipus on stage, to reject the innovative prismatic ending in which Jocasta and Oedipus become one[4].

Oedipus's last lines speak to the metamorphosis that occurs when "he/Oedipus" and "she/Jocasta" merge into an indeterminate other. At play's end, Oedipus, the "silent sea", the *mère/mer,* is awash in Jocasta, his ego dissolved and transmuted:

> It is you, my night, surging
> Over me
> As surely as I am the silent sea
> Whose flesh has just opened
> So that you may fill it.
> And we are entering each other
> My mother,
> My child.
> My flesh is restful here.
> I shall cease to suffer.
> I have forgotten everything.
> I no longer know who is dying[5].
> (Cixous 1994, tr. Makward and Miller: 326)

Watching the powerful and compelling male actor speaking those final lines at the conclusion of the New York performance, I felt that Cixous's effort in *The Name of Oedipus* to explode stultifying gendered positions had been foiled. I also realized that I was reacting like a theorist and translator – and not like a director. How, in fact, would one be able to *show* on stage Oedipus absorbing Jocasta into himself and becoming "us" – a new "bisexual" ideal?

Translating Cixous for the theater poses constantly this question: how to give shape on stage without trivializing it to what is unsayable yet said in her work – a space of conceptual newness or a space from which newness can emerge. Theater people, perhaps especially American-trained theater people, of which I am one, look for through lines, clear images, interpretative stances which fold down the text's multiple possibilities in order to offer to the audience something intense and graspable, in a defined time and space frame. My own efforts as theater translator have always led me to seek out from within the text the architecture of its potential stagings.

Mnouchkine herself unquestionably offers strong and unambiguous interpretations of Cixous. Nevertheless, she also always suggests the pregnancy of otherness through the theatrical forms and styles she deploys, her incursions into the performance practices of Asian theater having notably graced all of her recent *mises en scène*, including those of Cixous's texts, with a wondrous strangeness. Indeed, *Drums on the Dam*'s newness, its space of indecidability and openness lay in the decision taken by the Théâtre du Soleil, which reverberates throughout Cixous's text, to create a play inspired formally by various Asian puppet theaters[6]. Resonating with Japanese Bunraku theater – in which black-hooded non-speaking puppeteers manipulate puppets on stage – the actors of the Soleil performed both the roles of puppets (the *characters*) and of puppeteers working marionettes. Thus the production *looked like* puppet theater, while at the same time embodying the fascinating tension of live actors attempting to conform to the parameters of both clothed wooden puppets and *invisible* puppeteers.

Cixous's mandate – to create a language for puppets – finds a place among the ambitions of several major twentieth-century theater talents, from Alfred Jarry to Gordon Craig to Beckett – following Kleist – to Tadeusz Kantor and the South African Hand Spring Company. Puppet theater renders possible on stage a heightened metaphorization, an emptying out of psychological motivation, and a chiselling of physical imagery. Through outrageous stage action, puppet theater can make palpable the cruellest of farces. It can obviously, through the *thingness* of the puppet, also focus the dramatic inquiry on the nature of human will, consciousness, and agency. Searching for the right tone for the Soleil "puppets", Cixous read volumes of Noh theater in order to explore and adapt its alien quality. The richly oblique mood evoked through her language helped establish a singular dramatic universe as well as facilitating the actors' efforts to hold onto their puppet-ness.

Nonetheless, in my first version of *Drums on the Dam*, I ignored the question of puppets altogether and brought *characters* to center stage. I played out all the roles in my head, acted them with friends, and produced a coy version performable by American actors. In this I now realize I was not only influenced by my own American theatrical impulses and the energy of the performance but also by Mnouchkine's creation of a kind of hybrid performer – puppets, yes, but also actors giving psychological depth or at least personalities to their puppets through speech, clowning, and gesture. One might say that I departed from the ideal of the theatrical experiment to translate what actually happened when actors of differing abilities and approaches had the job of playing marionettes. Their physical presence thus slipped into the translation of Cixous's text.

Hence, I grounded the translated text in speaking bodies by adding filler words such as 'and', 'you know', 'now', or 'listen'. I finished sentences to make the dialogue clearer. I found American colloquialisms for clever or funny French terms that were not, however, colloquial. I also made contractions from subject pronouns and verbs, thus flattening the poetic intent overall. In what follows, I will examine several passages in both translated versions of *Drums on the Dam* in order to show how I initially strayed from Cixous's purposely defamiliarizing dramatic world, consequently producing a punchy play text, ripe for an American company.

Perhaps, unsurprisingly, the first misstep came in the translation of the title, an attempt which yielded *Duan and the Drummers: A Tale of Raging Waters in the Form of an Ancient Puppet Play, Performed by Actors*. This version avoided the vexing problem of translating "*la digue*", the term 'dyke' in English being too fraught to be used for a play title. However, by foregrounding in the title the character Duan (the *heroine* of the tale) and the Drummers (the collective *hero*, or the sentinels watching over the threatening river), I placed the emphasis immediately on character and on the characters' problem. In fact, *Drums on the Dam* is an allegory about unstoppable destruction wrought by greed and, more important, inattention to the need for environmental balance both among humans and between humans and the natural world. The drums – the instruments which call out, which awaken, which embody both the consciousness of a need for action as well as action itself – are more central to the meaning of the play than the drummers. They speak to the mystery of the inanimate become animate, a metamorphosis basic to the play's spiritual climate. They speak also to the power of art, in this case theater, to alert and to inspire action.

A second translating misstep, which helped determine the feel of the entire first version, came in rearranging lines. I reworked the order of sentences both in the more sustained poetic passages (of which there are few) and in the frequent rapid-fire exchanges among the some thirty-five characters. Rearranging lines resulted in a more fluent read in English. This type of stylistic manipulation, however, also lost the density of the original text and again, because it muffled the oddness of the dialogue, put 'persons' in the place of puppets.

The play begins, for example, with the Soothsayer recounting in a four-stanza poem what he had dreamed the previous evening: he saw himself and his daughter Duan peering down into the flooded ruins of their city.

> *Sous nos yeux*
> *Une rafle de jeunes enfants*
> *Enflés comme des outres*
> *Emportés par la mort*
> *Galop puissant, train d'enfer*
> *Le visage d'une mère*
> *Regarde*
> *Le Chapeau noir d'un lettré qui flotte, léger.*
> (Cixous 1999: 8)

I originally translated this introductory stanza of the Soothsayer's warning (that "The City of a Hundred Golden Doors" (Quan Ze) will soon be inundated) by collecting the verses in two movements:

> Under our very eyes
> A whirl of young children
> Swollen as if to burst,
> Carried off by death's
> Powerful gallop and hellish gait.
> The black hat of a scholar, floating lightly,
> Holds the attention
> Of a mother's gaze. (Cixous, tr. Miller, Up Ms: 2)

By regrouping words to establish a certain semantic logic, I changed the hesitant rhythm of the original French and lost the extended comparison between death and "a powerful gallop" and "hellish gait". These equine personifications of the raging and enraged waters flooding the city are, nevertheless, crucial in highlighting how the threat to the people of Quan Ze has taken on a life of its own.

The final translation, with Brian Mallet, retains the image of death bursting into multiple threatening forms. The slight disconnectedness of the verses re-establishes a more disembodied and nightmarish 'referential real'. And the final image of the last line, as in the French "the black hat of a scholar, floating lightly", reinforces the uncanny feel of the Soothsayer's vision and eliminates the potential sentimentality of ending with "a mother's gaze":

> Under our very eyes
> A swoop of young children
> Swollen like goatskin bottles,
> Carried off by death
> Powerful gallop, hellish gait.
> The face of a mother
> Watches
> The black hat of a scholar, floating lightly.
> (Cixous, tr. Mallet and Miller, Up Ms: 3; 2003: 192)

Throughout the second version of the entire translation, we effected similar changes, re-finding the feeling of the unexpected, creating a rhythm that disrupts and captures attention, taking care not to over-interpret the text.

Reworking the quickly paced dialogue between characters forced me to concentrate on giving life through phrasing and imagery to what is normally considered inanimate. This corrective insight was crucial for conveying the all-embracing world which is that of the play – a world endangered by those humans who learn to despise, denigrate, and otherwise distinguish themselves from it, a world in which ideas also pulse with life and power. In reworking the dialogue, particularly in light of Brian Mallet's insights, I also re-established the uncertainty characterizing the moral choices of those *characters* meant to be forces of authority. We also redoubled our efforts to foreground stylization, word play, and informing images.

A key early moment in the play that illustrates these transformations pits various parties against each other. What to do about the impending cataclysm holds some in thrall. Others act out of self-interest. The wisest, the Chancellor, frets over not finding an acceptable solution: he sees victims everywhere. The villains, Lord Hun – the nephew of ruler Lord Khang and aspirant to the throne – and the grasping Chief Intendant, have no such scruples. They plan to save the city and drown the peasants by blowing a hole in the dam where it protects the peasants' village:

> Le Chancelier
> *Le pays vacille au bord de l'eau trouble. La main gauche s'apprête à attaquer la main droite. L'Imminence attise les fureurs dans les frères, les fièvres, les appétits. Chacun devra choisir. Nord ou Sud, lui ou moi. L'homme vertueux sera celui qui... Et la campagne, le Devin pourtant en a parlé mais personne n'a entendu. [...] Quelle heure est-il?*
> Un Serviteur
> *Il est si tard, Seigneur, qu'il est bientôt très tôt.*
> Le Chancelier
> *Ce temps n'a déjà plus d'heure! Viens, allons sonder les coeurs simples sur la rive d'en face.*
> [Ils s'éloignent à travers la Ville. Entrent le Seigneur Hun et le Grand Intendant.]
> Le Seigneur Hun
> *Alors?*
> Le Grand Intendant
> *Il* [Lord Khang, the ruler] *est encore à balancer.*
> Le Seigneur Hun
> *Faut-il qu'il soit borné quand même. La solution est là, sous son nez. Cela vous crève les yeux, non?*
> (Cixous 1999: 15-16)

I first translated this expository exchange as follows:

> *The Chancellor*
> The country is wavering on the brink of troubled waters. The left hand is getting ready to attack the right. Imminent disaster is working brothers, appetites, and desires into a fury. Each must choose. North or South, him or me. What choice for the virtuous man? The City? And what about the countryside? The Soothsayer spoke about it too, but no one heard him [...]. What time is it?
> *A Servant*
> It's so late, my Lord, that soon it will be early.
> *Chancellor*
> What's time at a moment like this? Come, let's hear what the simple folk across the river have to say.
> *[They move away across the City. Lord Hun and the Chief Intendant enter.]*
> *Lord Hun*
> Well?
> *Chief Intendant*
> He's still weighing.
> *Lord Hun*
> Wouldn't you know he'd be so stubborn? The solution is right here, under his nose. It hits you right in the eye, doesn't it?
> (Cixous, tr. Miller, Up Ms: 6)

The second version, with Brian Mallet, offered several significant changes:

> *Chancellor*
> The country is wavering on the brink of troubled waters. The left hand is getting ready to attack the right. Imminent disaster is stirring up into a fury brothers, appetites, and desires. Each must choose. North or South, him or me. The virtuous man will be he who... And the countryside... The soothsayer has nevertheless spoke of it too, but no one heard him. [...]. What time is it?
> *A Servant*
> It is so late my Lord, that it will soon be very early.
> *Chancellor*
> This time no longer has any hour. Come, let us hear what the simple people across the river have to say.
> *[They move away across the city. Lord Hun and the chief intendant enter.]*
> *Lord Hun*
> Well?
> *Chief Intendant*
> He is still swaying back and forth.
> *Lord Hun*
> Yes, it is just like him to be short-sighted. The solution is here, under his nose. It strikes you right in the eye, does it not?
> (Cixous, tr. Mallet and Miller, Up Ms: 7; 2003: 194)

In the Chancellor's first lines, Cixous points through homophonic word play to the possible philosophical connotation of "imminence" – as a lack of metaphysical or other authority. Neither translated version keeps exactly this meaning; both explain "imminence" as "imminent disaster". However, the phrasing of the second version reinforces the active, nearly alive nature of "imminence" by using a more specific verb: "stirring up" – a verb associated with sorcery and magic – rather than the more prosaic "working into". "Imminence" consequently retains the sense of an independent and uncontrolled or supernatural force which is capable of bending people's will, a force not located in the known or rationally directed.

In the Chancellor's deliberation, he queries the role of the virtuous man, a query Cixous leaves open in the French text. My concern was that the audience would not, at this point, have held onto the sense of the city v. the countryside conflict: this is the central conflict that underlies the debate about what to do about the coming flood. In the first version, I thus oriented the answer to the question of the role of the virtuous man by adding a phrase ("The City?"). I focused the translation on the necessity of choosing to sacrifice either the city or the countryside. In version two, we put back into the text the unsolvable nature of Cixous's question, reintroducing the larger and more complicated dilemma facing all the characters, a dilemma not based merely in the choice between the seemingly dichotomous poles city and countryside, but rather on the ethical question of what it means to be virtuous.

Throughout this exchange, as well as throughout the entire second version, we eliminated contractions to make the dialogue more archaic, heightening a slightly old-fashioned and stylized feel. This is not a linguistic register that would include "folk" (a modern colloquialism) for "*coeurs simples*" – which we subsequently rendered without metonymy as "simple people". A major question for me in the first version was how to translate: "*Ce temps n'a déjà plus d'heure!*". I opted in version one for a rewriting which captures the sense of the absurdity of the concept of time when faced with the apocalypse. My translation, in the form of a question: "What's time at a moment like this?", added momentum to the Servant and Chancellor's exchange. It did not, however, retain the word play of "*temps*" (as in: "time" – 'hours and minutes' –, but also '*ambiance*, psychological climate, or historical period') and its multi-faceted relationship with "*plus d'heure*" (as in: 'no more hours – marking points, divisions –' but also: 'no more sense of an ending or never-endingness'). The second version, Brian Mallet's invention: "This time no longer has any hour", reintroduces the several interpretative levels suggested above.

Brian Mallet also retranslated the verb "*balancer*", "weighing", to "swaying back and forth" to pick up the physical movement used by the marionette Lord Khang each time he faces a choice. He rewrote "*borné*", "stubborn" in the first version, as "short-sighted" to maintain the focus on seeing (as in: 'understanding' or 'getting the picture'). In general, he helped locate an informing metaphor for each one of the play's twelve episodes, 'sight' and 'seeing' dominating in the episode in question.

Another key exchange between three fishermen, who eventually align their fate with the exploitative and environmentally scandalous Lord Hun, can also be examined to show how we reoriented the second version to lighten up American colloquialisms, to activate the anthropomorphic quality of the play's universe, and to keep the focus on 'money', a major trope underlying the play's violence. Tempted by bribery, the fishermen are about to renounce their principles in order to join the lumbermen cutting down the forest that holds up the River's banks. Their situation is dire, as all the fish, like many of the inhabitants of Quan Ze, seem to be "running away":

> Le Deuxième Pêcheur
> *Mon cousin, lui, s'est mieux débrouillé. Enrôlé par Hun, il est plus haut dans les collines et il coupe les forêts. Les arbres, eux, ne peuvent pas s'enfuir.*
> Le Premier Pêcheur
> *Justement, à propos de Hun, He Tao, son sombre lieutenant, m'a fait ce matin une proposition que je n'ai plus, ce soir, les moyens de refuser et que je vais vous dire. Pour nous ce serait de l'or.*
> Le Troisième Pêcheur
> *De l'or...* (Cixous 1999: 28-29)

For the first version of this exchange, I got slightly carried away in a *Godfather*-like riff:

> *Second Fisherman*
> My cousin's a lot smarter than us. He enlisted with Hun and is high up in the hills, where he cuts down the forests. Those trees can't run away.
> *First Fisherman*
> That's just what I wanted to talk to you about – Hun. His shadowy lieutenant He Tao made me an offer this morning I can't refuse – seeing the shape I'm in tonight. Listen, for us it's a golden opportunity.
> *Third Fisherman*
> Golden...
> (Cixous, tr. Miller, Up Ms: 12)

The second version downplayed the gangster mentality prominent in the language of the first:

> *Second Fisherman*
> My cousin has fended for himself much better than us. Recruited by Hun, he is high up in the hills, where he cuts the forests. Those trees cannot run away.
> *First Fisherman*
> Exactly, and speaking of Hun, this morning He Tao, his shadowy lieutenant, made me an offer which this evening I can no longer refuse and which I am going to share. For us it would be pure gold.
> *Third Fisherman*
> Gold...
> (Cixous, tr. Mallet and Miller, Up Ms: 2-13; 2003: 198)

The red-flag phrase: *"une proposition que je n'ai plus [...] les moyens de refuser"* prompted me to embroider, in the first version, upon the deal being made. The second version evacuates what is overly colloquial in the first version and brings out the formality in the fishermen's speech by keeping the frequent pauses of the French original.

In addition, whereas in the first version, the Second Fisherman says "cuts down the forest", in the second, he proclaims "cuts the forest". In the first version, the use of a standard verb for the work of a lumberjack draws no particular attention to the forest as a mysterious world of life and desire, capable, as Cixous would have it, of "running away". In the second version, the forest, which can be "cut", rather than "cut down", adopts a persona, a persona now unable to "run away". The second version helps maintain the anthropomorphization of the forest, which, like the River, the fish, the drums, and other natural and man-made objects in the play, does not sit in opposition to the human. Finally, by turning the slang expression "golden opportunity" into "gold", the second version places the emphasis on monetary gain and exchange value, in keeping both with this particular movement of the play, which emphasizes 'cashing in' and 'calculating' and with the sense throughout that 'capital' is abetting the destruction of a once cohesive universe.

Drums on the Dam, an enacted ritual of morality, lost some of its ceremonial quality in the first, more colloquial version of the translation. By paying more attention to central, determining images in the second, we helped reaffirm the spiritual struggle in the play. For example, during the last moments of the piece, the sympathetic Noodle Peddler, Madame Li, and her helper, Kisa, have fled the waters overrunning the city: the dam has collapsed. Escaping into the hills to find shelter with the peasants, they discover, nonetheless, that the segment of the dam holding back the waters from the peasants' village has also come under assault. Madame Li confronts the obvious: the flood waters are closing in everywhere; there is no where to go and yet she must try to move on.

> Madame Li
> À vue d'oeil fond l'espace pour le salut.
> Tout le pays est descendu par le fond.
> Fuyons encore plus loin, Kisa, nous finirons bien par
> nous mettre à l'abri.
> (Cixous 1999: 75)

This became in the first version:

> *Madame Li*
> The space of safety is disappearing as I look.
> The whole countryside is moving downwards.
> Let's run further, Kisa, we'll find something to shelter us.
> (Cixous, tr. Miller, Up Ms: 31)

In the second version, the choppy rhythm gives way to a more varied cadence:

> *Madame Li*
> As far as the eye goes, the space for salvation is disappearing.
> The entire country has descended to the bottom.
> Let us flee even further, Kisa, we will find somewhere
> to shelter in the end.
> (Cixous, tr. Mallet and Miller, Up Ms: 32; 2003: 212)

This second version restores a ritual connotation to the first sentence by underscoring the notion of "salvation", rather than "safety". By selecting the verb 'to descend', this latter version also reinforces the double nature of the country's decline, both a physical movement and a moral slide. These last lines also prepare the triumphant return of the character of the River, whose thunderous condemnation of "the sin of negligence" ("*péché d'inattention*") and the "sloth of souls" ("*paresse de l'âme*") brings the play to its watery and vengeful close.

These examples of transformations in rhythm, syntax, choice and thickness of imagery, linguistic stylization, and spiritual and psychological coloration from version one to two of *Drums on the Dam* illustrate the work that was necessary to move the first version of *Drums* to a register that would derange, jolt, and intrigue. We sought a final translation that would bring us as close as possible to the original work without attempting to replace it. We also wanted a translation that would value mood and hesitancy over character and action. The final effort is, all the same, weighted by the time period in which it was executed and by the current conditions of doing theater in English. Even consciously trying to sideline these concerns the second time around, I was never able to stop visualizing a performance, hearing a rhythmic delivery, and feeling the immediacy of words becoming flesh.

Spanish philosopher Ortega y Gasset's thoughts on translation resume, albeit with a slightly different slant, my own uneasiness about translating Cixous: "What will [the translator] do with a rebellious text? Isn't it too much to ask that he [sic] also be rebellious, particularly since the text is someone else's? He will be ruled by cowardice [...], he will place the translated author in the prison of normal experience; that is, he will betray" (Venuti 2000: 50). Perhaps betrayal is the normal lot of the translator of literary texts, even those less demanding than Cixous's. Perhaps, however, what I have always faced in attempting to translate Hélène Cixous is a confounding incompatibility in personal languages. My style is vigorous and forthright. I am not an ambiguous, playful, polysemic writer. I look to rhythm for effect and to make a point. Is this the American asserting herself in me? Am I not able to submit my own writer's ego to the force of the writer I am translating?

In the two translations I completed, these questions thankfully and eventually became moot. In each case there was another mind, another ego at work, altering, shifting, joining with mine: French (and American) for *Oedipus*, British (and Swiss and Colombian) for *Drums*. I have come to see that it takes that kind of collaboration for me to claim a part in translating Cixous, to get in my own language to where her language takes us, to find the "ineffable" without worrying about awkwardness or pretension.

---

[1] Ariane Mnouchkine has directed four plays by Hélène Cixous – all of which Cixous developed in collaboration with the Théâtre du Soleil. These include: *L'histoire terrible mais inachevée de Norodom Sihanouk, roi du Cambodge* (1985); *L'Indiade ou l'Inde de leurs rêves* (1987), *La ville parjure ou le réveil des Érinyes* (1994), and *Tambours sur la digue: Sous forme de pièce ancienne pour marionnettes jouée par des acteurs* (1999). Mnouchkine has also worked with Cixous on another three productions: Cixous translated Aeschylus's *Eumenides* for the Soleil's

House of Atreus Cycle (1990-1992), contributed to the film *La nuit miraculeuse* (1989) and to the Soleil's collective creation *Et soudain des nuits d'éveil* (1997), a project termed "in harmony" with Hélène Cixous.

[2] Brian Mallet passed away in December 2000, after a short and valiant struggle with cancer. I am deeply sorry we will never again be able to discuss translating Cixous and I am deeply appreciative of his insights.

[3] This "otherness" is obviously not merely the otherness always potentially present in a translated text. Cixous's texts are already 'other' in French.

[4] Marya Mazor, founder and director of Voices and Vision, developed the project *The Name of Oedipus* over a number of years. She showcased it in June 1998 in a small theater on East 4th street in New York.

[5] The original French reads as follows:

> *C'est toi ma nuit qui déferle*
> *Sur moi*
> *Et c'est bien moi cette mer*
> *Silencieuse qui vient d'ouvrir*
> *Sa chair pour que tu t'épanches*
> *Et nous entrons l'un dans l'autre,*
> *ma mère,*
> *Mon enfant.*
> *Ma chair est calme ici.*
> *Je vais cesser de souffrir.*
> *Je viens de tout oublier.*
> *Je ne sais plus qui mourir*
> (Cixous 1978: 86)

[6] For an in-depth analysis of the Soleil's production of *Tambours sur la digue*, see Béatrice Picon-Vallin's excellent article 'Les longs cheminements de la troupe du Soleil' in *Théâtre/Public* 152 (Fall 2000): 5-13. See also for a discussion of the genesis of *Tambours sur la digue*, Jean-François Dusigne. 2002. 'Travels with the Soleil' in Bradby, David and Maria Degado (eds) *The Paris Jigsaw*. Manchester: Manchester University Press. 131-145.

References

Cixous, Hélène. 1978. *Le Nom d'Oedipe: Chant du corps interdit*. Paris: des femmes.
—. 1994. *The Name of Oedipus: Song of the Forbidden Body* (tr. Christiane Makward and Judith Miller) in Makward, Christiane and Judith Miller (eds) *Plays by French and Francophone Women: A Critical Anthology*. Ann Arbor, MI: The University of Michigan Press. 253-326.
—. 1999. *Tambours sur la digue: Sous forme de pièce ancienne pour marionnettes jouée par des acteurs*. Paris: Théâtre du Soleil.
—. 2003. *Drums on the Dam: In the Form of an Ancient Puppet Play, Performed by Actors* (tr. Brian J. Mallet and Judith Miller) in Prenowitz, Eric (ed.) *Selected Plays of Hélène Cixous*. London and New York, NY: Routledge.
Venuti, Lawrence (ed.). 2000. *The Translation Studies Reader*. London and New York, NY: Routledge.

Hélène Cixous, Translator of History and Legend: *"Ce transport vertigineux"*

Deborah Jenson

Many readers of early theoretical texts by Cixous were disconcerted by her later plays and asked themselves how both types of writing could be reconciled. After her own translation of *La prise de l'école de Madhubaï* into English, Deborah Jenson relates Cixous's own "translation" from history into legend as effected in this play (whose protagonist is the contemporary Indian woman "bandit" Phoolan Devi) to the "global maternity" and the "writing of the body", two seminal concepts developed in these Cixous's famous theoretical texts.
Key-words: theory, drama, legend, writing of the body, *La prise de l'école de Madhubaï*.

How does "writing the body", a concept familiar from readings of Hélène Cixous's early theories of *"l'écriture féminine"*, translate to "writing historical others", a problem that imposes itself especially in Cixous's plays? "Writing the body" for Cixous has from the start included the act of writing the life of others within one's body, or of giving birth to others within one's texts: "And in the wake of the child, a squall of Breath! A longing for text!... The milky taste of ink!" (Cixous 1991: 31) cries the narrator in the 1977 *Coming to Writing* (*La venue à l'écriture*) in a typical cross-fertilization of feminine literary and reproductive tropes. This maternity does not involve a narcissistic mother/child genealogy, but rather an elated mimesis of the *souffle* ['breath'/'inspiration'] of others. It is a global maternity, in relation to which the "body" is not an island, but a sea of related alterity. In her essay "Going to the Sea" ("Aller à la mer"), also from 1977, Cixous theorized a writing of theater in which *"la mère"* ['mother'] and "la mer" ['sea'] are the homophonic site of "a body decoding and naming itself in one long, slow push; the song of women being brought into the world, of the infinite patience of woman expecting Woman. All it requires is one woman who stays beyond the bounds of prohibition, experiencing herself as many, the totality of those she has been, could have been, or wants to be..." (Cixous 1984b: 547). By contrast Cixous describes her first play, the 1972 *Portrait de Dora*, as a sort of dialogue with tradition, "a scene with the Father", even if it is "a scene in which the relationship is broken off". She predicts that in her future theater, woman will be not so much a voice in dialogue with the Father, as a "stage-body [that] will not hesitate to come up close, close enough to be in danger – of life. A body in labour".

In December of 1983, Cixous's first play about a living woman, *La prise de l'école de Madhubaï* [*The Conquest of the School at Madhubaï*], was performed at the *Petit Odéon*, several months prior to its March 1984 publication in *L'Avant-Scène Théâtre*. (This engagement with contemporary historical personages silhouetted against the anonymity of the present by the force of legend came to full fruition with her masterpiece *L'Histoire terrible mais inachevée de Norodom Sihanouk, roi du Cambodge* [*The Terrible But Unfinished Story of Norodom Sihanouk, King of Cambodia*], also from 1983.) *The Conquest* fulfilled various conditions of theatrical femininity as predicated in "Aller à la mer". The heroine of the play, Sakundeva, was based on a living Indian woman bandit, Phoolan Devi, and there was no question but that Phoolan Devi was "close enough to be in danger: of life", in her status as a living, endangered, and dangerous woman.

The play was an astonishing feat of nearly simultaneous translation of the 1983 events that made the life Phoolan Devi legendary. Cixous had first come across the news of Phoolan Devi's spectacularly staged February 1983 surrender for her role in a group massacre of upper caste men in an Indian village in a *fait divers* in a newspaper. But by the time the play was performed, she had managed to acquire a detailed knowledge of the case that continues to square to a surprising degree – surprising in relation to the poetic nature of the play – with subsequent in-depth journalistic investigations of Phoolan Devi's life. Cixous's writing of a play about a woman so alive that her historical death is far in the future of the play contextualized history as a living theater in which the bodies of theatrical characters, their historical models, and the actors who play them, carry out parallel (but different) lives in the historical production and reception of legend. Phoolan Devi's life, and my relation to it as translator, will be my point of departure in exploring Cixous's theatrical *"transport vertigineux"* (Cixous 1984a: 4) ["vertiginous transport"] of body and history onto the stage. The Latin '*translatio*' encompassed the idea of transport and transference, and Cixous's translation of history and legend exemplifies this vertiginous movement in the *translatio* of stories from one culture to another and the performance of legend from the subject to the actor of legend.

I first translated *The Conquest of the School at Madhubaï* in 1986 for the journal *Women and Performance* (now defunct), when I had just finished a year attending Cixous's *Études féminines* seminar at Vincennes. This put me, like many translators of Cixous's work, in a double and unusual relation to literary contemporaneity: first to Hélène Cixous herself as a contemporary author/teacher whose epic literary achievements, quasi-autobiographical inscriptions, and sense of personal drama have made her legendary in her own right, and secondly, through translation, to legendary characters in contemporary world history. Recently I revised that earlier translation of the play. During my revision work I opened the paper one morning to find a brief news item reporting the shooting death of Phoolan Devi, no longer a bandit but a member of Parliament, on July 25th, 2001, by four men outside her house in New Delhi. The mortality of this contemporary literary heroine, who was close to my own age, hit me hard, right where my translation of Hélène Cixous meets Hélène Cixous's translation of history and legend, which is to say where coming to writing meets life in history and legend. It prompted me to try to understand the trope of global maternity in the writing of the body as a problem of the real, in the *oeuvre* of a writer who can be characterized as anything but *realist*.

Cixous is strongly interested in the phenomenological translations of story to embodied performance in theater, and yet one cannot argue that her theatrical investment in the biographical reality of notable world figures was catalyzed by that interest, since some of her *real* characters are novelistic, as in Nelson and Winnie Mandela in South Africa in the 1988 *Manne aux Mandelstams aux Mandelas* [*Manna: For the Mandlestams for the Mandelas*]. But it is plausible that her literary engagement with history in the 1980s was deepened by her fascination with the reality of bodies in theater, and vice versa. In "From the Scene of the Unconscious to the Scene of History", first presented in 1986, Cixous suggests that her history (perhaps like her maternity), is global because in the hybridity of her marginal affiliations – Jewish, Algerian, woman, French, and a native speaker of German – she could never really know "which History is mine" (1989: 11)[1]. Rather than "choosing" a history, Cixous chose theater as a means of "'*démoïsation*', this state of without me, of depossession of the self, that will make possible the *possession* of the author by the characters" (*ibid.*: 13). This unegoification of the authorial enterprise relies on the "saintly" ability of actors to "jump across the gap left by the ego" (15), even while they "give us the whole body that we don't have to invent. And everything is lived and everything is true. This is the present that theater makes to the author: incarnation" (*id.*). In theater, "the *immediate* site of desire of the other" (12), the historical reality of bodies is performed materially as well as discursively. History is not materially represented – the reality of the actor, however saintly, never coincides with the reality of the character –, but the question of history is materially posed.

That materiality of history coincides in Cixous's work with the performance of what is at stake in maternity as a translation of the body. In *The Conquest,* historical and legendary material emerges precisely in terms of "the infinite patience of woman expecting woman", as described in "Aller à la mer". A fictional old woman, Pandala, has a maternal presentiment of Sakundeva's arrival: "I'm like a woman who feels the coming of the child.

I'm exactly like a woman whom the child warns: 'Watch out! This is the day I arrive'"[2]. Pandala is the midwife in Cixous's literary birthing of Sakundeva, the "bandit queen" who emerges from the jungle to negotiate the terms of her surrender with the Chief Minister of Madhya Pradesh. Sakundeva in turn formulates the conditions of her surrender partly on the basis of her own oneiric birthing of a child whose special needs she must satisfy. Sakundeva pawns her freedom in exchange for many things, including a school where her brother and sisters – "my children" – can be educated, in the company of "a one-eyed child that I don't know". This child she doesn't know is an orphan who in her dream walks over to her and burrows into her womb, causing her to reflect "no one told me that you could have children this way". Cixous's theatrical incarnation of the raped woman criminal involves a backwards maternity in which a disabled child moves from the outside world to inside the abused womb for mutual protection and regeneration.

Linguistically, the play is marked by simplicity. Cixous shows no interest in putting complicated neologisms in the mouths of characters who have never been to school. Yet their speech is subject to a poetry deriving both from the absence of casual conversational "fillers" and from the characters' beliefs that their bodily states *figure* other realities. When Pandala says "My body is moved as if I were awaiting Sakundeva", her body becomes the space of analogy, the site of a correspondence between bodily stimulation and waiting, but for Pandala the correspondence is not rhetorical but visionary. For me as translator, the greatest dilemma presented by the text was whether to aim for colloquial and *realistic* speech or instead to preserve the sparse poetic tonality of the characters' utterances.

I chose to preserve poeticity in the rhythms of the characters' speech at the expense of colloquial authenticity in part because the typographic conventions of the text clearly indicate a fusing of formally poetic and less poetic speech. Free verse, rather than prose, is at stake in lines such as these:

> The radio said: despite the new troops from Delhi
> despite the dogs from Germany
> despite the helicopters
> despite the special forces
> despite all efforts.

There is frequently an almost La Fontainean quality, a fabulatory or proverbial speech, in characters' references to the natural world:

> *If you don't see the tree that exists in the seed*
> *Or the woman that lives in the child*
> *How would you see the step in front of the door?*

Sakundeva finds it natural to spin off comparisons between people and objects from the natural world with those from the domain of the sacred: "My father was born a potter. And the father of Durga was also born a potter. The father of Durga touched his daughter as though she were a vase. But me, I have never seen my father's hands touch me as though I were a vase". Repetition of terms underscores this poeticity, especially when characters segue from one subject to another within the same tropological parenthesis, as in the following temporal trope:

> SAKUNDEVA: The police know very well that I'm alive. And Malik?
> PANDALA: He barks no more since twelve months ago.
> SAKUNDEVA: Two or three days, maybe less.
> PANDALA: As short or as long a time as you desire.

Cixous's theatrical characters arguably speak like inhabitants of a country of poetry who are foreign to any given geo-political state, and I have tried to preserve this foreignness. It resonates with what Cixous has described of her own experiences in texts like "Coming to Writing": "I have no roots: from what sources could I take in enough to nourish a text? Diaspora effect. I have no legitimate tongue. In German I sing; in English I disguise myself; in French I fly, I thieve" (1991: 15). In effect, despite the extraordinary biographical variety of Cixous's *real-life* theatrical characters, Cixous brings them into the world as autobiographical narrators of linguistic denaturalization.

The poetics of maternal mimesis in the story of Sakundeva in *The Conquest* does not preclude visceral engagement with the violence that she endured and inflicted. Cixous's Sakundeva surrenders after being hunted day and night because of her participation in the massacre of twenty-one men in Behmaï. The massacre, in which Sakundeva's direct role is obscure, is in retaliation for her earlier group rape and torture in the village. "I closed my eyes and saw it over and over. I saw myself between their thighs... O Pandala, I was pestilent. I was slithering with worms! What I would have liked, Pandala, was to tear out their eyes". Cixous's maternal poetics in *The Conquest* brings to life the potential violence for women of staying "beyond the bounds of prohibition" (1984b: 547).

The real-life terrible story of Phoolan Devi is documented in sources ranging from her ghost written autobiography (Devy and Cuny 1996) to the excellent article in the *Atlantic* by Mary Anne Weaver. Phoolan Devi was born in the Chambal River Valley in August 1963 (a birthdate which only came to light in recent years; she had apparently believed she was a few years older) to a lower caste, illiterate family. The family had become impoverished through a land dispute with a cousin, and Phoolan braved cultural interdiction by publicly seeking revenge from that cousin. Perhaps in retaliation, she was forcibly married at the age of eleven to an abusive much older man named Putti Lal. Phoolan escaped from her married household at the age of twelve and returned in disgrace to her family.

After years of marginalized and rebellious existence in her village, including further experiences of rape, Phoolan either was kidnapped by or left voluntarily with a group of bandits in 1979. She was raped over the course of several days by the upper caste leader of the group before a lower caste bandit, Vikram Mallah, shot the leader, replaced him in the hierarchy of the group, and became Phoolan's lover. In 1980, men linked to the assassinated leader shot Phoolan's lover and kidnapped her to Behmaï, where they raped and tortured her for three weeks. Phoolan escaped and became the leader of her own group of bandits, holding up trains, robbing banks, and committing an array of other crimes. In February 1981 she returned to Behmaï and led the so-called Valentine's Day Massacre in which twenty-one upper caste village men were shot dead and nine others were wounded.

In February 1983, after two years in which the popular dissemination of her legend had made her a celebrity in among the lower castes of the region, she negotiated the terms of her surrender with the chief minister of Madhya Pradesh, Arjun Singh. The surrender took the form of a gala public ceremony in the village of Bhind. With her lover of the time and her gang co-leader, Man Singh, Phoolan mounted a brightly decorated dais, armed and dressed as a police officer, and bowed first to images of Ghandi and of the goddess Durga, and then to the chief minister. She had negotiated among other things that she and her gang members would not be hanged, that they would be released after eight years, that her father's land would be returned to him by the cousin, and that her brother would be given a government job. The negotiation of a school is not a prominent detail in accounts of the surrender, although it is consistent with Phoolan's later political goals.

She was then jailed in Gwalior not for the eight years she had negotiated, but until February of 1994. That year she was freed by Mulayam Singh Yadav, the lower-caste chief minister of Uttar Pradesh who was trying to mobilize the lower castes as a political constituency. In 1995 her autobiography was published in France, and she began to campaign under the political mentorship of Singh Yadav, who was now the leader of the Samajwadi Party. Despite her illiteracy and an ongoing predilection for disrupting scheduled train routes and storming prisons to see old friends, she was elected to Parliament and remained a controversial but popular MP at the time of her assassination.

In Cixous's 1983 play, the time frame does not extend beyond 1983. Sakundeva has difficulty envisioning the year 1995, the year when, according to the play, she will be freed. "In 1995! I will be... a hundred years old. And I will be dead". In real life, Phoolan Devi was released from prison at the age of thirty-one, after which her election to parliament would confirm the truism that reality is stranger than fiction. It is largely accepted that the distinction between reality and fiction in the life of Phoolan Devi has been permanently obscured, that she and her family were the first to spin her life out of the space of documentarity and into that of legend or myth. Mary Anne Weaver (1996) quotes Sunil Sethi's description of Phoolan as "tailor-made for the Indian imagination: since ancient times we have had an inordinate capacity to make a myth out of any story... Phoolan is a do-it-yourself goddess who can rapidly demonize"[3].

But Cixous, in "Le droit de légende" ["The Right to Legend"] that accompanies the play in *L'Avant-Scène Théâtre*, speaks of legend not disparagingly as an obfuscation or manipulation of history, but rather as the chance to escape from the terms that have been "so implacably programmed by the great social machines" (1984a: 4). Her theatrical translation of history relies on legend as a *Gestalt* of the present that may or may not later add up to material worthy of being sanctioned as history. Her use of contemporary history does not predict the future, and indeed, an obvious risk in writing about living legends is that Robin Hoods may become corrupt, eternal lovers may divorce, and deposed kings may remain on the sidelines. A fierce insistence on the present tense of theater means that the 'epic' dimensions of history may be realized only momentarily without losing their validity.

When Cixous says in "Le droit de légende" that theatre "must always be in the present", and that this presence is "life itself" (1984a: 5), she demonstrates a tremendous desire to *make real* bodies and stories whose existence that would otherwise be inaccessible to phenomenological confirmation. If, as I happened to, a reader reads a work such as *The Conquest* at the time of its publication, and then follows the ongoing events of the historical model's life and death as measured on the continuum of the reader's own life, a sense of an approximation of *real time*, of virtual communication between the reader's life and the character's historical life, is produced. Yet Cixous's literary love of real bodies and real time, her desire to make real, is unlike the literary realism in which the reality effect is the guarantee of the author's stylistic success in competing with the real. Instead, it is realism as the imitation of the experience of someone/something being born, emerging as its own organic imperative with all the problems of social agency that attend that miracle. "One immediately recognizes the character who has been defended by love – writes Cixous in "From the Scene of the Unconscious" – for he becomes the world's child" (1989: 13-14). The global maternity of writing the body, leading to the theatrical birth of the world's child, perhaps in the most idealistic sense is done to make readers aware of their own right to legend, their own chance to escape the implacable programming of the great social machines. Or one could argue that it allows readers to play the role of the one-eyed orphan in *The Conquest*, burrowing from worldly existence back into the womb, translating damaged childhood into healing maternity. In either case, Cixous's theatrical (anti)realism makes the bodily experiences of Phoolan Devi into a phenomenological obstacle to cultural self-containment.

---

[1] The essay was initially given as a talk at the Institut français in Copenhagen on May 6, 1986.
[2] My quotes are from my revised translation of *The Conquest of the School at Madhubaï*.
[3] The text is also at www.theatlantic.com//issues/96nov/bandit/bandit.htm, and the above quote is on p. 5 of that version.

References

Cixous, Hélène. 1984a. 'Le droit de légende' in *L'Avant-Scène Théâtre* 745 (March): 4.
—. 1984b. 'Aller à la mer' (tr. Barbara Kerslake) in *Modern Drama* 27(4) (December): 547.
—. 1986. *The Conquest of the School at Madhubaï* (tr. Deborah Carpenter) in *Women and Performance: A Journal of Feminist Theory* 3(1): 59-96.
—. 1989. 'From the Scene of the Unconscious to the Scene of History' (tr. Deborah W. Carpenter) in Ralph Cohen (ed.) *The Future of Literary Theory*. London and New York, NY: Routledge.
—. 1991. *'Coming to Writing' and Other Essays* (ed. Deborah Jenson). Cambridge, MA: Harvard University Press.
Devi, Phoolan and Marie-Thérèse Cuny. 1996. *Moi, Phoolan Devi, reine des bandits*. Paris: Fixot.
Weaver, Mary Anne. 1996. 'India's Bandit Queen' in *The Atlantic Monthly* 278(5) (November): 89-104.

Beyond the Text, into the Realm of Live Performance: Working on the *Portrait de Dora*

Liliana Alexandrescu

> The author, who directed a version of *Portrait de Dora* in Dutch, speaks of translation in a theatrical and cultural sense: putting a written text on the stage is also a kind of translation, from words to bodies, and here complicated by the *real* or linguistic – and cultural – translation from the original French into Dutch. In the particular case of Dora's character, body language is far from negligible, as it sometimes supports and at other times negates her spoken discourse. This fact convinced the director to employ two different actresses to incarnate Dora as a child and as a young woman.
>
> Key words: Freud, Dora's case, performance, body language.

>> Translating: rediscovering the simple violence of dreams. (Cixous 1987: 262)
>> Language: forest with all its roots / audible. (Cixous 1994: 93)

I leaf again through the small volume I bought years ago at a bookshop on the Herengracht: *Portret van Dora*, published in 1983 by Editions SUA in Amsterdam (the Dutch version of *Portrait de Dora* by Hélène Cixous, translated by Josée Kuijpers, Isolde Landman and Camille Mortagne). The voices of the play, the gestures, the steps, the cries, the entangled bodies carve out for themselves a way outside the enclosure of the pages, climb again to the surface, emerge with their vehemence of yesteryear:

> *Als u me durft te kussen...*
>   If you dare to kiss me...
> *In Wenen is een deur [...] Vaak droom ik dat [...]*
>   There is a door in Vienna [...] I often dream that [...]
> *Ik zal een brief schrijven [...] Jij hebt me gedood [...]*
>   I will write a letter[...] You killed me[1]

I enter the labyrinth of this bilingual whispering, this double passionate breathlessness, which along winding ways bring me back to Dora – Cixous's Dora, Freud's Dora. Her own language was German. The language of Hélène's mother, Eva Klein, born in Osnabrück, was German. As it was her grandmother's, for whom, at the beginning of the 20th century, "the Kaiser existed" (Calle-Gruber and Cixous 1994: 187). And her grandfather's, who died on the Russian front as a German soldier. I look at their photograph as a young couple: they could have appeared in a family album from the time of the B.'s or the K.'s. Her maternal grandfather was born in a village not far from Vienna. Dora's Vienna of forbidden doors... But: "I have a passion for doors. It comes no doubt from a magic door of Osnabrück" (Cixous 1999: 19).

Hélène's mother, *die Mutter*, says to her daughter: *vernünftig*. She says: *der Tod* (*non, la mort* [death], cries Hélène). She says: *Wohnzimmer* [livingroom], *trennen* [*untstich*], *Tränen* [tears]. Like a far echo, I hear in Dutch: *vernuftig... dood... tranen...* I pursue the words and their resemblances, I gather them, like incantations: "All my affinities are nordic" (Calle-Gruber and Cixous 1994: 183). Choosing Dora, taking her out of the pages of *Brüchstück einer Hysterie-Analyse* (1905) by Freud, her face pale after such a long sleep, placing her tenderly in her text, perhaps for Cixous this also was climbing toward the North star, toward the "snowy landscape" of her mother (Calle-Gruber and Cixous 1994: 195). As she did too in her epic play *L'Histoire (qu'on ne connaîtra jamais)* from 1994, making the heroes of the most Germanic of legends: Hagen, Gunther, Edda, Brunhild, Kriemhild, Sigfrid, "king of the Low Countries" speak on stage – in French, of course!

*

Eugenio Barba (1993: 7): "There exists a homeland of perpetual transition, a *Heimat* made of time, without territory". It is that of the theatre artists, no matter what country they come from, no matter what community. The stage is full of worlds – exclaims Hélène Cixous as she watches the rehearsals at the Théâtre du Soleil –, minor or great, each actor has the universe as his audience. "Each one reigns on his own planet, the stage is occupied with regions" (Cixous 1987: 276).

And in this open space, it is the "burning body" that speaks (*ibid.*: 261). It is up to it, above all, to express its truth, to go beyond the barrier of words. With a simple look of his deaf and mute actor, Robert Wilson, in his performance *Deafman Glance* (from 1970), opens the doors to a world of silence of terrifying intensity, where there is only gesture, slow displacement, menacing objects.

This eloquence of body language is also Dora's, supporting or negating her spoken discourse. She coughs several times in the course of the conversation: "The unsaid, lost, in the bodies, among the bodies" (Cixous 1976: 23). She keeps fiddling with her purse. Freud: "He whose lips are still, talks with the tips of his fingers"(*ibid.*: 53).

Two or three years ago, in Amsterdam, I saw a performance based on the letters of Vincent van Gogh to his brother Theo, played by deaf-mute actors. The spectators too were for the most deaf-mute. During the performance, one heard nothing, *I* heard nothing except, now and then, the grating of a chair being pushed back, a sigh, a rustling of cloth, the sole of a shoe inadvertently hitting against the floor, a glass broken on the stage, or a table violently thrown over by an actor, unaware of the crashing sound of his gesture. (Brook 1988: 133: "direct communication through signs [...], into the strange area where what to a hearing person is a vibrating sound, to a deaf person is a vibrating movement".) All these small noises coming out of the silence, accompanying my visual participation in the scene, acquired, for me, the quality of a second language, which made me even more sensitive to this *other* system of signs, this *other* alphabet, into which I had been plunged. In the extreme concentration of this silent hall, all around me, in me, there passed large currents, which carried us away in a shared emotion. The drama of Vincent, this misunderstood, isolated being, this "suicide of society" (Artaud), became, for this public, its own drama. At the end, at the moment for applause, my instinct was to clap my hands loudly, then I realized that the actors would hear nothing of my enthusiasm. I then joined the others who all, standing, raised their arms in the air, waving their hands, as if beneath a gust of invisible wind.

Dora's muteness: "My body is concealed. In the forest. It is dark. I have no voice" (Cixous 1976: 29).

*

Antonin Artaud (1974: 29):

> *Un bougeoir sur une chaise, un fauteuil de paille verte tressée,*
> *Un livre sur le fauteuil*
> *Et voilà le drame éclairé.*
> *Qui va entrer?*
> *Sera-ce Gauguin ou un autre fantôme?*
>
> A candlestick on a seat, an easy chair of woven green straw,
> A book on the easy chair
> And behold, the drama illuminated.
> Who is going to enter?
> Will it be Gauguin or another phantom?

Artaud believed that theatre has to act not as the Double of immediate, daily reality, but of another reality, dangerous and meaningful (*Le théâtre et son double*). And, in contemplating a canvas by Van Gogh, he sensed in the painted image, and beyond, not the stillness of a lonely room, but the tension of an empty stage setting, anxiously awaiting the arrival of the characters.

*

On my knees there is a script. I am seated, my eyes closed, my hands resting on the text – a blind person before her Braille feeling her way in her pursuit of the visible: forms, colours, distances. It is dark.

"There is a door in Vienna..."

Someone, a man, enters into an unknown space and lights a lamp. Soft, filtered light, peaceful.

Vienna, January 1, 1900. Snow-covered streets, passers-by who walk and laugh in their heavy winter clothes, cabs, horses, the cry of newspapers vendors. A dog barks.

But here inside, all is calm. This closed room is a cocoon of silence. The man sits in his chair and smokes.

A gradual change of atmosphere: a young woman enters, takes off her coat and stretches out on the coach. She fiddles with her small purse, coughs, opens her mouth and speaks. The man listens and smokes. From time to time, he asks a brief question. I do not hear what they say, there is no sound.

But then the voices begin. And with the voices, the ghosts appear. They enter into the conversation, interrupt, cut off words – out of the past come obtrusive shadows, of dreams and memories.

I look into the distance, through binoculars held the wrong way round, at the illuminated room and its occupants, suspended somewhere in the night, at the edge of another time, another place.

*

Hélène Cixous:

> We are tiny-bodies-in-a-great-cube-of-light.
> ("Entre tiens", in Calle-Gruber and Cixous 1994: 31)
>
> I love dialogue (that is why I love theatre) – work, dance, rectification, repentance, misunderstandings – (portraits of dialogues) – blows and injuries – duet. (*ibid*.: 26)

*

And look, the play's two principal speakers are in place: Freud in his chair, in the back, seen from behind, and Dora on the famous coach, sometimes seated, sometimes lying down, sometimes rising, facing the public at the front of the stage, her face exposed, vulnerable, fully illuminated. The third firm point of this (almost) empty space, without sheltering curtains, is a coat stand, marking Dora's entrances and departures, a protective sign of the threshold, a separation of worlds (outside/within). Cixous's scenario includes three other characters: Monsieur B. (Dora's father), Monsieur K. (Monsieur B.'s friend), and Madame K. Echoes of another time, phantoms, memories, like Pirandello's characters, they will come to claim their right to this brief fictive existence, in order to expose their own version of events, to justify themselves, to be absolved.

Time, so complex and supple in this structure, so typical of Hélène Cixous, is thus not linear. It is multiple and fluid, protean, sliding imperceptibly from one level to another: the past of memory and dream, the present of scenic dialogue, and an even closer present, that of Freud's account and his reflections on the "Dora's case", punctuating and concluding the action. There are two predominant seasons in the play: the Viennese winter of 1899, with Dora's visits to Freud, and the summer days of the adolescence, the walks in the woods and along the lakefront (a lake boarded by white flowers whose image and several oneiric variants recur in Dora's words: something happened there, near the lilies-of-the-valley, between Monsieur K. and the young girl...). Included in the category of adults, Monsieur B., Monsieur K. and the seductive Madame K. are all linked to Dora's past and the summer atmosphere. Freud's character functions both as a partner in the discussion with Dora and as narrator and a final commentator in his own text, but also as a depersonalized (false) witness behind the oracular mask of the "Voice of the Play", to diffuse all emotional transfer:

> Le docteur Freud aurait pu faire ce rêve, à la fin du mois de décembre 1899. Dora est alors une jeune fille florissante [...] Elle a quelque chose de contradictoire et d'étrange qui fait son charme. Une chair épanouie mais une bouche dure, un front de jeune fille, des yeux glacés fixes. [...]
> Il n'est pas de plus grande douleur que de se souvenir de l'amour.
> Et cela Freud le savait. (Cixous 1976: 62-63; 105)

> Doctor Freud could have had this dream at the end of the month December 1899. Dora is at that time a blossoming young girl [...] She has a contradictory quality about her and a strangeness, which gives her charm. Bright skin but a hard mouth, the brow of a young girl, her eyes frozen, fixed [...]
> There is no greater pain than to remember love.
> And Freud knew that.

Dora herself oscillates unceasingly, in a perpetual coming and going, between two ages: the young woman seated in Freud's office and the pubescent girl of memory. It is she who connects the different lays of time. Her words, like invocations, call back to the stage the characters of her choice. In the undefined space that separates Freud's chair, placed back to the right, and Dora's couch, to the left in front, on this diagonal of the imaginary, on this lunar path, the ghosts appear and move, dressed in white, smiling, indifferent. They walk with nonchalance. Exchange cunning, deceitful glances.

*

Hélène Cixous:

> *Mais le théâtre est invocation. L'appel retentit de toutes parts: libération des voix, des gestes, je suis cernée. D'un côté les spectateurs, de l'autre les acteurs, autour, dedans après devant, les personnages, toute l'humanité [...]*
> *[I]l faut que les paroles livrées par l'auteur au personnage soient les paroles mêmes que les lèvres vivantes et pensantes pétrissent et insufflent. [...]*
> *Annoncer, désigner, nommer. Mais ne pas décrire: cela c'est le comédien qui le fera avec son corps.*
> *[...]*
> *J'écoute et je traduis. Ma traduction des passions doit être d'une extrême fidélité.*
> *[...]*
> *Quand l'inconscient remonte aux lèvres, il se précipite dans des gestes, des aveux, qui ouvrent aux personnages des visions bouleversantes: ils se voient ramper, sangloter, vomir, fuir, dévorer. Ils vivent et laissent voir tous les grands événements intérieurs, les supplices, les incendies, les assassinats, les suicides, les étreintes qui forment notre vie intérieure et secrète. Traduire: retrouver la simple violence du rêve.* ('L'Incarnation' in Cixous 1987: 261-262)

> But theatre is invocation. The call resounds from all sides: liberation of voices, gestures, I am surrounded. On one side the spectators, on the other the actors, around, inside then in front, the characters, all humanity [...]
> The words given by the author to the character must be the same words that living and thinking lips shape and breathe life into. [...]
> Announce, designate, name. But do not describe: this the actor will do with his body.
> [...]
> I listen and translate. My translation of passions must be extremely faithful.
> [...]
> When the unconscious rises to the lips, it precipitates into the gestures, the confessions, which reveal overwhelming visions to the characters: they see themselves crawl, sob, vomit, flee, devour. They live and expose all the great interior events, the tortures, the conflagrations, the assassinations, the suicides, the embraces that form our interior, secret life. Translating: rediscovering the simple violence of dreams.

*

The arena where these austere battles first take place is the rehearsal hall. It is there that our body engages in hand to hand combat with these "paper beings" (Pavis 1980: 292), the textual prototypes of drama. Lying in wait between the pages, they spy on us. Virtually, they are already projected into space: "The theatre is written vertically" (Cixous 1990: 32). Their hungry, importunate looks burn through the page: they ask no more or less than for our flesh and blood! We submit, we commit this beneficial vampirism, conscious of being responsible for their survival. The fictional takes possession of the real. Gorged with life, the characters rise and take their place on stage. "It is not the character that becomes *real* inside the actor, it is the actor who becomes *unreal* inside the character". It seems to me that this remark by Sartre (1940: 368) subtly defines the ambivalence of this process of incarnation commonly called "getting into the skin of the character" – an expression that almost always makes me think of Mayan ritual sacrifices during which the priest, celebrating the spring festival, covered himself with the skin of a flayed victim and mounted the altar before the believers, to assure them with this act, both physical and symbolic, the perpetuation of the cycles of life and death.

*

Hélène Cixous:

> We are always in the multiple register. The mono-vocal register does not exist.
> ('Entre tiens' in Calle-Gruber and Cixous 1994: 29)

*

> *DORA*
> *Osez m'embrasser, je vous donnerai une gifle!*
> *FREUD*
> *Oui, vous me raconterez. Dans tous les détails.*
> *DORA*
> *[...]*
> *Si vous voulez. Et après?*
> *FREUD*
> *Vous me raconterez la scène du lac, dans tous les détails.*
> (Cixous, 1976: 9-10)

> DORA
> Try to kiss me and I'll slap you!
> FREUD
> Yes, you will tell me. In detail.
> DORA
> [...]
> If you wish. And then?
> FREUD
> You will tell me about the scene at the lake, in detail.

One immediately perceives, at the beginning of the play, the different levels of time and place: in her first line, Dora is speaking to Monsieur K., in the second, to Freud. She must, after all, be present simultaneously in her own account and in the doctor's office. She will be played by two actresses, each one acting as the double (*Doppelgänger*) of the other. "Tell me", says Freud, and this act of speaking extends from the one to the other, along winding ways or through textual short cuts.

We call them Dora 1 and Dora 2, the "grown-up" and the "little" Dora. The second is always near the first, as a younger sister, asking for protection but also ready to intervene, to be actively supportive. Curled up next to the couch, she gets up suddenly, speaks, stamps her foot, cries out, throws shoes at her father's head (out of jealousy), kisses him, writes letters, is tormented by her amorous desires (towards Madame K.) and attacked physically by Monsieur K., returns next to the couch, is quiet, falls asleep. If Dora 1 is talking, Dora 2 is implicated in all physical actions. This division of the role, which in Cixous's play was one, and consequently the division of the text and its attribution to two persons, depended mainly on the perspective of the events "before" and/or "now". But both Doras together experience time as a continuity of past and present. Carried away by the flux of memories, they sometimes begin to talk at the same time, their discourse become superimposed, the tempo accelerates, the barriers fade. But it is the solo of Dora 1, the narrator, that unifies and controls everything.

This latent polyphony bursts through to the surface more than once in Hélène Cixous's writing, showing itself to the reader in a graphic dualism on the page where, at moments of crisis, the printed phrases follow one another and become entangled in two different letter types, a visible expression of disorder, of scission, of splitting. At one point of the play, Dora tells a dream. A man tries to force open the door to her room, she struggles, resists him and finally grabs him by the neck and strangles him. This reliving of the dream is intense like a vision: a traumatic image, buried in memory, has erupted and explodes. The character's panic is manifested in the layout of the text, where the perfect visual dualism (normal letters alternating with letters in italics) underscore her deviations. Cixous repeats this double typographic movement of the two voices in several sequences in the play. And each time, the appearance of italics in the text is a cry of alarm, a signal sent by the double.

In working on this scene, we were immediately carried away by its enormous physical impact. The active bodies imposed their language on us, the spoken text was swept along by an irresistible undercurrent. Gruff voices, tensed muscles, eager bodies are blindly mixed in a supreme effort to satisfy their desires, to ignore their repulsions, culminating in an orgasm of love and destruction.

"It is dark here...", says the little Dora near the couch. The stage space has disappeared in the shadows, with the exception of one point. There, in the spotlight, Monsieur K' s silhouette becomes visible. The two Doras start walking, they turn toward him in step. They embrace him, they immobilize him between them. He takes the little Dora in his arms and presses against her. He does not notice the other Dora, she belongs to another time. She clings to him from behind, caresses him with feverish fingers. Heads, hands, legs seek each other, touch, hold one another within the limits of the circle of light, in the unrestrained passion of this three-headed embrace. And throughout this time, the two feminine voices speak, whisper, sigh, cry out unceasingly. Furious, frightened, joyful, ecstatic. In the end, while the little Dora pushes him away with all her might, the grown up Dora, with a gesture of the hand, cuts his throat. The man's body slackens abruptly, he is heavy, he slumps against the two Doras, who hold him with difficulty. Then they release him, throwing him to the floor. He falls to his knees. The light changes, the entire stage is again visible. They cough, return to the couch.

"I had a bad pain in my throat. It's hard for me to speak", Dora explains to Freud.

*

I leaf through a book by Peter Brook (1989: 3): "When I begin to work on a play, I start with a deep, formless hunch which is like a smell, a colour, a shadow. [...] There's a formless hunch that is my relationship to the play".

*

DORA
J'ai rêvé qu'il me rejetait et que je le voyais pour la dernière fois. [...] Et les larmes roulaient sur mes joues, mais je disais oui, oui [...] puis il a dit cette phrase: "Je reprends mes perles!" [...] et aussi: "Je t'avais donné la clé du coffre; je la retire". À quoi servait-il de pleurer? Au milieu des phrases bizarres? Et je disais oui, oui – comme si je voulais mourir. Mais quelle clé?
MONSIEUR K
Quelle clé?
FREUD
Quel coffre?
DORA
Monsieur K. m'avait fait cadeau quelque temps auparavant d'un très précieux petit coffre à bijoux. Pour mon anniversaire.
(Cixous 1976: 45-46)

DORA
I dreamt that he rejected me and that I was seeing him for the last time [...] And the tears ran down my cheeks, but I said yes, yes [...] then he said these words: "I'm reclaiming my pearls!" [...] and also: "I gave you the key to the box; I'm taking it back". What was the use of crying? In the middle of these bizarre phrases? And I said yes, yes – as if I wanted to die. But which key?
MONSIEUR K
Which key?

FREUD
Which box?
DORA
Some time before, Monsieur K. had given me a very fine little jewellery box as a gift
For my birthday.

Rejection, wishing to die, tears, pearls, birthday, gift, jewellery box, here are so many words that project this sequence against an overcharged background. Inside this odd puzzle there is hidden a blocked mental image, which one must try to uncover. It is especially the word 'birthday' that I keep stumbling over, an unknown threshold, which will lead me where? Somewhere, to a flawed party. I must reinvent this party. I imagine Monsieur K.'s friendly gesture, as he offers the young Dora her gift, Madame K.'s gentle grace, Monsieur B.'s fatherly tenderness. All seem to be showering the adolescent girl with attention; in fact, they are uniquely preoccupied with their own petty affairs. For Dora, suffering is at hand, lying in wait behind the false joy. It is a scene without words, which in the performance will be a pantomime, (deceptively) celebrated by waves of sublime music, an ambiguous commentary on the action. I can already hear the magnificent clucking of Mozart's plumed bird-catchers, Papageno and Papagena:

Pa, Pa, Pa, Pa...
Nun, so sei mein liebes Weibchen!
Nun, so sei mein Herzenstäubchen!

A beam of gleaming solar light suddenly crosses the stage diagonally from left to right, at the very moment when the love duet begins (*The Magic Flute*, act II, scene 10). Along this imaginary path, the beautiful Madame K., in a white moiré dress, advances carrying a birthday cake covered with a thick layer of Chantilly cream and decorated with lighted candles. A joyous group in the centre of the stage. Surrounded, the pampered Dora blows out the candles. A festive atmosphere. She receives the jewellery box from Monsieur K. and wants to show it to the others, but in the meantime Madame K., taking away the cake, has drawn Monsieur B., Dora's father, toward the front of the stage. She plunges her finger into the cream and puts it into Monsieur B.'s mouth; he licks it. Stiffly, Dora and Monsieur K. watch. Entwined, Madame K. and Monsieur B. disappear into the wings, laughing. The music ends too, the last trills fade and the light goes out.

We are again in Doctor's Freud room. Monsieur K. and little Dora each go to their respective corners. Still seated on the couch, in her sombre red velvet dress, grown up Dora looks out, a painful grimace distorting her face.

FREUD
Well, then. And the key?

[Translated from the French by Cornelia Golna]

---

[1] *Portret van Dora* was played by the FRI theatre group of the University of Amsterdam, under the direction of Liliana Alexandrescu. Translation in Dutch: José Kuijpers, Isolde Landman and Camille Mortagne. First night: April 6, 1995, at the Studio C (Amsterdam). Video of the performance: Marty de Bruijn and Anne-Mieke Zaat (92 minutes, PAL System).

References

Artaud, Antonin. 1964. *Le théâtre et son double*. Paris: Gallimard.
—. 1974. 'Van Gogh le suicidé de la société' in *Œuvres complètes*. Paris: NRF-Gallimard. 9-64.
Barba, Eugenio. 1993. *Le Canoë de papier. Traité d'anthropologie théâtrale*. Paris: Bouffonneries.
Brook, Peter. 1989. *The Shifting Point. Forty Years of Theatrical Exploration. 1946-1987*. London and New York, NY: Methuen Drama.
Calle-Gruber, Mireille and Hélène Cixous. 1994. *Hélène Cixous, photos de racines*. Paris: des femmes.
Cixous, Hélène. 1976. *Portrait de Dora*. Paris: des femmes, 1986.
—. 1987. *L'Indiade ou l'Inde de leurs rêves et quelques écrits sur le théâtre*. Paris: Théâtre du Soleil.
—. 1990. 'De la scène de l'Inconscient à la scène de l'Histoire: Chemin d'une écriture' in van Rossum-Guyon, Françoise and Myriam Díaz-Diocaretz (eds) *Hélène Cixous, chemins d'une écriture*. Amsterdam-Paris: Rodopi-PUV.
—. 1994. *L'Histoire (qu'on ne connaîtra jamais)*. Paris: des femmes.
—. 1999. *Osnabrück*. Paris: des femmes.
Pavis, Patrice. 1980. *Dictionnaire du théâtre*. Paris: Éditions sociales.
Sartre, Jean-Paul. 1940. *L'Imaginaire*. Paris: NRF-Gallimard.
Wilson, Robert. 1970. *Deafman glance* [script and stage direction]. First night: December 15, at the University Theater of the Iowa University. On tour in Brooklyn, Nancy, Rome Paris and Amsterdam.

[English translations of all fragments of works cited in the text are by Cornelia Golna.]

Bibliography

1. Books in French by Hélène Cixous

1967. *Le prénom de Dieu*. Paris: Grasset.
1968. *L'exil de James Joyce ou l'art du remplacement*. Paris: Grasset.
1969. *Dedans*. Paris: Grasset; des femmes, 1986.
1970a. *Le troisième corps*. Paris: Grasset.
1970b. *Les commencements*. Paris: Grasset; des femmes, 1999.
1971. *Un vrai jardin*. Paris: L'Herne; des femmes, 1998.
1972. *Neutre*. Paris: Grasset; des femmes, 1998.
1973a. *Tombe*. Paris: Seuil.
1973b. *Portrait du soleil*. Paris: Denoël; des femmes, 1999.
1974. *Prénoms de personne*. París: Seuil.
1975a. *La Jeune née* (with C. Clément). Paris: U.G.E.
1975b. *Révolution pour plus d'un Faust*. Paris: Seuil.
1975c. *Un K. incompréhensible: Pierre Goldman*. Paris: Christian Bourgois.
1975d. *Souffles*. Paris: des femmes, 1998.
1976a. *La*. Paris: Gallimard; des femmes, 1979.
1976b. *Portrait de Dora*. Paris: des femmes.
1977a. *Angst*. Paris: des femmes, 1998.
1977b. *La venue à l'écriture* (with Madeleine Gagnon and Annie Leclerc). Paris: U.G.E.
1978a. *La pupille*. Paris: Cahiers Renaud-Barrault.
1978b. *Préparatifs de noces au-delà de l'abîme*. Paris: des femmes.
1978c. *Le nom d'Oedipe: Chant du corps interdit*. Paris: des femmes
1979a. *Partie*. Paris: des femmes.
1979b. *Vivre l'orange*. Paris: des femmes.
1979c. *Ananké*. Paris: des femmes.
1980. *Illa*. Paris: des femmes.
1981. *With ou l'art de l'innocence*. Paris: des femmes.
1982. *Limonade tout était si infini*. Paris: des femmes.
1983. *Le livre de Promethea*. Paris: Gallimard.
1985. *L'histoire terrible mais inachevée de Norodom Sihanouk, roi du Cambodge*. Paris: Théâtre du Soleil.

1986a. *Entre l'écriture*. Paris: des femmes.
1986b. *La bataille d'Arcachon*. Québec: Trois.
1986c. *Théâtre* (includes *La prise de l'école de Madhubaï*). Paris: des femmes.
1987. *L'Indiade, ou l'Inde de leurs rêves*. Paris: Théâtre du Soleil.
1988. *Manne aux Mandelstams aux Mandelas*. Paris: des femmes.
1989. *L'heure de Clarice Lispector*. Paris: des femmes.
1990. *Jours de l'an*. Paris: des femmes.
1991. *L'ange au secret*. Paris: des femmes.
1992a. *Déluge*. Paris: des femmes.
1992b. *On ne part pas, on ne revient pas*. Paris: des femmes.
1993. *Beethoven à jamais*. Paris: des femmes.
1994a. *La ville parjure ou le réveil des Érinyes*. Paris: Théâtre du Soleil.
1994b. *L'histoire (qu'on ne connaîtra jamais)*. Paris: des femmes.
1994c. *Photos de racines* (with Mireille Calle-Gruber). Paris: des femmes.
1995a. *La fiancée juive*. Paris: des femmes.
1995b. *Messie*. Paris: des femmes.
1997. *OR les lettres de mon père*. Paris: des femmes.
1998. *Voiles* (with Jacques Derrida). Paris: Galilée.
1999a. *Osnabrück*. Paris: des femmes.
1999b. *Tambours sur la digue*. Paris: Théâtre du Soleil.
2000a. *Le jour où je n'étais pas là*. Paris: Galilée.
2000b. *Les rêveries de la femme sauvage: Scènes primitives*. Paris: Galilée.
2001a. *Benjamin à Montaigne. Il ne faut pas le dire*. Paris: Galilée.
2001b. *Rouen, la Trentième Nuit de Mai '31*. Paris: Galilée.
2001c. *Portrait de Jacques Derrida en Jeune Saint Juif*. Paris: Galilée.
2002. *Manhattan. Lettres de la préhistoire*. Paris: Galilée.
2003a. *Rêve je te dis*. Paris: Galilée.
2003b. *L'amour du loup et autres remords*. Paris: Galilée.

2. Books in English
(compiled by Marguerite Sandré and Eric Prenowitz)[1]

1972. *The Exile of James Joyce* (tr. Sally A. J. Purcell). New York, NY: David Lewis; London: John Calder, 1976.
1977. *Portrait of Dora* (tr. Anita Barrows) in *Gambit International Theatre Review* 8(30): 27-67; (tr. Sarah Burd) in *Diacritics* (Spring 1983): 2-32.
1979. *To Live the Orange* (tr. Ann Liddle and Sarah Cornell) in *Vivre l'orange* (bilingual). Paris: des femmes.
1985. *Angst* (tr. Jo Levy). London: John Calder; New York, NY: Riverrun.
1986a. *Inside* (tr. Carol Barko). New York, NY: Schocken Books.

1986b. *The Conquest of the School at Madhubaï* (tr. Deborah W. Carpenter) in *Women and Performance* 3: 59-95.
1986c. *The Newly Born Woman* (tr. Betsy Wing). Minneapolis, MN: University of Minnesota Press; Manchester: Manchester University Press, Theory and History of Literature, vol. 24.
1990. *Reading with Clarice Lispector* (ed. and tr. Verena Andermatt Conley). Minneapolis, MN: University of Minnesota Press; London: Harvester Wheatsheaf.
1991a. *Readings: The Poetics of Blanchot, Joyce, Kafka, Lispector, Tsvetaeva* (ed. and tr. Verena Andermatt Conley). Minneapolis, MN: University of Minnesota Press.
1991b. *'Coming to Writing' and other Essays* (tr. Sarah Cornell, Deborah Jenson, Ann Liddle, and Susan Sellers; ed. Deborah Jenson). Cambridge, MA: Harvard University Press.
1991c. *The Book of Promethea* (tr. Betsy Wing). Lincoln, NB: University of Nebraska Press.
1993. *Three Steps on the Ladder of Writing* (tr. Sarah Cornell and Susan Sellers). New York, NY: Columbia University Press.
1994a. *The Name of Oedipus: Song of the Forbidden Body* (tr. Christiane Makward and Judith Miller) in Makward, Christiane and Judith Miller (eds) *Plays by French and Francophone Women: A Critical Anthology*. Ann Arbor, MI: The University of Michigan Press. 253-326.
1994b. *The Terrible but Unfinished Story of Norodom Sihanouk, King of Cambodia* (tr. Judith Flower MacCannell, Judith Pike and Lollie Groth). Lincoln, NB: University of Nebraska Press.
1994c. *Manna, for the Mandelstams for the Mandelas* (tr. Catherine A.F. MacGillivray). Minneapolis, MN: University of Minnesota Press.
1994d. *The Hélène Cixous Reader* (ed. and tr. Susan Sellers). London: Routledge.
1997. *Rootprints* (tr. Eric Prenowitz). London: Routledge.
1998a. *First Days of the Year* (tr. Catherine A.F. MacGillivray). Minneapolis, MN: University of Minnesota Press.
1998b. *Stigmata: Escaping Texts*. London: Routledge.
1999. *The Third Body* (tr. Keith Cohen). Evanston, IL: Hydra Books-Northwestern University Press.
2001. *Veils* (with Jacques Derrida) (tr. Geoffrey Bennington). Stanford, CA: Stanford University Press.
2003a. *Selected Plays of Hélène Cixous* (ed. Eric Prenowitz). London and New York, NY: Routledge. Includes: *Portrait of Dora* (tr. Ann Liddle); *Black Sail White Sail* (tr. Donald Watson); *The Perjured City* (tr. Bernadette Fort); *Drums on the Dam* (tr. Judith G. Miller and Brian J. Mallet).

2003b. *Portrait of Jacques Derrida as a Young Jewish Saint* (tr. Beverley Bie Brahic). New York, NY: Columbia University Press.

3. Translations of Hélène Cixous's Texts by our Contributors
(in alphabetical order)

3.1. Liliana Alexandrescu (researcher and stage director, The Netherlands):
1996. 'Portretul Dorei, Hélène Cixous și Freud' in *Secolul 20* 7-9: 216-231. [Article including two excerpts of "La jeune née" and *Portrait de Dora*.]

3.2. Anu Aneja (Ohio Wesleyan University, USA):
1997. *Sapnõ Ki Adhoori Dastaan* [*L'Indiade ou l'Inde de mes rêves*]. New Delhi: Radha Krishna Prakashan.

3.3. Verena Andermatt Conley (Harvard University, USA):
1989. 'How to write agua viva' [Introduction to Clarice Lispector *Agua viva*]. Minneapolis, MN: University of Minnesota Press, Emergent Literatures Series.
1990. *Reading with Clarice Lispector*. Minneapolis, MN: University of Minnesota Press, Theory and History of Literature Series, v. 73.
1991. *Readings: The Poetics of Blanchot, Joyce, Kafka, Kleist, Lispector, and Tsvetaeva*. Minneapolis, MN: University of Minnesota Press, Theory and History of Literature Series, v. 77.

3.4. Monica Fiorini (Università degli Studi di Bologna, Italy):
1998a. 'Is a Book a Tomb?' in *Poetiche. Letteratura e altro* 3: 33-41. [Excerpt from an unpublished text in French.]
1998b. 'La venuta alla scrittura' in *Studi di Estetica* 17: 7-53.
1998-1999. *OR le lettere di mio padre* [unpublished].
2000a. 'Ostetriche crudeli' in *Autodafé* 1: 103-116.
2000b 'L'ultimo quadro o il ritratto di Dio' [for the catalog of the exhibit *Oeuvres d'être... works of beings... pere d'essere*, Rome, October 30-November 24].
2001. *Osnabrück*. Ferrara: Luciana Tufani.

3.5. Deborah Jenson (University of Wisconsin, USA):
1986. *The Conquest of the School at Madhubaï* in *Women and Performance* 3: 59-95.
1990. 'Interview with Hélène Cixous' [by H. Cixous and Alice Jardine] in Jardine, Alice and Anne Menke (eds) *Shifting Scenes: Interviews on Women, Writing and Politics in Post 1968 France*. New York, NY: Columbia University Press. 32-50.

1994. 'Sonia Rykiel in Translation' in Benstock, Shari and Suzanne Ferris (eds) *On Fashion*. New Brunswick, NJ: Rutgers University Press. 95-99.

3.6. Sissel Lie (Norges Teknisk-Naturvitenskapelige Universitet, Norway):
1991. 'Medusas latter' in Kittang, Atle et al. (eds) *Moderne litteraturteori. En antologi*. Oslo: Universitetsforlaget.
1998. *Nattspråk* (ed. and tr.). Oslo: Pax. [Includes: 'La venue à l'écriture', 'Le lieu du crime, le lieu du pardon', 'L'incarnation', 'L'auteur en vérité', *Jours de l'an* (excerpt), 'Demasqués!'.]

3.7. Isako Matsumoto (University of Nagoya, Japan):
1993. *Medhusa-no warai* (with Sonoko Kokuryo and Keiko Tokura). Tokyo: Kinokuniya. [Includes: 'Le rire de la Méduse', 'Le sexe ou la tête?', 'La jeune née' (excerpt), 'La venue à l'écriture' (excerpt).]
1995. *Ookami-no-ai*. Tokyo: Kinokuniya. [Includes: 'L'amour du loup', 'En octobre 1991...', 'Quelle heure-est-il? ou la porte (celle qu'on ne passe pas)', 'Contes de la différence sexuelle', and 'Fourmis' by Jacques Derrida.]
1997a. 'Mohmoku-de-kaku' ['Écrire aveugle'] in *Gendai-sisoh* (September). Tokyo: Seidosya.
1997b. 'Watashi-no Algériance' ['Mon Algériance'] in *Gendai-sisoh* (December). Tokyo: Seidosya.
1998. 'Hélène Cixous, rutu-wo-toru' [*Hélène Cixous, photos de racines*, excerpt] in *Onnatachi-no-furansu-siso*. Tokyo: Keiso Shobo.
2001. *Dora-no-Syozo* (with Koharu Kisaragi). Tokyo: Shinsuisya. [Includes: *Portrait de Dora*, *La prise de l'école de Madhubai*, 'L'auteur entre texte et théâtre', 'Démasqués!'.]

3.8. Judith G. Miller (New York University, USA):
1994. *The Name of Oedipus: Song of the Forbidden Body* (with Christiane Makward) in *Plays by French and Francophone Women: A Critical Anthology*. Ann Arbor, MI: University of Michigan Press.
2003. *Drums on the Dam: In the Form of an Ancient Puppet Play, Performed by Actors* (with Brian J. Mallet) in Prenowitz, Eric (ed.) *Selected Plays of Hélène Cixous*. London and New York, NY: Routledge.

3.9. Mara Negrón (Universidad de Puerto Rico):
1997. 'Cuentos de la diferencia sexual' in *Bordes* 4 (May).
2001. *Velos* (with Jacques Derrida). Mexico: Siglo XXI.

3.10. Lynn K. Penrod:
2003-2004. *The Jewish Bride* (to be published).

3.11. Maribel Peñalver Vicea (Universidad de Alicante, Spain):
2000a. 'Apariciones' in *Debats* 69 (July): 48-57.
2000b. 'Cronología'; 'Álbumes y leyendas'; 'Los nombres de Orán'; 'Amaneceres. Vistas sobre mi tierra' in *Quimera* 190 (April): 22-24; 25-32; 33-39; 40-49.
2000c. 'Obstetricias crueles' in *Autodafe* 1. Barcelona: Anagrama.
2000d. 'Mi argeliancia' in *Revista de Occidente* 234 (November): 120-147.
2000e 'Un verdadero jardín' in *Anales* 9. Murcia: Universidad de Murcia.
2001. '¡Al carAjo, Haider! – No hay que decirlo –' in *Lateral* 73 (January): 39-41.
2002a. *Los ensueños de la mujer salvaje* (unpublished).
2002b. 'Estigmas'; 'Carta a Zhora Drif'; 'La piel de más' in *Lectora* 7: 189-194; 203-210; 211-217.

3.12. Eric Prenowitz (University of Leeds, UK):
1995 'The Place of Crime, the Place of Pardon' in Drain, Richard (ed.) *Theatre Anthology*. London: Routledge.
1996a. '"Mamãe, disse ele" or Joyce's Second Hand' in *Poetics Today* 17(3) (Fall): 339-366. [Reprinted in Cixous, Hélène. 1998. *Stigmata: Escaping Texts*. London and New York, NY: Routledge. 101-128.]
1996b. 'An Error of Calculation' in *Yale French Studies* 89: 151-154.
1996c. 'Writing Blind' in *TriQuarterly* 97 (Fall): 7-20. [Reprinted in Cixous, Hélène. 1998. *Stigmata: Escaping Texts*. London and New York, NY: Routledge. 139-152.]
1996-97. 'Guardian of Language: An Interview with Hélène Cixous' in *Women's Education des Femmes* 12(4) (Winter): 6-10.
1997a. *Hélène Cixous: Rootprints* (with Mireille Calle-Gruber). London and New York, NY: Routledge.
1997b. 'Stigmata: Job the Dog' in *Philosophy Today* (Spring): 12-17. [Reprinted in Cixous, Hélène. 1998. *Stigmata: Escaping Texts*. London and New York, NY: Routledge. 181-194.]
1997c. 'Attacks of the Castle' in Leach, Neil (ed.) *Rethinking Architecture: A Reader in Cultural Theory*. London and New York, NY: Routledge. 303-307.
1997d. 'My Algeriance' in *TriQuarterly* 100 (Fall). [Reprinted in Cixous, Hélène. 1998. *Stigmata: Escaping Texts*. London and New York, NY: Routledge. 151-172.]
1998. 'Letter to Zohra Drif' in *Parallax* 7 (April-June): 189-196.
1999. 'Post-Word' in McQuillan, M., G. MacDonald, R. Purves and S. Thomson. *Post-Theory: New Directions in Criticism*. Edinburgh: Edinburgh University Press. 209-213.
2002. 'The Towers: Les tours' in *Signs* 28: 431-433.

2003. 'On Theatre' [interview] in Prenowitz, Eric (ed.) *Selected Plays of Hélène Cixous*. London and New York, NY: Routledge. 1-24.

3.13. Susan Sellers (The University of Saint Andrews, UK):

1988. 'Extreme Fidelity'; 'Tancredi Continues' (tr. with Ann Liddle) in Sellers, Susan (ed.) *Writing Differences: Readings from the Seminar of Helene Cixous'*. New York, NY: Open University Press, Milton Keynes, St. Martin's Press. 9-36; 37-53.

1989. 'The "Double World" of Writing'; 'Listening to the Truth'; 'A Realm of Characters'; 'Writing as a Second Heart' in Sellers, Susan (ed.) *Delighting the Heart: A Notebook by Women Writers*. London: The Women's Press. 18; 69; 126-128; 198.

1991. 'The Last Painting or the Portrait of God' (tr. with Sarah Cornell) in Jenson, Deborah (ed.) *'Coming to Writing' and Other Essays*. Cambridge, MA: Harvard University Press. 104-131.

1993. *Three Steps on the Ladder of Writing* (tr. with Sarah Cornell). New York, NY: Columbia University Press.

1994. 'Neutral'; 'Breaths'; 'The (Feminine)'; 'FirstDays of the Year'; 'Deluge' in Sellers, Susan (ed.) *The Hélène Cixous Reader*. London and New York, NY: Routledge. 6-16; 49-55; 59-67; 183-187; 191-196.

2004 (forthcoming). *The Writing Notebooks of Hélène Cixous*. London and New York, NY: Continuum Press.

3.14. Nadia Setti (Études féminines, Université de Paris VIII, France):

1988. 'L'approccio di Clarice Lispector' in *Donnawomanfemme* 7 (December): 35-45.

1992. *Il teatro del cuore*. Parma: Pratiche Editrice. [Anthology of texts and interviews on theatre, ed., tr. and introd. N. Setti.]

1998. 'Corpi e visioni, la magia del teatro' [excerpts from 'Apparitions'] in *Il Manifesto*, Thursday, November 19.

1999a. 'La marionetta sublime" [interview] in *DWF* 1(41): 14-18.

1999b. 'La mia Algeriance' in *DWF, Passioni di scena* (January-March): 70-92.

1999c. 'Lettera a Zohra Drif'; 'Da un velo all'altro' ['Mue', and three poems from *Le Butin* de Hamida Ait El Hadji] in *Leggendaria* 14 (April): 4-9; 10-11.

2000. 'Apparizioni'; 'Tancredi continua' in Bono, Paola (ed.) *Scritture del corpo*. Napoli: Sossella.

2004 (forthcoming). *Le fantasticherie della donna selvaggia, scene primitive*. Torino: Bollati Boringhieri.

---

[1] We are grateful to M. Sandré and E. Prenowitz for accepting to reproduce here this part of their work.